Against the background of the global financial crisis which has left a legacy of political turmoil and a populist surge across Europe, this book could not be more timely. The contributors offer the reader a comparative understanding of youth inequalities in difficult times. Labour market, family transitions and intergenerational relationships are described and explained from a life course perspective and firmly located in an era of increasing social inequality. The editors are to be commended on pulling together such an excellent collection.

Fiona Devine, *Head of Alliance Manchester Business School and Professor of Sociology at The University of Manchester, UK*

Social change is complicated! This book brilliantly shows and explains how a new generation of young Europeans are living through the consequences of the global financial crisis, recalibrating their expectations and optimising their resources in ways that compound inequality. Empirically robust, theoretically nuanced and rooted in a range of European contexts, this is state of the art youth studies, providing a sense of how we got into this situation, offering the starting point for navigating a more socially just future.

Rachel Thomson, *Professor of Childhood & Youth Studies, University of Sussex, UK*

Transitions to Adulthood Through Recession

Long-running trends towards increasing inequality between the rich and poor across Europe have been exacerbated by the 2008 global financial crisis and its aftermath. As employment opportunities for young people diminish and as the welfare state is pulled back, pathways to adulthood change and become more difficult to navigate.

Transitions to Adulthood Through Recession consists of a collection of papers by researchers from Britain, Norway, Germany, Portugal, Italy and Greece, locating young people's transitions to adulthood in their national social, economic and political contexts. It explores young adulthood with reference to generational continuity and change and intergenerational support. With a cross-national comparative framework, this volume highlights the importance of variations in structural contexts for young people's transitions.

Bringing together authors across sub-disciplines such as the sociology of youth, family and kinship, class and inequality and life-course studies, *Transitions to Adulthood Through Recession* will appeal to academic social scientists as well as final-year undergraduate and postgraduate students interested in fields such as political science, sociology, youth studies, social policy, anthropology and psychology; and a wider public readership.

Sarah Irwin is Professor of Sociology at the University of Leeds, UK.

Ann Nilsen is Professor of Sociology at the University of Bergen, Norway.

Youth, Young Adulthood and Society

Series editor: Andy Furlong, University of Glasgow, UK

The **Youth, Young Adulthood and Society** series brings together social scientists from many disciplines to present research monographs and collections, seeking to further research into youth in our changing societies around the world today. The books in this series advance the field of youth studies by presenting original, exciting research, with strongly theoretically- and empirically-grounded analysis.

For a full list of titles in this series, please visit https://www.routledge.com/Youth-Young-Adulthood-and-Society/book-series/YYAS

Published:

Youth, Class and Everyday Struggles
Steven Threadgold

Youth Homelessness and Survival Sex
Intimate Relationships and Gendered Subjectivities
Juliet Watson

Spaces of Youth
Work, Citizenship and Culture in a Global Context
David Farrugia

Transitions to Adulthood Through Recession
Youth and Inequality in a European Comparative Perspective
Edited by Sarah Irwin and Ann Nilsen

Forthcoming:

Rethinking Young People's Marginalisation
Beyond Neo-Liberal Futures?
Perri Campbell, Lyn Harrison, Chris Hickey and Peter Kelly

Transitions to Adulthood Through Recession

Youth and Inequality in a European Comparative Perspective

Edited by
Sarah Irwin and Ann Nilsen

Routledge
Taylor & Francis Group

LONDON AND NEW YORK

First published 2018
by Routledge
2 Park Square, Milton Park, Abingdon, Oxon OX14 4RN

and by Routledge
711 Third Avenue, New York, NY 10017

Routledge is an imprint of the Taylor & Francis Group, an informa business

British Library Cataloguing in Publication Data
A catalogue record for this book is available from the British Library

Library of Congress Cataloging in Publication Data
Names: Irwin, Sarah, 1961- author. | Nilsen, Ann, author.
Title: Transitions to adulthood through recession : youth and inequality in a European comparative perspective / Sarah Irwin and Ann Nilsen.
Description: Abingdon, Oxon ; New York, NY : Routledge, 2018. | Series: Youth, young adulthood and society | Includes bibliographical references and index.
Identifiers: LCCN 2017047046 | ISBN 9781138294288 (hardback)
Subjects: LCSH: Youth--Europe--Social conditions--21st century. | Youth--Europe--Economic conditions--21st century. | Adulthood--Europe. | Equality--Europe.
Classification: LCC HQ799.E9 I79 2018 | DDC 305.242094--dc23
LC record available at https://lccn.loc.gov/2017047046

ISBN: 978-1-138-29428-8 (hbk)
ISBN: 978-1-315-23168-6 (ebk)

Typeset in Times New Roman
by Taylor & Francis Books

Contents

Illustrations

Figures

Tables

About the authors

Nuno de Almeida Alves is Associate Professor and Head of Social Research Methods at ISCTE-IUL. His research interests are in the area of youth studies and the sociology of work. His most recent publications include: Cairns, David, Nuno de Almeida Alves, Ana Alexandre e Augusta Correia (2016), *Youth Unemployment and Job Precariousness: Political Participation in the Austerity Era*, Basingstoke, Palgrave-Macmillan. Carmo, Renato Miguel do, Frederico Cantante e Nuno de Almeida Alves (2014), Time projections: Youth and precarious employment", *Time & Society* 23(3), pp: 337–357. DOI: 10.1177/0961463X14549505. Cairns, David, Katarzyna Growiec and Nuno de Almeida Alves (2014), "Another 'Missing Middle'? The marginalised majority of tertiary- educated youth in Portugal during the economic crisis", *Journal of Youth Studies* 17(8), pp: 1046–1060. DOI: 10.1080/13676261.2013.878789

Julia Brannen is Professor of Sociology of the Family, Thomas Coram Research Unit, UCL Institute of Education, London and Adjunct Professor at the University of Bergen. She has an international reputation for her methodological contributions and for ESRC and EU-funded research on family life and intergenerational relationships. She recently published *Fathers and Sons: Generations, families and migration* (2015) Palgrave.

Patrick Heady joined the Max Planck Institute for Social Anthropology in 1999. His research interests centre on the connections between cognition, identity and cooperation – with applications to kinship organisation and anthropological demography. Between 2004 and 2010 he led an EU-funded collaborative project on Kinship and Social Security in Europe (KASS). The findings of this study were published in 2010 as *Family, Kinship and State in Contemporary Europe* (eds. P. Heady, H. Grandits, M. Kohli, P. Schweitzer) Frankfurt/New York: Campus Verlag.

Sarah Irwin (co-editor) is Professor of Sociology at the University of Leeds. She is Director of the Centre for Research into Families, the Life Course and Generations. She has published extensively in the areas of family, youth, parenting and social inequalities, and has a long standing interest in research methods. Relevant publications include: Irwin, S. and Elley, S. (2013)

'Parents' hopes and expectations for their children's future occupations', *The Sociological Review* 61 [1]: 111–30. Irwin, S. and Elley, S. (2011) 'Concerted cultivation? Parenting values, education and class diversity', *Sociology* 45(3): 480–495. Also relevant is her 1995 publication: *Rights of passage: social change and the transition from youth to adulthood*, UCL Press.

Abigail Knight is a Research Officer at the Thomas Coram Research Unit, UCL Institute of Education, where she specialises in qualitative research with children, young people and families. She has worked on a number of studies, including those funded by central government, ESRC and ERC.

Alexandra Koronaiou is a Professor of sociology and teaches sociology of work and leisure as well as sociology of media at Panteion University, Department of Psychology and Introduction to Adult Education at the Greek Open University. She has been coordinating EU projects (FP7 & Horizon 2020) at Panteion University since 2011 on young people's socio-political engagement, young people's well-being and the evaluation of innovative social policies. Her recent publications include: "Women and Golden Dawn: Reproducing the nationalist habitus", *Gender & Education* (with A. Sakellariou), Volume 29, Issue 2, 2017, pp. 258–275; "Singing for Race and Nation: Fascism and Racism in Greek Youth Music" (with A. Sakellariou and E.Lagos), in P. Simpson and H. Druxes (eds.), *Digital Media Strategies of the Far Right in Europe and the United States*, Lanham: Lexington Books, 2015, pp. 193–213; "Golden Dawn, Austerity and Young People: The Rise of Fascist Extremism among Young People in Contemporary Greek Society" (with A.Sakellariou, E. Lagos, I. Chiotaki-Poulou & S. Kymionis), in H. Pilkington and G. Pollock (eds.), *Radical Futures? Youth, Politics and Activism in Contemporary Europe*, West Sussex: Wiley-Blackwell, 2015, pp. 231–249.

Nicola De Luigi is Assistant Professor of Sociology at the Department of Sociology and Business Law of the University of Bologna. He has carried out numerous research studies at national and European level and published in the area of youth studies, focusing in particular on school to work transitions, social inequalities, gender relationships, problem behaviours during adolescence and early adulthood. He is currently involved in the European research project PARTISPACE – 'Spaces and Styles of Participation. Formal, non-formal and informal possibilities of young people's participation in European cities' (Horizon 2020 UE Program). Recent publications include De Luigi, N. and Martelli, A., (2015), Attitudes and practices of parents: disadvantage and access to education, in *European Education*, Vol. 47, issue 1, 2015, pp. 46-60 and De Luigi, N., Barberis, E. and Buchowicz, I. (2016) 'Producing Accessibility through Discretionary Practices of Educational Professionals', in *Governance of Educational Trajectories in Europe*, W., A., Parreira do Amaral, M., Cuconato, M. and Dale, R. (eds), New York, NY: Bloomsbury Academic, pp. 117–138.

Robert MacDonald is Professor of Sociology at Teesside University. He is also currently the Obel Foundation Visiting Professor at the Danish Centre for Youth Research, Aalborg University and Deputy Editor of the *Journal of Youth Studies*. His research interests cross sociology, social policy, criminology and youth studies. Relevant publications include MacDonald, R, Shildrick, T. and Furlong, A (2013). 'In search of "intergenerational cultures of work-lessness": Hunting Yetis and Shooting Zombies', *Critical Social Policy*, 34: 2 199–220.

Elena Mattioli is currently Research Fellow at the Department of Sociology and Business Law, University of Bologna. She successfully completed her Ph.D. in Sociology in May 2015 at the School of Political and Social Sciences, University of Bologna. Her main areas of interests concern housing, transitions to adulthood, social inequalities and class analysis, disadvantaged groups and social exclusion processes. She has taken part in several studies concerning young people, both at a local and national levels, on these issues. Her main publications are *Intersectionality at work. Reflections from a study on intergenerational negotiation of independent living in working classes families,* in *"Rassegna italiana di sociologia"*, n.3 (with Nicola De Luigi) (2016), *Intergenerational negotiations of independent living in working class context*, [Dissertation thesis], Alma Mater Studiorum Università di Bologna. Dottorato di ricerca in *Sociologia*, 27 Ciclo. DOI 10.6092/unibo/amsdottorato/7014; (2014), and "Famiglie, insegnanti e vita scolastica: le relazioni all'interno dei *local school spaces"* (with Stella Volturo), in *Cuconato M., (a cura di), Il tempo delle medie. Esperienze scolastiche e transizioni generazionali*, Carocci, Roma, pp. 124–144 (book chapter).

Ann Nilsen (co-editor) is Professor of Sociology at the Department of Sociology, University of Bergen, Norway. Her main research areas are life course and biographical studies. Her research projects have received funding from the EU and the Norwegian Research Council (NFR). She is currently leader of the NFR funded study *Intergenerational Transmission in the Transition to Adulthood*. Recent publications include Nilsen, A and J Brannen (2014) An Intergenerational Approach to Transitions to Adulthood: The Importance of History and Biography *Sociological Research Online*, 19(2) 9, and Scott, J, Nilsen A (eds) (2013) *C.Wright Mills and the Sociological Imagination. Contemporary Perspectives*

Ken Roberts is Professor of Sociology at the University of Liverpool. His major research areas are the sociology of leisure, and the sociology of young people's life stage transitions. Since 1991 he has coordinated a series of research projects in East-Central Europe and the former Soviet Union. These have investigated how various social groups' circumstances have changed during the political and economic transformations of their countries. His current research is into youth in south and east Mediterranean countries. Professor Roberts' books include *Surviving Post-Communism:*

Young People in the Former Soviet Union (2000), *Youth in Eastern Europe and in the West* (2009), *Class in Contemporary Britain* (2011), *Sociology: An Introduction* (2012), *The Business of Leisure* (2016), and *Social Theory, Sport, Leisure* (2016).

Alexandros Sakellariou is currently teaching sociology at the Greek Open University and is a post-doctoral researcher at Panteion University of Athens. He earned his PhD on Sociology from the Department of Sociology of Panteion University. Since 2011 he has worked as a researcher at Panteion University in EU Projects on young people's socio-political engagement, young people's well-being and the evaluation of innovative social policies. His recent publications include: "Women and Golden Dawn: Reproducing the nationalist habitus", *Gender & Education* (with A. Koronaiou), Volume 29, Issue 2, 2017, pp. 258–275, "Singing for Race and Nation: Fascism and Racism in Greek Youth Music" (with A.Koronaiou and E. Lagos) in P Simpson and H.Druxes (eds.), *Digital Media Strategies of the Far Right in Europe and the United States*, Lanham: Lexington Books, 2015, pp. 193–213; "Golden Dawn, Austerity and Young People: The Rise of Fascist Extremism among Young People in Contemporary Greek Society" (With A.Koronaiou, E. Lagos, I. Chiotaki-Poulou & S. Kymionis), in H. Pilkington and G. Pollock (eds.), *Radical Futures? Youth, Politics and Activism in Contemporary Europe*, West Sussex: Wiley-Blackwell, 2015, pp.231-249.

Tracy Shildrick is Professor of Sociology and Social Policy at University of Leeds. She has written widely on young people's transitions to adulthood and she recently led two projects for the Joseph Rowntree Foundation. She has been involved in the development of the forthcoming JRF UK anti-poverty strategy and is Deputy Editor of the Journal of Youth Studies and Co-Editor of the Journal of Poverty and Social Justice. Her research interests are young people social class and intergenerational inequalities. Relevant publications include: Shildrick, et al (2012) '*Poverty and Insecurity: Life in low pay, no pay Britain*' Bristol Policy Press

Kristoffer Chelsom Vogt is Associate Professor at the Department of Sociology, University of Bergen (Norway) and is affiliated with the project *Intergenerational Transmission in the Transition to Adulthood* (funded by the Norwegian Research Council). His research interests lie at the intersection between life course research and research about education, work, class, family and gender. Recent publications include the articles 'The postindustrial society: from utopia to ideology' in *Work, Employment & Society* (2016), 'The concept of the work situation in class analysis' in *Current Sociology* (2017), 'Age norms and early school leaving' in *European Societies* (2017), "The timing of a time out: the gap year in life course context" in *Journal of Education and Work*, and the monograph "*Men in Manual Occupations: Changing Lives in Times of Change*" published with Nordic Open Access (Cappelen Damm Akademisk).

Acknowledgements

The editors and some of the chapter authors participated in a workshop entitled *Intergenerational Transmission and the Transition to Adulthood: the relationship between empirical analysis and theoretical conceptualisations* in Bergen, Norway in October 2015 as part of the study *Intergenerational Relations in the Transition to Adulthood*. We acknowledge the funding from *The Norwegian Research Council* for the study under the Independent Projects (FRI-HUMSAM) scheme. Such funding is extremely helpful for creating the opportunity for researchers to discuss their work and to exchange ideas. The edited book is one outcome of such collaborative endeavours. The initiative to write an edited volume came up during the workshop and we were fortunate to secure a contract from Routledge in the Youth Series edited by the late Professor Andy Furlong. It is very sad that he is no longer with us.

Most of the chapters in this book are based on interviews with informants from the respective countries. All authors are indebted to the anonymous interviewees who have taken the time to meet with us and tell us about their lives, making the chapters in this volume possible.

Gratitude is also due to the editorial team at Routledge, Elena Chiu and Emily Briggs, and to the reviewers of our initial proposal and of our final book manuscript.

1 Understanding youth transitions in difficult times

Sarah Irwin and Ann Nilsen

Introduction

This book explores continuities and changes in youth and the transition to adulthood in diverse European country contexts. It explores recent developments in light of the global financial crisis of 2008 and the subsequent recession, social crises and austerity policies and situates their relevancies with reference to the long-term restructuring of youth and young adulthood. We bring together authors from across various sociological sub-disciplines specialising in youth, family and kinship, class and inequality and life course studies. They analyse developments across six European nations: Norway, the UK, Germany, Portugal, Italy and Greece. Each chapter investigates country-specific institutional, cultural and economic processes reshaping the life course phases of youth and early adulthood and how transitions are experienced, negotiated and authored by young people and their families. In most country case studies we offer new analyses of qualitative data. The contributors explore generational dynamics as an important analytic lens on youth and transitions, interrogating continuities and changes across generations as well as the interdependencies that bind familial generations. Most also focus on social class as a key dimension of their analyses of young people's pathways and transitions. Whilst the analyses derive from distinct projects they are complementary and sit in dialogue with one another. In this introductory chapter, we trace some general developments through the latter part of the twentieth century, identify and explore some recent changes in the framing of young people's pathways and transitions with reference to our country case study contexts, and discuss the conceptual value of the transitions approach and of a contextualist life course approach.

Notions of progress have underlain ideas about historical development in the Western world for hundreds of years (Kumar 1978). These ideas inspired the belief that conditions would improve from one generation to the next. The three decades of economic growth after World War II and the establishment of welfare states and poverty reduction along with expansion in education and employment for all were understood to be the new standard for development that fitted into the notion of progress (Hobsbawm 1994). In northern and western Europe post-war growth, investment, full employment, welfare state development and growing prosperity (particularly relative to the hardships of previous decades) underlay the long boom described by Hobsbawm. Extremely diverse sets of welfare arrangements and linked rights, responsibilities and gendered divisions of labour were built across these European nations in the post-war decades. Full employment meant that young people's pathways to independent living were strongly underpinned by access to jobs, improving relative earnings and the resources deemed necessary for family formation. This period was also 'the age of the housewife' (Oakley 1974; Wærness 1978) and the male breadwinner model was the standard in most families. The transition to adulthood was strongly gendered and influenced by social class. Young working-class men were expected to get a job and earn a living as soon as compulsory schooling was over. A long period spent in university education was a privilege for the few. The post-war decades of inclusive growth saw increases in absolute if not relative upward social mobility (Breen 2004; Goldthorpe and Mills 2008). Through the post-war era family background remained a strong indicator of young people's life chances in education and future employment. Therefore, although the era is often described as one of inclusive growth it was marked by strongly classed pathways from families of origin to destination. Nevertheless, the institutional structures of welfare, education and labour market regulation, and full (male) employment buttressed relatively standardised transitions across northern Europe.

From 1973 the era of inclusive and seemingly continuous growth faltered and gave way to recessions and rising unemployment across Europe (Hobsbawm 1994; Blanchard 2006). Anticipated by the policies of the Thatcher Conservative government in the UK, the 1980s saw a broader move away from the Keynesian policy strategies of the post-war decades and a new ascendancy of market-oriented policies. This period also saw an intensification of a process of globalisation with its deepening international economic interdependencies. Buchholz and colleagues, for example, identify interrelated social trends which engender greater connectedness across nations, including a growing internationalisation of markets and linked growth in economic competition across countries, a tendency to internal deregulation and reliance on market mechanisms in the provision of goods and services, and a linked increase in interdependence rendering nations more vulnerable to common crises (Buchholz et al 2009). Within nations these developments have heightened risks and precarity for those in vulnerable positions. Indeed, restructuring has itself altered the distribution of vulnerability across and within different population groups and life course stages.

Another important trend across European nations is the marked expansion of education. The number of years in compulsory schooling has increased and whilst in 2016 it was on average nine years (European Commission 2015), there has been growing concern over young people who do not complete 12 years of schooling, the so-called 'drop-outs' (Vogt 2017). Early school leaving is defined by the European Commission as completing school at the point of lower secondary education (typically at 16 years old). From 2002 to 2016 early school leaving rates continued to decline across the EU and fell from 17% to 11% (Eurostat 2017). Across Europe, participation in tertiary education has increased across the same time period from 24% to 39% (Eurostat 2017). This is a remarkable social change across a short historical period, and leads to interesting patterns of contrast in levels of education across population cohorts. For example, Germany manifests extensive similarities across generations in their levels of educational attainment. In stark contrast, Portugal manifests a very large generational gap in levels of formal education due to the low base of secondary education amongst currently retiring cohorts and very significant recent increases in educational participation amongst successor cohorts (Allmendinger and von den Driesch 2014). The marked increase in educational participation across many nations also raises important questions relating to the effectiveness of skills strategies and the fit between labour supply and demand. Some commentators highlight risks of credential inflation, widely seen to engender increased difficulties for more highly educated young people (eg Brown et al 2010). Systemic pressures also mean that those with few educational qualifications are increasingly marginalised and are less likely to overcome a difficult labour market start than in the past (eg George et al 2015).

In seeking to shed light on the macro-level framing of transition and country-specific diversity, many writers define and draw on typologies of regime types relating to welfare, education and labour market arrangements, and school to work transition patterns (eg Esping Andersen 1990; Walther 2006; Buchholz et al 2009; Buchmann and Kriesi 2011; Eurofound 2014). Such typologies form useful organisational and framing devices for social analysis. They foreground some of the ways in which contrasting institutional and cultural contexts profoundly shape the experiences and opportunities confronting young people and their lifetime implications. In their analyses of restructuring life course processes and the position of young people, Buchholz and colleagues (2009) very effectively show how diverse country-specific institutional structures mediate wider trends and translate them very differently at national, meso and individual levels. Although national contexts frame life course processes and social inequalities very differently, the authors argue that young adults are 'the losers of the globalization process' (p.67). Recent cohorts of young adults have been disproportionately undermined due to their life course stage and relatively vulnerable position in the labour market in an era of significant economic and social changes; times which differ markedly from those experienced by their parents and grandparents.

In the opening decade of the twenty-first century, all European countries were affected by the global financial crisis in 2008. Whilst public funds in many countries were spent on bailing out the banking sector after the crash, economic recession was used to justify spending cuts and policies of austerity (Stiglitz 2012). This is evident in some countries represented in this book: the UK, Portugal, Italy and Greece. The consequences of these policies have been dire on many fronts in these societies. Where austerity policies have been vigorously pursued and welfare and public services subject to retrenchment (Stiglitz 2012), intergenerational support for the transition to adulthood from family, friends and the wider community has gained new relevance, including within Mediterranean countries which already had a strong tradition of family support. Countries manifest significant diversity in how they provide support for early labour market transitions (O'Reilly et al 2015) and in the inter-generational inheritances, support and commitment which influence young adults' experience (Allmendinger and von den Driesch 2014). Southern European nations have seen significant outward migration as a response to shrinking labour market opportunities. Throughout this book the diversity and variety of experiences, perceptions and practices are contextualised and demon-strated. Within the chapters our contributors situate recession and related developments alongside analyses of longer-run trends in the shaping of youth and early adulthood as life course stages.

Whilst the era from the 1970s/80s onwards has a longer duration now than the so-called post-war era of inclusive growth (eg Taylor-Gooby 2013) that preceded it, it nevertheless provides a common counterpoint in descriptions of current arrangements. For example, many commentators contrast the experience of youth and young adulthood today with that which was obtained in the post-war decades until the 1970s. They particularly highlight that youth and the transition to adulthood has become less linear, more protracted and more precarious (eg Buchholz et al 2009; Heinz et al 2009; Buchmann and Kriesi 2011; Antonucci et al 2014; Raffe 2014). Billari and Liefbroer (2010) describe the emergence of 'a new European pattern of transition to adulthood' (p.73), characterised as late, protracted and complex in contrast to the early, con-tracted and simple transitions which characterised the post-war period. These new characteristics and how they manifest across country contexts are well illuminated through the chapters. We turn now to illustrating some continuities and changes in youth and early adulthood across our country contexts.

Youth transitions in changing social and economic contexts

In this section we highlight some trends in the youth labour market, familial transitions and relationships across generations and we flag some key themes to be explored through the book. Positioned at the margins of the labour market, young people have been especially vulnerable to unemployment with low recruitment and exposure to last in, first out, policies in economic reces-sion. They have also been undermined by the trend for employers to devolve risks to their employees, particularly through the use of casual and temporary labour (cf Bukodi et al 2008). Across Europe, unemployment rates vary sig-nificantly. In 2013 the EU-28 unemployment rate of young people aged 15–24 was 23%, reaching 40% in Italy and 58% in Greece (O'Reilly et al 2015). EU youth unemployment rates have since improved slightly to 2017 and stand at 19% (European Commission 2017). Such rates compare unemployed and employed youth, whilst the unemployment *ratio* measures unemployment as a proportion of the cohort as a whole. On this measure the 2013 EU average stood at 10%, varying from 4% and 5% in Germany and Norway to 13% in Portugal and 17% in Greece (O'Reilly et al 2015).

The EU employment rate of 15–24 year olds declined from 37% in 2008 to 33% in 2012 (Eurofound 2014), and then manifested a slight rise to 34% in 2016 (European Commission 2017). Employment rates vary significantly across northern and southern European nations. For example, in 2016 employment rates amongst young men aged 25 to 29 remained fairly constant at above 80% in the UK and Germany. In contrast, equivalent employment rates fell from 88% to 73% in Portugal and from 82% to 63% in Greece between 2000 and 2016 (Eurostat, Data Explorer). These are important reasons for the emigration discussed in the Portuguese and Greek chapters in the current volume.

National labour markets vary greatly in the kinds of employment available to young people and the extent to which early jobs comprise 'cul-de-sac' (dead-end) jobs or routes to labour market integration and a decent career (cf Bukodi et al 2008). There is a trend towards a polarisation of jobs with increased relative shares of high and low-skill jobs across many countries and a shrinking of the share of middle-skill jobs over recent decades (OECD 2017). It is widely observed that the youth labour market has become much more precarious than in the past. Across Europe, whilst 10% of the workforce aged 25–64 were on temporary contracts, this was the case for 42% of those aged under 25 (Eurofound 2014). Germany was relatively insulated from the consequences of economic recession (see Burda and Hunt 2011). Indeed, unemployment rates there fell between 2008 and 2011 (OECD 2011). In their study of the life course in Germany, Buchholz and Kolb (2011) highlight the particular vulnerability of young people (and women generally) due to a trend towards flexible employment practices, more widely found since the 1980s. With over 25% of young people under 30 on fixed-term contracts in Germany, this exemplifies the widespread vulnerability of those at the start of their careers (Buchholz and Kolb 2011). Nevertheless, Germany still manages an economy which integrates its young workers relatively successfully through its training and education systems (Eurofound 2014). This stands in contrast to several other country examples explored in this book. Growing labour market difficulties for young adults are widely seen to compromise pathways to autonomy and social independence, and to undermine psychological and subjective wellbeing (Antonucci et al 2014). Our chapters highlight the question of young people's experiences and orientations across diverse national, regional and class-related contexts.

European nations may be experiencing a slow return to economic and employment growth from 2013/14 onwards, yet low and middle earnings remain static, and evidence points to inequalities becoming more marked (OECD 2017). Several researchers suggest that family background has maintained its grip on young people's life chances (Antonucci et al 2014; Biggart et al 2015; O'Reilly et al 2015). Allmendinger and von den Driesch point to a deepening divide between the haves and have-nots and argue that '...through inheritance, the opportunities and risks accumulate dramatically on both sides' (2014, p.99; see also O'Reilly et al 2015). The prospects of those with low qualifications is a particular concern. Many have very little chance of employment beyond short-term or zero-hour contracts at the low-pay end of the labour market. Across Europe, amongst 25 to 39 year olds with no more than lower secondary education, employment rates remained steady from 2000 to 2008 but then declined markedly, from 66% in 2007 to 56% in 2013 (European Commission 2017, p.72), suggesting particular difficulties for the least qualified. Young people's early experiences of the labour market are crucial components in their future employment trajectories and wider wellbeing, for example through the scarring effects of early unemployment (O'Reilly et al 2015). Thus, although there may be a slow resumption of economic growth there are extensive concerns that this will be exclusionary and further marginalise disadvantaged youth. Conditions for young people with little or no formal education beyond compulsory schooling are remarkably similar across national contexts, signifying the importance of supranational trends in skills demands related to processes of both globalisation and national policies that we have pointed to and which will be further elaborated in individual chapters

There are gender differences across countries in employment participation, with the highest rates amongst women in the Nordic countries and the lowest in southern Europe (European Commission 2017, p.32). The highest female participation rates are amongst older women, especially those with higher education and seniority in workplaces. The gender employment and pay gap continues and remains an important issue across EU nations although now, notably, women are more highly qualified than men across the EU (European Commission 2017). Despite their higher qualifications on average young women earn less than young men and are more commonly in part-time and temporary jobs (Loi et al 2017).

Uncertainty over the future is a fundamental factor influencing pathways to independent living and to taking on financial commitments of one's own, particularly through family formation. We next consider patterns of leaving home across Europe and offer some brief observations relating to changing fertility patterns. In northern European countries with strong welfare states, especially in Scandinavia, the family is generally less important as a direct source of support than in southern Europe (Buchholz et al 2009; Nilsen et al 2012). However, as the chapters in this book demonstrate, extended family and intergenerational relations remain very important for young people during the transition to adulthood. Their nature and importance vary by country, by social class and by gender. Across European nations, a comparison of ages at leaving the parental home reveals marked differences relating to welfare arrangements, familial interdependencies and cultural expectations, patterns of support across generations, and the nature and availability of housing. Nordic countries manifest the lowest ages at leaving the parental home (the early 20s) whilst southern European nations have the highest at around 30 (Eurofound 2014). Ages at leaving the parental home have manifested some considerable constancy over the long term (Billari and Liefbroer 2010; Eurofound 2014). More recently, from 2000 to 2016, across the EU 28, the average age of leaving the parental home remained steady for males at 27.1 and increased amongst females from 24.7 to 25.1. Italy manifests especially late ages at leaving home, in 2016 on average just over 31 years for men and 29 years amongst women (Eurostat, Data Explorer). The headline figures hide great diversity and some complexity. In their study of the UK, Stone et al (2011) show an extensive prolonging of the period of partially dependent co-residence within the parental home, particularly influenced by increased house prices and reduced financial security and especially marked for disadvantaged groups. For example, approximately one-quarter of those without qualifications and aged 30–34 co-reside with their parents (Stone et al 2011). In Italy, acquiring independent housing is often a family project, with complex negotiations which mark young people's pathways and familial exchanges. Linked subjectivities, values and practices amongst working-class young adults in Italy are taken up in Chapter 8 in this volume by Mattioli and de Luigi.

There is a widely articulated concern that the undermining of economic security for young adults additionally leads to delayed family formation, reduced fertility and increased childlessness. Sobotka and colleagues (2011) urge caution in presuming evidence of causation between economic recession and fertility decline. An adequate economic analysis requires in-depth understanding of diverse opportunity costs to childbearing, costs which cannot be straightforwardly read off from recession, and which vary by gender, education and employment status (Sobotka et al 2011; see also Miettinen 2015). Furthermore, any assessment of economic influences on fertility needs to be informed by an understanding of the cultural contexts in which relevant values, judgements and practices take place (cf. Szreter 1996; Bernardi and Keim 2017). Across European nations there had been some upturn in fertility rates from 2000 onwards, explained in part by an end to the trend of relative postponement, as well as by more family-friendly policies in some countries (Goldstein et al 2013). Patterns of fertility decline have re-occurred since the onset of the recession and these authors conclude that extensive unemployment and uncertainty is manifest in new delays in the timing of first births evidenced across many EU countries from 2009 onwards (Goldstein et al 2013; see also Sobotka et al 2011). In Chapter 10 of this volume, Heady explores the cultural embeddedness of economic and other considerations relevant to fertility decision-making and behaviours.

These questions about transition from the parental home to independent housing and from family of origin to family of destination bring into sharp focus some issues which are under-explored within youth research relating to exchange, support and inter-relatedness across generations. These issues are examined in several chapters in this collection. Relationships across generations have distinct, if overlapping, relevancies in shaping youth-to-adulthood transitions. Firstly, family background and parental socio-economic circumstances are crucial influences on children's life chances. The reproduction of inequalities across generations relates to the economic, social and cultural resources which are passed on within families. This pattern and its manifestation and causality has been the subject of extensive sociological traditions of research and writing since at least the 1960s (eg Bourdieu 1986; Bertaux and Thompson 1997; Bernstein 2000). There is an overlapping question which is sometimes sidelined in empirical research so it is important to identify it separately: specifically, the question of how familial generations share a common social and economic position in respect of labour market and social opportunities (see eg O'Reilly et al 2015). These inequalities – of resource and position – manifest throughout young adults' pathways and transitions in their diverse educational, training and early labour market experiences and in their wider social and cultural participation and agency. These themes are taken up particularly in the chapters by Brannen and colleagues (Chapter 3), Irwin (Chapter 4), MacDonald and Shildrick (Chapter 5), and Jentsch and Reiter (Chapter 6).

The second area in which generational relationships bear on youth as a life course stage and youth transitions is through the familial relations of care and commitment, which lie at the heart of how generational interdependencies are experienced. These interdependencies connecting children and their parents (and grandparents) are shaped through historical, cultural and institutional arrangements. Indeed, the prolonged partial dependence of youth is partly contingent on its accommodation through familial support and parental obligations to support young adult children (cf Irwin 1995). There are interesting and important questions relating to the articulation of subjective orientations and social structural arrangements, and some argue that there has been a long-run shift to a more normative, 'obvious' expectation of parental support in enabling young people towards social independence (eg Brannen 2004). New norms, however, can exclude those whose circumstances do not fit (for example, those who are estranged from their parents or need to support them). Furthermore, everyday practices do not simply follow 'norms' but are contextually embedded and often subject to negotiation. The analysis of pathways to independent housing in Italy by Mattioli and de Luigi in Chapter 8 of this volume neatly exemplifies some of the linked challenges.

Youth transitions have been a recurring theme in the social sciences, studied from a number of perspectives. Theoretical designs and approaches that lend themselves to analysing and examining such questions where the *temporal dimension* is prominent are described below.

Youth studies and a contextualist life course approach across national contexts

In this section we will give a brief outline of methodological themes that are important across the chapters. We also seek to provide a framework that invites a cumulative and comparative reading of the country case study chapters. They all relate to the school-to-work transitions of young men and women, and demonstrate the diversity in transitions that are specific to national contexts but also link to wider structural dimensions that cut across national boundaries. The discussion in the chapters emerges from different but related theoretical and methodological approaches. In the literature, there is a dividing line between youth studies and life course research. However, these two approaches engage with temporal dimensions and address structural aspects of societies as well as individual agency. They thus demonstrate that taking a view across sub-field divides is helpful for providing a richer insight into processes that involve both 'history and biography' (Mills 1959).

Youth studies pay particular attention to the age groups defined as youth and topics related mainly to that life course phase. MacDonald (2011) discusses two main approaches in youth studies and makes a distinction between a *cultural* approach engaged with local youth cultures and a *transitions* approach, which primarily studies transitions from school to work (MacDonald 2011). He takes a long view, discussing the development of youth research in the UK over a 30-year period and suggesting that in order for youth research to gain more relevance in discussions of important social and political issues such as youth unemployment, it would be helpful to bridge the gap between the two perspectives. Furlong et al (2011) discuss the same divide and suggest a social generation approach in order to bridge the gap. Roberts' chapter in the current volume (Chapter 2) traces the traditions of the transitions perspective, whilst MacDonald and Shildrick (Chapter 5) engage with the transitions perspective with reference to a specific set of empirical cases.

There are many definitions and approaches within life course research. Heinz et al (2009, p.15) define life course research as follows:

> As a proper methodological basis for the analysis of social processes, [the life course approach] denotes an interrelationship between individuals and society that evolves as a time-dependent, dynamic linkage between social structure, institutions, and individual action from birth to death.

Elder et al (2006) adopt a term from Merton (1968, cited in Elder et al 2006) and discuss the life course perspective in terms of a *theoretical orientation* and see 'the life course as consisting of age-graded patterns that are embedded in social institutions and history. This view is grounded in a contextualist perspective and emphasises the implications of social pathways in historical time and place for human development and ageing' (p. 4). Elder's definition of the life course is more specifically engaged with the historical context than other definitions, hence a *contextualist* approach.

Historical change happens in a complex process of interactions between social, economic and political factors. It is not the result of inevitable forces of nature. This becomes particularly evident when studying intergenerational processes from a contextualist life course approach. Elder's (1974/1999) study of two cohorts who were children under the Great Depression in the United States, bears testament to the importance of political intervention for what happened in people's lives after the deprivation brought on by the social and economic situation during the 1930s. The Keynesian economic policies after the war created conditions of affluence in Western countries that contributed to lessen the impact of hardship and unemployment some had known in their childhood years during the Great Depression.[1] Combining cross-national perspectives with comparisons across time gives a broader outlook on conditions in the present. Blossfeld (2009), commenting on the usefulness of a life course approach in cross-national comparisons, states that life course studies 'tend to deepen our understanding of cross-national differences when we give a convincing explanation of the impact of institutional and social-cultural conditions on the life course in various nations' (p. 281). In this book, where the life course phase of youth transitions is centre stage, comparisons across contexts give insight into variations and diversity over historical time and across countries.

Throughout this book, the chapters are organised and written in a way that set them in a comparative 'dialogue'. Thematically their specific focus varies dependent on country-level concerns that come across in the research projects. For the purpose of this book, these differences are important dimensions that we have used to identify them as 'cases' located in specific contexts at a particular moment in their history. Hammersley and Gomm (2000) observed that one of the problems with the term 'case study' is that it is used in many different ways. Ragin (1992) wrote about the process of 'casing' in social research and discussed it in terms of a practical activity that is ongoing in any research project. Putting together chapters for a cross-national book is not a research project, but in the framing of the whole the chapters are 'cased' as instances that can be compared and contrasted in order to give insight beyond the single chapters. When we invite a comparative reading across chapters, we emphasise the usefulness of cross-national comparisons. The chapters are written by authors who have situated their research in 'countries as contexts' (Kohn 1987; Brannen and Nilsen 2011); as 'cases of' youth transitions, generational relationships and class-related inequalities that are temporal and spatially bound.

The chapters may be considered as 'cases' of questions that are specific to particular national contexts within the overarching theme of youth transitions and social inequality. We have arranged them in an order that reflects this dimension. The next chapter in the volume is devoted to an overview of the theoretical approaches in youth studies, by one of the leading names and a pioneer in the field, Ken Roberts. In Chapter 2, *Youth research meets life course terminology: the transitions paradigm revisited*, Roberts explores broad theoretical discussions informing youth research. He outlines the development of 'the transitions paradigm', and its association with sociology's claim to being the lead discipline in the study of youth. Roberts considers the distinctive merits of 'transitions' vis-à-vis other paradigms and the challenges involved in extending its use beyond education-to-employment transitions. For Roberts, a key research challenge is to generate understanding of how the period of youth is critical for framing life course trajectories and how this varies across historical and social contexts. Roberts advocates 'transitions' as the lead paradigm for advancing knowledge and describes its merits vis-à-vis alternative conceptual framings. The centrality of the history-biography dynamic is thus underlined in Roberts' discussion of the transitions paradigm.

Chapter 3, *Transitions from school to work in Norway and Britain among three family generations of working-class men* (Brannen, Vogt, Nilsen, and Knight), provides a cross-national comparison of the school-to-work transition of working-class men in the two countries. Based on biographical interviews with members of three generations in each family, it discusses working-class men's transitions set in the contexts of historical change and intergenerational relations. Theoretically the chapter relates to a contextualist life course approach. The data shows both differences and similarities between the two countries over time. The overall changes in employment opportunities for working-class men in the youngest generation are similar and reflect the increase in manufacturing jobs being moved to other parts of the world and the processes of globalisation analysed by Buchholz et al (2009). Although public spending on education and welfare is relatively higher in Norway than in Britain, the role of intergenerational support for young men has gained in importance in both contexts.

In Chapter 4, *How parents see their children's future: education, work and social change in England*, Irwin explores the perspectives of parents as their children grow up and approach young adulthood. She considers changing educational arrangements, the restructuring of youth labour market opportunities and rewards, recession and longer-run economic changes. How are young people and their families positioned in these changing contexts and how is change experienced and negotiated across diverse class circumstances? Irwin draws on qualitative longitudinal data generated when the parents' children were approaching young adulthood in the context of recession and austerity. She explores parents' perspectives on their teenage children's educational and labour market prospects and on their wider chances for securing a decent living. In so doing, she illuminates commonalities and class-related differences in the experiences, orientations and practices of parents supporting their children's progression to adulthood.

The focus is still on Britain in Chapter 5, *Biography, history and place: understanding youth transitions in Teeside* (Shildrick and MacDonald), but this time on a very specific place that is emblematic of de-industrialisation, Teesside. The chapter brings together and discusses a series of research projects first begun in the late 1990s – *the Teesside Studies of Youth Transitions and Social Exclusion*. The focus is on the way in which young people make transitions to adulthood in the context of declining opportunities for secure employment, reduced social security for young adults and austerity cuts to youth services, in a place that has high levels of multiple deprivation. The chapter describes these studies and offers a summary overview of their main thematic insights, then offers analysis of the social, economic, geographic, historical and political contexts shaping the biographies and transitions of economically marginalised youth. The authors explore the processes and decisions that result in the economic marginality of places and populations, and argue for the necessity of a form of sociological analysis capable of making sense of the complexities of individual biographies and addressing the pressing policy problems that relate to 'socially excluded youth'.

In contrast to many of the other countries, Germany saw a more limited impact of the 2008 crisis. Chapter 6, *Social inequality and the transition to education and training: the significance of family background in Germany* (Jentsch and Reiter), explores problems of inequality from a different angle that demonstrates how the tie between family background and educational achievement is strong compared to other European countries, a pattern linked to early tracking in the schooling system. The chapter provides an overview of the highly specialised German education system and highlights the importance of family background at different points of selection throughout young people's education trajectories, and how these processes are important in the reproduction of social inequality. Despite the widely admired and vaunted status which is attached to German vocational training, the least qualified encounter increasing difficulty securing a foothold in vocational education and training (VET) and the labour market.

Chapter 7, *Youth transitions and generations in Portugal: examining change between baby-boomers and millennials* (Alves), explores patterns of change in youth transitions in Portugal against the backdrop of the country's contemporary history which sets it apart from most of its EU partner countries. Portugal had an extremely long period of autocratic rule (1926–1974) during which time it was a colonial power but had a fragile economy and a limited welfare state, especially in public policies and benefits relevant for young people. The specific history that still informs many of its economic and social characteristics has been responsible for the wide gap between rich and poor, and for prolonging already difficult transitions of young people, which were exacerbated by the 2008 crisis. This chapter analyses a set of historical statistics relating to the age group 15–29 in different periods with special reference to education and employment. It also draws on qualitative interviews with this age group in 2012–2013 during the most difficult years of the crisis to give an in-depth understanding of conditions for Portuguese youth. The topic of emigration comes up in the interviews and in the statistical material, demonstrating that Portugal has a long history of people emigrating during difficult times; it is not a phenomenon restricted to the last years of crisis.

Chapter 8, *Young people and housing transitions: the role of intergenerational support in an Italian working-class context* (Mattioli and De Luigi), explores morals and practices relating to extreme shortages of independent housing for young people as well as intergenerational support in working-class families when young adults seek to leave home. The global financial crisis of 2008, austerity policies and a weakening of welfare provision further increased young people's structural dependency on their families. Based on qualitative interviews with parents and young people, the authors explore the specific contexts where support is provided and negotiated, and examine ideas of independence, moral values and intergenerational relationships in times of increasing inequality. The chapter analyses the subjective experiences of parents who give financial and in-kind support and of adult children who receive it and offers insights into some of the ways in which moral obligations between generations are translated into actions and tensions which can arise.

Chapter 9, *Young people and recession in Greece: searching for a better future* (Sakellariou and Koronaiou), explores young people's perceptions and attitudes towards aspects of the economic crisis in Greece, asking how young people reflect on and respond to the circumstances in the society in which they live. The chapter examines young people's viewpoints, emotions and values during a crucial period of their lives and under the exceptional circumstances of deep crisis – economic, social and political – in Greek society. Based on qualitative research conducted at the peak of the crisis in 2013, the chapter explores how young people were affected by the crisis, how they saw Greek society under crisis and what futures they saw for themselves. Additionally, the authors consider how young people perceived the role of the family and intergenerational relations, and their perspectives on the extensive outward migration pursued by many young adults.

Chapter 10, *Kinship, community and the transition to adulthood – geographical differences and recent changes in European society* (Heady), addresses transitions to adulthood from a social anthropological approach with reference to two aspects: economic and socio-spatial placement. The first part focuses on processes of socio-spatial placement as coherent social sub-systems and as aspects of a wider socio-economic reality. The second part explores how these systems are affected by economic transformation and the resources which they offer for dealing with economic and social stress. A series of comparative statistical studies over the past decades have demonstrated that the timing of the transition to adulthood, and the order in which the different steps take place, vary considerably between different European regions – and that these differences are correlated with aspects of spatial and kinship organisation in the regions concerned, demonstrating the complex and embedded nature of transition processes.

Note

1 Elder's study was groundbreaking at the time since most longitudinal research in psychology aimed to arrive at knowledge that would transcend time and space. Elder's study rather emphasised the importance of the historical context (Nilsen and Brannen 2010). The contextualist approach takes the historical period into the study as an important dimension and thus demonstrates how social processes are embedded in a specific time and place.

References

Allmendinger, J. and von den Driesch, E. (2014) *Social inequalities in Europe: facing the challenges*, Berlin Social Science Center (WZB) Discussion Paper P2014–2005. Berlin: Berlin Social Science Center

Antonucci, L., Hamilton, M. and Roberts, S. (2014) 'Constructing a theory of youth and social policy', in Antonucci, L., Hamilton, M. and Roberts, S. (eds) *Young people and social policy in Europe: dealing with risk, inequality and precarity in times of crisis*. Houndmills: Palgrave Macmillan, Chapter 2

Bernardi, L. and Keim, S. (2017) 'Childlessness at age 30: a qualitative study of the life course plans of working women in East and West Germany', in Kreyenfeld, M. and Konietzka, D. (eds) *Childlessness in Europe: contexts, causes and consequences*, Demographic Research Monographs, pp. 253–267. Open Access. doi:10.1007/978-3-319-44667-7_12

Bernstein, B. (2000) *Pedagogy, symbolic control and identity: theory, research, critiques*. Oxford: Rowman and Littlefield

Bertaux, D. and ThompsonP. (1997) *Pathways to social class: a qualitative approach to social mobility*. Oxford: Clarendon Press

Biggart, A., Jarvinen, T. and Parreira do Amaral, M. (2015) 'Institutional frameworks and structural factors relating to educational access across Europe', *European Education*, 47(1), 26–45

Billari, F.C. and Liefbroer, A.C. (2010) 'Towards a new pattern of transition to adulthood?', *Advances in Life Course Research*, 15, 59–75

Blanchard, O. (2006) 'European unemployment: the evolution of facts and ideas', *Economic Policy*, 21(45), 6–59

Blossfeld, H-P (2009) 'Comparative life course research: a cross-national and longitudinal perspective', in Elder, G. and Giele, J. (eds) *The craft of life course research*. New York: Guilford Press, pp. 280–306

Bourdieu, P. (1986) 'The forms of capital', in Samson, J. (ed.) *Handbook of theory and research for the sociology of education*. New York: Greenwood, pp. 241–258.

Brannen, J. (2004) 'Cultures of intergenerational transmission in four-generation families', *Sociological Review*, 54(1), 133–154

Brannen, J. and Nilsen, A. (2011) 'Comparative biographies in case-based cross-national research: methodological considerations', *Sociology*, 45(4), 603–618

Breen, R. (ed) (2004) *Social mobility in Europe*. Oxford: Oxford University Press

Brown, P., Lauder, H. and Ashton, D. (2011) *The global auction: the broken promises of education, jobs and incomes*. New York: Oxford University Press

Buchholz, S., Hofäcker, D., Mills, M., Blossfeld, H-P., Kurz, K. and Hofmeister, H. (2009) 'Life courses in the globalisation process: the development of social inequalities in modern societies', *European Sociological Review*, 25(1), 53–71

Buchholz, S. and Kolb, K. (2011) 'Selective flexibilization and deregulation of the labour market: the German answer to increased needs for employment flexibility and its consequences for social inequalities', in Blossfeld, H-P., Buchholz, S., Hofacker, D. and Kolb, K. (eds) *Globalized labour markets and social inequality in Europe*, Basingstoke: Palgrave Macmillan, pp. 25–45

Buchmann, M. and Kriesi, I. (2011) 'Transition to adulthood in Europe', *Annual Review of Sociology*, 37, 481–403

Bukodi, E., Ebralidze, E., Schmelzer, P. and Blossfeld, H-P. (2008) 'Struggling to become an insider: does increasing flexibility at labor market entry affect early careers? A theoretical framework', in Blossfeld, H-P., Buchholz, S., Bukodi, E. and Kurz, K. (eds) *Young workers, globalization and the labor market*. Cheltenham: Edward Elgar

Burda, M.C. and Hunt, J. (2011) 'What explains the German labour market miracle in the Great Recession?' *Brookings Papers on Economic Activity*, Spring, Brookings Institute

Elder, G. (1999 [1974]) *Children of the Great Depression: social change in life experience*. Boulder, CO: Westview Press

Elder, G., JohnsonM.K. and CrosnoeR. (2006) 'The emergence and development of life course research', in Mortimer, J.T. and Shanahan, M. (eds) *Handbook of the life course*. New York: Springer, pp. 3–22

Esping Andersen, G. (1990) *The three worlds of welfare capitalism*. Princeton, NJ: Princeton University Press

Eurofound (2014) *Mapping youth transitions in Europe*. Luxembourg: Publications Office of the European Union.

European Commission (2015) *Compulsory education in Europe – 2015/2016. Eurydice facts and figures*. Luxembourg: Publication Office of the European Union

European Commission (2017) *Employment and social developments in Europe: Annual Review 2017*. Brussels: European Union

Eurostat (2017) 'Europe 2020 Indicators'. Retrieved from http://ec.europa.eu/eurostat/statistics-explained/index.php/Europe_2020_indicators_-_education

Eurostat (n.d.) *Data explorer*. Retrieved from http://ec.europa.eu/eurostat/data/database

Furlong, A., Woodman, D. and Wyn, J. (2011) 'Changing times, changing perspectives: reconciling 'transition' and 'cultural' perspectives on youth and young adulthood', *Journal of Sociology*, 47(4), 355–370

George, A., Metcalf, H., Tufekci, L. and Wilkinson, D. (2015) *Understanding age and the labour market*. York: Joseph Rowntree Foundation

Goldstein, J.R., Kreyenfeld, M., Jasilioniene, A. and Orsal, D.K. (2013) 'Fertility reactions to the Great Recession in Europe: recent evidence from order-specific data', *Demographic Research*, 29(4), 85–104

Goldthorpe, J. and Mills, C. (2008) 'Trends in intergenerational class mobility in modern Britain: evidence from national surveys 1972–2005'. *National Institute Economic Review*, 205, 83–100

Hammersley, M. and Gomm, R. (2000) 'Introduction', in Gomm, R., Hammersley, M. and Foster, P. (eds) *Case study method*. London: Sage, pp. 1–16.

Heinz, W., Huinink, J., Swader, C.S. and Weyman, A. (eds) (2009) *The life course reader*. Frankfurt/Main: Campus Verlag, pp. 15–30

Hobsbawm, E. (1994) *Age of extremes: the short twentieth century*. London: Michael Joseph

Irwin, S. (1995) *Rights of passage: social change and the transition from youth to adulthood*. London: UCL Press

Kohn, M.L. (1987) 'Cross-national research as an analytic strategy: American Sociological Association 1987 presidential address', *American Sociological Review*, 52(6), 713–731

Kumar, K. (1978) *Prophecy and progress: the sociology of industrial and post-industrial*. London: Penguin Press

Loi, D., Patrizio, M. and Lodovici, M.S. (2017) *Young women's unemployment in EU*, EU Policy Department for Citizens' Rights and Constitutional Affairs, www.europarl.europa.eu/RegData/etudes/BRIE/2017/583125/IPOL_BRI(2017)583125_EN.pdf

MacDonald, R. (2011) 'Youth transitions, unemployment and underemployment: plus ça change, plus c'est la même chose?' *Journal of Sociology*, 47(4), 427–444

Miettinen, A., Rotkirch, A., Szalma, I., Donno, A. and Tanturri, M. (2015) *Increasing childlessness in Europe: time trends and country differences*. Families and Societies Working Paper Series. Retrieved from www.familiesandsocieties.eu/wp-content/up loads/2015/03/WP33MiettinenEtAl2015.pdf

Mills, C.W. (1980 [1959]) *The sociological imagination*. London: Penguin

Nilsen, A. and Brannen, J. (2010) 'The use of mixed methods in biographical research', in Tashakkori, A. and Teddlie, C. (eds), *Sage handbook in social and behavioural research*. London: Sage, pp. 677–697

Nilsen, A., Brannen, J. and Lewis, S. (eds) (2012) *Transitions to parenthood in Europe: a comparative life course perspective*. Bristol: Policy Press

Oakley, A. (1974) *Housewife*. London: Allen Lane

OECD (2011) *Divided we stand: why inequality keeps rising*, OECD country note: Germany, www.oecd.org/els/social/inequality

OECD (2017) *Employment outlook 2017*. Paris: OECD Publishing. http://dx.doi.org/10.1787/empl_outlook-2017-en

O'Reilly, J., Eicchhorst, W., Gabos, A. et al (2015) 'Five characteristics of youth unemployment in Europe: flexibility, education, migration, family legacies and EU policy', *Sage Open*, Jan–March 2015, 1–19, *Creative Commons*

Raffe, D. (2014) 'Explaining national differences in education-work transitions', *European Societies*, 16(2), 175–193

Ragin, C.C. (1992) '"Casing" and the process of social inquiry', in Becker, H.C. (ed) *What is a case? Exploring the foundations of social inquiry*. Cambridge: Cambridge University Press, pp. 217–226.

Sobotka, T., Skirbekk, V. and Philipov, D. (2011) 'Economic recession and fertility in the developed world', *Population and Development Review*, 37(2), 267–306

Stiglitz, J. (2012) *The price of inequality*. London: Penguin

Stone, J., Berrington, A. and Falkingham, J. (2011) 'The changing determinants of UK young adults' living arrangements', *Demographic Research*, 25(20), 629–666. doi:10.4054/DemRes.2011. 25. 20

Szreter, S. (1996) *Fertility, class and gender in Britain, 1860–1940*. Cambridge: Cambridge University Press.

Taylor-Gooby, P. (2013) 'Why do people stigmatise the poor at a time of rapidly increasing inequality, and what can be done about it?' *The Political Quarterly*, 84(1), 31–42

Vogt, K. (2017) 'Age norms and early school leaving', *European Societies*. http://dx.doi.org/10.1080/14616696.2017.1358391

Walther, A. (2006) 'Regimes of youth transitions: choice, flexibility and security in young people's experiences across European contexts', *Young. Nordic Journal of Youth Research*, 14(2), 119–139

Wærness, K. (1978) 'The invisible welfare state: women's work at home', *Acta Sociologica*, 21, 193–207

2 Youth research meets life course terminology

The transitions paradigm revisited

Ken Roberts

Introduction

Today's youth researchers are likely to define their field as the study of youth transitions, or more fully, the study of youth life stage transitions. However. 'transitions' is just one of several paradigms that are available, that have been and are still employed in the study of youth. 'Paradigm' is used here in Thomas Kuhn's sense (Kuhn, 1962): a prescribed set of problems to be investigated, questions asked, and methods to be adopted in a scientific field. Kuhn argued that in periods of 'normal science', one dominant paradigm prevailed, but this has never been the case in sociology, and among youth researchers there are several paradigms, all complementary. It is unnecessary to reject all others in order to highlight and exploit the special merits of any one. The key advantage of the transitions paradigm lies in its ability to embed the study of youth within the longer life course. The paradigm involves the application of an origins-routes-destinations model, thereby establishing connections to longer-term life stories. Youth follows childhood and is followed by adulthood, which is followed by later life. Each life stage is a transition. Adults have youth as their origin: adulthood is the origin of seniors. Every life stage involves a set of journeys from entrance to exit. With the exceptions of birth and death, points of entry and exit cannot be specified as precise moments in time, though such moments must be selected for operational purposes in order to focus on and analyse any selected stage in life of which youth is one.

In youth research, the transitions paradigm has been pioneered in the study of transitions from education into employment. The following passages outline the development of the paradigm, and how its adoption was associated with sociology replacing psychology as the lead discipline in the study of youth. We then consider the distinctive merits of 'transitions' vis-à-vis other paradigms that are available for use by youth researchers, and the challenges involved in extending its use beyond education-to-employment transitions. We then look forward to a time when the youth transitions paradigm will establish whether youth is *the* critical life stage when life courses become irrevocably set or reset, and if so and when, exactly how and for whom. We shall see that the answers are likely to vary depending on the life domain, place and time. This chapter is defending and advocating 'transitions' as the lead paradigm for the sociology of youth as the lead discipline in the youth field. The pre-eminence of sociology is merited because of the extent to which youth, like all other life stages, is a social construct rather than a universal whose main features are dictated by human biology. The pre-eminence of the transitions paradigm is merited because, above all else, youth is a transitional life stage, and application of the transitions paradigm offers a more true-to-life portrait than one of the alternative paradigms, once dominant but now visibly out-of-date, which is to define and profile youth as an age group.

First, we must distinguish between the real-life social transitions that sociology examines and legal transitions. In all countries there are precise ages when young people become able to vote, to be elected or appointed to a public office, to open a bank account, to obtain a bank loan, to be subject to adult courts and adult judicial penalties, able to marry, consent to sexual intimacy, to claim welfare benefits as independent citizens, to purchase alcohol and tobacco, and to terminate their formal education. Until the 1970s it was normal for young people in Britain to quit education forever as soon as they were legally able to do so (at age 15 until 1972). At that time most of these school-leavers soon became established in occupations that they could hope to retain indefinitely. It is still the case that some young people in Britain exit education forever as soon as this becomes legally possible (now age 18). They are unlikely today to step directly into occupations that they might wish to occupy or are able to retain for the long term, and it has always been the case that the process of developing career aims and gaining work experience has begun long before the point of terminating education. Likewise, young people can begin to develop political opinions and identities long before they are able to vote. Alternatively, they may remain politically inactive and indifferent long after they become eligible to vote in elections. Similarly, many young people become sexually active before this is legally permissible while others remain inactive for many years beyond. In all these examples, real-life youth transitions occur across extended time spans. They do not take place abruptly, at precise ages, by legal command. Changes in the law may or may not lead to, and may or may not follow, changes in young people's actual behaviour. Youth transitions are processes – series of movements in positions and changes in internal psychological states that normally extend over many years, from occupying typically child-like positions and possessing child-like dispositions, to occupying positions and possessing dispositions that are typical of adults in the societies in which they live. These are the processes on which the youth transitions paradigm focuses. This does not merely offer the most authentic descriptions of youth at particular points in historical time and in specific places, but enhances comparisons, the identification of differences and similarities between the youth life stage in different places and at different points in history.

Historical background

The psychology of the adolescent

Throughout most of the 20th century, psychology was the lead discipline in youth studies. The field was founded when the American psychologist, G Stanley Hall, 'discovered' the adolescent at the beginning of the century (Hall, 1904). Subsequently, the standard approach to explaining all distinctive youthful behaviour including delinquency and youth cultures was in terms of the bio-psychological challenges posed by growing through adolescence. Youth became an age group, the adolescent age group. In America the term 'youth' has remained anchored to the high school years (12–18). In the UK it became 14–21, the age group for which statutory youth services were made available by the 1918 Education Act. During the late 20th century and subsequently, adulthood has been reached at later ages, and American researchers have been coining new concepts to describe a post-youth life stage: arrested adulthood (Cote, 2000) and emerging adulthood (Arnett, 2005). In southern Europe and North Africa, this new post-youth life stage is often called 'waithood' (Dhillon and Yousef, 2009).

Before the Second World War, youth (then called juvenile) unemployment and blind alley, dead-end jobs, and their implications for adolescent development, were leading public and research issues. Then after 1945 full employment and the high profile of affluent young workers demoted, indeed banished, youth unemployment from youth research agendas. However, psychology remained the lead discipline in such school-leaving research as was conducted. Its core issues were whether school-leavers were being adequately prepared to make momentous occupational choices (Carter, 1962; Maizels, 1970; Veness, 1962) and whether they could cope with the potentially traumatic change from being seniors in their secondary schools to the most junior employees in adult workplaces (Tenen, 1947). This was the central issue in the infamous but now recovered 'lost Elias project' (Goodwin and O'Connor, 2006).

The sociology of youth

The studies that have become part of present-day sociology's collective memory which stressed how easily entry into employment difficulties were normally resolved, and explained this in terms of family and educational backgrounds aligning expectations and ambitions with the opportunities that were available (Ashton and Field, 1976; Roberts, 1968; Willis, 1977), were not core contributions to either that era's school-leaving research or its sociology of youth. Delinquency and youth cultures were the hot issues for sociologists who studied young people, and where psychology's hold on the field was first challenged The initial challenges were launched before 1945 by American social anthropologists and sociologists. Margaret Mead explained that youth was very different in Samoa (Mead, 1928). Chicago sociologists argued that boy gangs and delinquency were sub-cultural – normal behaviour in the age group within the relevant ethnic and neighbourhood communities (Thrasher, 1936; Whyte, 1943). These arguments were taken up by British sociologists in the 1950s and 60s, initially in relation to delinquency by John Mays (1954), then in the interpretations of post-war youth cultures that emanated from Birmingham University's Centre for Contemporary Cultural Studies (Hall and Jefferson, 1976).

Between the 1950s and 70s, Britain became the lead site for studies of youth cultures. This can be explained in terms of Britain having more early school-leavers (at age 15 until 1972), who could progress rapidly to adult earnings in non-skilled jobs, than either other European countries or North America. Britain's affluent young workers had money to spend on distinctive fashions, recorded music and transport (motor bikes and scooters). These were the decades when London became a serious rival to New York as a centre for music publishing. This has given American and UK artists an enduring advantage in reaching global audiences.

In Britain, sociology decisively dislodged psychology from prime ownership of youth studies only in the 1970s when mass youth unemployment returned and the school-to-work transition once more became *the* hot public and youth research issue, a position retained to the present day. Youth's new condition was clearly not explicable in terms of, and could not be 'solved', by addressing the bio-psychological dramas of adolescence, though this has not inhibited psychology-based researchers from investigating whether 'resilience' and persistence enable individuals to overcome setbacks (for example, Schoon, 2006). Social psychology has responded energetically to Ulrich Beck's claim that globalisation and economic restructuring are creating a new kind of 'risk society' (Beck, 1992). Socio-economic structures are said to be loosening, creating scope for an 'entrepreneurial self' (Kelly, 2006) and for individuals to construct their own 'choice biographies' (Peters, 1995) via the paths that they select at 'critical moments' in their lives (Thomson et al, 2002). However, this neglects the economic and social psychological support that continued to flow reciprocally between generations (see Irwin, 1995; Nilsen and Brannen, 2014). Also, entrepreneurial selves can navigate only through the opportunities that are immediately available to young people such as themselves, of a specific sex and age, with specific qualifications, and in particular places. They can head only towards employment that is on offer in the labour markets to which their searches are confined. The net effect of boosting young unemployed people's efforts to obtain work is either greater crush, congestion and frustration at ports of job entry, or more 'churning' on the fringes of the labour market (see Worth, 2005).

However, throughout the 1970s and 80s youth remained an age group in public discourse and for research purposes. In the mid-1980s Britain's Economic and Social Research Council launched a programme of research, the *16–19 Initiative*, which was to identify and clarify the operation of teenagers' old and new routes through post-compulsory education and training (Banks et al,

1992). A (mistaken) assumption in the mid-1980s was that by age 19 individuals' adult occupational destinations would be known. Those progressing through higher education were believed (mistakenly) to be assured of privileged futures.

Britain's investigators began treating youth as an extended life stage only when its youth research was Europeanised during the 1980s. Germany and adjacent countries had always been comfortable with an extended notion of youth encompassing everyone serving apprenticeships and in higher education. Southern Europe was equally at ease with an extended definition of youth: individuals were treated as remaining in the life stage until they exited their parents' homes, typically only on marriage in their late 20s or beyond. Communist countries' youth organisations mobilised 16–28 year olds (Wallace and Kovacheva, 1998). Transnational research networks began to classify countries according to their youth transition regimes, each comprising a distinctive set of routes through upper secondary and higher education and vocational training (see Raffe, 2008, 2014). Attempts were made to link these youth transition regimes to employment regimes, distinguishing those that were occupationalised from others (Gangl, 2001), and to Esping-Andersen's (1990) typology of welfare regimes (Hammer, 2003). At that time, typologies of youth life stage regimes were based on, and have remained largely confined to, education-to-work transitions. A question and challenge for the transitions paradigm (which is considered below) is whether the paradigm can be applied in other life domains – families, housing, welfare, leisure and politics.

Merits of the transitions paradigm

The appeal of the transitions paradigm among education-to-work researchers becomes evident when contrasted with the age group profiling that it has challenged. When youth is treated as an age group, its investigators profile its members in terms of their positions in education and training, whether they are living at home or have moved out, and uses of free time and money (see, for example, Emmett, 1971; Park et al, 2005). They can show how these profiles change each year as individuals grow older. Profiles of an age group can be disaggregated by gender, ethnicity, family social class, prior education attainments and so on. Snapshot profiles can take us this far. If repeated they can chart any changes over time and indicate whether government interventions are making a difference, by boosting levels of sport participation and much else. The transitions paradigm adds to this by offering a more realistic, more fluid, more dynamic portrait of youth. A transitions paradigm seeks typical sequences of positions in education, training and employment, and we shall see below that it may do the same with residential arrangements and intimate relationships. Youth becomes a process rather than a state. The paradigm recognises that lives change while successive positions remain interconnected in stable or changing ways. There are not three stable states: childhood, youth and adulthood. There is movement throughout all three. Young people aged 16–20 do not want to hang out in places used by younger kids. Those in their late-20s may prefer not to be confused with students. In 2017 it was interesting, and highly policy relevant and challenging, to be shown that the under-35s were the sole working age group whose incomes had not recovered to levels prior to the 2008 banking crisis, and that the age group had been progressivly forced out of home ownership by low wages and rising house prices (Corlett et al, 2017). It would cost more, but add significant value, to learn which 25–35 year olds in 2008 had experienced increases in their real incomes by 2017, how this had been achieved, and whether the eventual winners could have been predicted from their childhood origins.

This is what the transitions paradigm can add. It seeks to identify and separate young people into different 'career groups', each characterised by a typical sequence of positions and experiences. Up to now the careers usually handled by the transitions paradigm have been from education into employment, but in principle other life domains can be treated in the same manner (see below). The origins and destinations of different career groups can be compared. Both origins and destinations may vary in specificity, which can be measured: whether those recruited into youth career groups share common origins, and whether they are all delivered to very similar destinations. It can be shown that the ages when transitions start and end vary by time and place. This applies whether the transitions are from education into working life, family and housing situations, or leisure practices. Historical changes over time can be identified: how since the mid-20th century youth transitions have typically lengthened. Investigators can also assess the extent to which youth transitions have been destandardised, meaning a collapse or weakening of normative sequences such as obtaining an adult job prior to embarking on parenting. 'Individualisation' – greater variety in transitional experiences within socio-demographic groups – can also be assessed. In all these ways, the transitions paradigm clearly offers advances beyond what can be achieved by profiling an age group.

The transitions paradigm's associated merit arises from embedding youth in the longer-term life course. It thereby promises to establish whether youth really is *the* critical life stage that is often assumed. Initiatives are commonly targeted at young people. The assumption is that if given the right youth education or training, adult employment careers will flourish. It is regularly claimed, or hoped, that if captured during youth, which is possible given the fluidity of young people's lives, then individuals will remain in sport, or the arts, or politically engaged, for the rest of their lives. This is indeed possible but as yet unproven. It will remain forever unproven if youth research simply profiles the age group. The other possibility is that youth careers in sport, the arts and politics are likely to be short-lived unless they are built on foundations laid in childhood. Another possibility is that adult behaviour responds to circumstances and opportunities that arise at the time. The future lives of America's children of the Great Depression of the 1930s were rescued by the Second World War, then the full employment and economic growth that followed (Elder, 1974). Many young people in Britain who believed that apprenticeships served in the 1950s and 60s would make them 'skilled for life' discovered otherwise during the economic restructuring that occurred in the following decades (Goodwin and O'Connor, 2007, 2009). That said, we now know that prolonged unemployment invariably has some long-term scarring effects, and these effects are especially severe when those concerned are young people (Tumino, 2015). Youth researchers routinely justify claims for research funds and proclaim the importance of their field in terms of the role of the life stage in laying foundations on which future lives are based. The transitions paradigm offers the means to test and thereby substantiate this claim or, more likely, to become more precise about the types of interventions, when and for whom the claims can be justified.

The case for the transitions paradigm is not new (see Elder et al, 2003; Heinz, 2009). This case needs to be restated repeatedly because the relevant research is more expensive in terms of time and money than snapshot profiling, and the rewards still remain mainly potential rather than accomplishments.

Other paradigms: complementary or competitors?

Generations

Transitions can be used alongside other youth research paradigms. There is some value in profiles, but identifying transition sequences adds enormous value. The same applies to a generations paradigm, which involves identifying changes over historical time in the youth life stage. This is simply different, complementary to using a transitions paradigm. Wyn and Woodman (2006), Woodman and Wyn (2015), and Woodman and Bennett (2015a, 2015b) have been powerful advocates in promoting 'generation' as a core concept in youth research. The position argued below is that 'transitions' and 'generations' are best kept as alternative, complementary but distinct paradigms. Alone or when used jointly, each is strongest when not blended. Youth cultures is likewise best kept as an alternative, complementary paradigm, but one which can be strengthened by aligning it with youth 'transitions' and 'generations' perspectives.

Change over time is certainly not a neglected feature in youth research. In the 1950s and 60s, youth pre-1939 was usually an implicit comparison group. Since the 1970s the comparison group has been youth in the 1950s and 60s. The evidence is available in Britain to chart historical changes using a transitions paradigm. The necessary data has been collected in the successive birth cohort studies, starting with those born in 1946, then 1958, then 1970, and youth transitions data from those born in 2000 is now becoming available. The data sets of the oldest cohorts now cover the samples' lives through childhood, then youth and into adulthood, and into later life in the case of the 1946 birth cohort. Data that captures historical youth transitions is also available in the life histories collected in the *British Household Panel Study* which began in 1991 and has now been assimilated into the larger *Understanding Society* panel.

Identifying changes over time is uncontroversial, but there are serious as yet unresolved and indeed barely addressed difficulties in importing the generation concept into youth research (see Nilsen and Brannen, 2014). There is something different about young people's experiences and opportunities in every decade. Youth is never exactly the same as before. So exactly what needs to change, and by how much, before an upcoming cohort is announced as the vanguard of a new generation? The term loses its power when used interchangeably with cohort. It is easy to apply the term generation to families – children, their siblings and cousins, then their parents, aunts and uncles, then grandparents and then great-grandparents. Generations can be identified in politics when new ideas are worked into policies by politicians and used to mobilise support. However, the authors of the new ideas, the politicians and their supporters, can be from any age group. A new political generation is defined not by age but in relation to its predecessor.

In relation to youth, talk of new generations is most easily justified following major historical ruptures like the World Wars in 20th-century Europe when those who fought and then returned, and those who grew up afterwards, experienced different conditions, or experienced the old conditions differently, to those who grew up earlier. Communist generations were formed after 1917 in the Soviet Union and after 1945 in Central and South-East Europe. Post-communist generations have been in formation since 1989. These are comparable to the post-independence generations in former colonies and the post-apartheid generation in South Africa. Those who have grown up subsequently treat national independence, democracy, a market economy or whatever applies as simply normal rather than achievements for which those who fought deserve perpetual gratitude. Set against these ruptures, rock 'n roll and the internet look like minor ripples rather than generation-making innovations. Globalisation, de-industrialisation and the expansion of higher education have occurred too gradually to act in a similar way in separating a new vanguard from an earlier generation. These changes began before the 1970s, but it was only then that they began to disrupt what had become normal post-1945 education-to-employment transitions. The first to be affected were the least qualified earliest school-leavers in Western Europe's weaker economies. Subsequently, disruption has spread gradually throughout Europe, from 16–18 year olds, to those up to age 21, then 25 and currently beyond. It has affected young people with intermediate qualifications and nowadays those with higher education. It seems still too soon to declare complete the formation of a successor to the post-1945 generation.

Youth cultures

This is another paradigm, used by many youth researchers. Like generations, it is entirely compatible with a transitions paradigm. Occasional outbursts of sparring are due mainly to differences in preferred research methods and types of evidence, as when Cohen and Ainley (2000) urged rejection of transitions in favour of studying youth cultures. Actually the two paradigms provide complementary evidence so there is really no need to make an either/or choice. However, it is true that these paradigms prioritise different kinds of evidence. Transitions are identified from sequences of positions that individuals occupy. Young people are seen as following routes that are pre-structured by the stratification of families, the organisation of education, the operation of labour and housing markets, the leisure opportunities to which they have access, and so on. Individuals are able to be agentic, to navigate, but only within limits. Exploring the cultural dimension (which pervades the whole of people's lives, not just leisure and youth cultures as commonly understood) involves probing inside individuals' minds. Cultures may prove common throughout, unifying and distinguishing socio-demographic groups, but they can be accessed only through how individuals think, and the meanings that they attach to their own and other people's behaviour.

People can recall positions that they occupied in the past, so 'careers' in education, employment, housing and in structured leisure activities such as sports can be accessed retrospectively. In contrast, individuals cannot be relied on to recall how they felt and what they believed years or even months ago. Longitudinal evidence needs to be collected prospectively and 'soft' qualitative research methods enjoy advantages. It is simply impossible to cover samples of the size and to extend this type of research over the periods of time that would be necessary to build the equivalent of 'objective' career data. There have been exceptions (for example, Henderson et al, 2007), but most studies of youth cultures are snapshots. They are best used, and most useful, alongside evidence from transitions and generations paradigms, illustrating states of mind during specific episodes and at specific historical time periods within career tracks. Standing alone, studies of youth cultures have the same limitations as all snapshots. There are no sensible grounds for abandoning the transitions paradigm and relying wholly on cultural studies. This is despite still unresolved problems in operationalising the transitions paradigm and extending its use across all life domains.

Challenges for the transitions paradigm

Start and end points

This is a challenge that all youth researchers confront. It has become impossible to identify precise start and end points for youth in present-day biographies. This is the change that has made snapshot profiling obsolete. Woodman and Wyn (2015) follow Cohen and Ainley (2000) in focusing on present-day cases where individuals become 30-something without establishing themselves in long-term career occupations. They note that what was once 'youth' employment and, in many cases, broader youth lifestyles, have spread into and become indistinguishable from adults' jobs and ways of living.

In practice, all paradigms have no difficulty in coping with fuzzy beginnings and ends to youth. For operational purposes, education-to-work transitions can be considered complete once individuals have exited and not returned to full-time, normally pre-career education and training. Otherwise 'now' can always be the default destination for everyone who has left education and training and who has moved out of the parental home. 'Now' can be their default adult destinations in employment, housing, family situations, politics, leisure practices and as recipients of state welfare. A mixture of temporary, part-time jobs and unemployment can be an adult destination. All paradigms can cope routinely with different start and end points in different life domains. Start points can be first optional courses in education, first romantic attachment, first exit from the parental home, first politically significant act (defined by the individual), first independent claim for state welfare, and first friends, activities and purchases without adult supervision or guidance. Selecting operationally appropriate start and end points to what are now fuzzy beginnings and exits from youth is a challenge that must be confronted, and is easily met, by whoever studies *youth* cultures, historical changes in the life stage, and routes from childhood origins to adult destinations

Classifying origins, routes and destinations

The real and special challenges for the transitions paradigm are to develop suitable classifications of childhood origins and adult destinations, and routes followed in-between. This development work is necessary in order to apply an origins-routes-destinations model. It is only for transitions through post-compulsory education and training that satisfactory classifications of youth routes, pathways or careers have already been developed. For classifying origins and destinations, conventional occupational class schemes may be out-of-date. As regards family origins and destinations, has marriage been replaced by cohabitation, and is parenthood any longer a necessary accomplishment for achieving full adulthood? Or is exiting the parental home sufficient? Classifications need constant review and periodic revision in order to keep pace with historical changes.

Leisure participation is the one domain where existing classifications look satisfactory. The main division in adult sport/physically energetic recreation is simply between the active and inactive. The same applies to consumption of the arts defined as attendance at live performances and visits to museums, galleries and exhibitions. In politics, adults may be divided into those pursuing professional careers in politics, others who are active as members of parties or other 'political' groups, loyal voters, floating and irregular voters, and the disengaged. In relation to state welfare, adults can be classified into those in receipt of means-tested benefits, other benefits (maybe split into those claimed while in-work and those for citizens who are out-of-work) and non-claimants. Housing origins and destinations can be classified using a combination of types of dwellings and tenure. An unresolvable problem in applying a youth transitions paradigm is that information collected years and decades ago in, for example, the UK's ongoing birth cohort studies, and life histories collected elsewhere, evidence that we would now like to have at our disposal was simply not sought. The further challenge facing the transitions paradigm is to develop classifications of youth routes through life domains other than education, training and employment, and in all cases the classifications of routes need periodic review and updating to keep abreast of historical changes. The challenge is never-ending.

Tackling other life domains

Researchers have analysed the short youth housing careers of specific socio-demographic groups: for example, residential university students in Britain (Rugg et al, 2004), and graduates and others in full-time employment who transition into shared private sector housing (Heath and Kenyon, 2001). However, major studies comparing all socio-demographic groups of young people's entwined careers in housing and intimate relationships spanning the entire youth life stage are still awaited. Short youth careers in various kinds of leisure have been identified in gambling (Edgerton et al, 2015), drug use (Liegregts et al, 2015), alcohol consumption (Seaman and Ikegwuonu, 2011), and crime (MacDonald and Shildrick, 2007). The consistent message is that young people have careers in all these domains. Life does not stand still during the youth life stage. Snapshot profiles of an age group are inherently misleading, whether the focus is on education, work, housing or any type of leisure.

Critical life stages

However, the big and unique rewards from the transitions paradigm arise when youth careers are set in a full life course context thereby identifying when, how, and for whom youth is *the* critical life stage.

We know that youth careers through upper secondary and higher education and vocational training feed into different adult occupational careers. We also know that the links vary by country on account of their different economies, and occupational profiles and employment regimes, as well as their distinctive education and training systems. We also know that in all countries for which we have evidence these links have changed over time alongside changes in education and training provisions, and in the economies. For example, in Germany the Hauptschule has been enrolling declining proportions of the 10–16 age group and has become, in practice, a residual route that is unlikely to feed straight into employer-based apprentice training. There are fewer craft occupations in Germany's increasingly post-industrial economy, and apprenticeships leading to higher-skilled occupations go to young people from higher education, gymnasium or Realschule (Solga, 2002). In Britain the expansion of higher education alongside wider income and wealth inequalities since the 1980s has been accompanied by the separation of a high-salary upper middle class from the rest of the middle class, and direct entry into the upper middle class has become strongly related to graduation from a limited number of elite universities that recruit above-the-norm proportions of their students from independent secondary schools (Friedman et al, 2015; Savage, 2015; Wakeling and Savage, 2015).

We also know the profiles of youth sport participation that predict long-term adult careers in participant sport (Roberts et al, 1991), and likewise in most other structured leisure activities (McGuire et al, 1987; Scott and Willits, 1989). Musical tastes that are nurtured during youth are often retained indefinitely and expressed in ways that are adapted to the fans' changed family and work situations (see Bennett, 2006; Bennett and Hodkinson, 2012; Hodkinson, 2011). All this evidence will support the view of youth as the critical life stage when the foundations of adult lives are built, but we need to pause before settling for this conclusion.

Youth careers of most types are associated with childhood origins, albeit to varying extents, and the childhood origins often prove almost as good and sometimes superior as predictors of adult outcomes. Rates of relative social mobility have remained little changed in Britain (and in all other modern societies) since at least the early 20th century despite all the changes in youth education and training (see Bukodi et al, 2014). Childhood measurements of family circumstances and educational progress prove good predictors of risks of future homeless episodes in the United States and probably elsewhere (see Brakenhoff et al, 2015). Family support has always been important in assisting young adults when establishing themselves in child-rearing households (see, for example, Bell, 1968). Childhood experiences of sport are good predictors of adult participation (though adult family circumstances and types of employment are the best predictors). The rise in sport participation during the teenage years proves temporary. Individuals tend to lapse if childhood foundations have not been laid (see Green et al, 2015; Haycock and Smith, 2014; Parry, 2015; Smith et al, 2015). Youth careers in many life domains channel individuals towards whatever childhood indicators suggested would be their most likely adult destinations.

The transitions paradigm is most obviously successful when it can reveal strong links between, on the one side, childhood origins and youth careers, and on the other side, between youth careers and adult outcomes. In all modern societies, children from the higher socio-economic strata are over-represented among university students, and higher education qualifications increase their chances of obtaining high-level employment. This is our best, proven example of strong links. While parading this evidence we must acknowledge the possibility of youth acting as a moratorium life stage during which individuals can try out different abilities and identities, taste different kinds of employment and experience successive intimate relationships which have no long-term consequences. The mixtures of strong links to childhood and adulthood, and moratorium, are likely to vary between different life domains, and by time and place. Post-Second World War cohorts in Britain were able to construct adult housing careers depending solely on their adult incomes. Since then the cost of housing (to rent and to buy) has outpaced earnings, which has made young people's access to independent transitional and then adult housing increasingly dependent on the 'bank of mum and dad'. Tastes in music and dress acquired during youth may or may not be retained for life. A taste for high culture appears difficult to acquire unless acquisition begins in childhood (Nagel, 2010). This kind of evidence does not diminish the value of the transitions paradigm. Rather, it demonstrates the paradigm's ability to identify for whom, at which times and in which places, and in which life domains, youth really is *the* critical life stage.

There are issues of huge public and political interest that require examination using a transitions paradigm which remain almost evidence-free while hypothesis rich. For example, in Britain there is an unresolved debate about the inter-generational transmission of worklessness and welfare dependence. We now know that despite the most thorough efforts it has been impossible to locate any households where no family member has worked for three generations (Shildrick et al, 2012). There are very few such sole individuals once the chronically ill and disabled and recent entrants to the workforce are excluded. However, there will be children and young people who grow up in households that are normally in receipt of out-of-work or in-work means-tested benefits (tax credits and/or housing benefit in the UK). Some of these young people may become adults who regard these benefits as normal components of a livelihood. Other children and young people grow up in households whose only welfare dependence is on universal benefits and who acquire scant if any knowledge of out-of-work and in-work means-tested welfare. They may regard the recipients of such benefits as 'not one of us' and a burden on tax-paying workers.

Political careers are another topic on which there is a serious evidence deficit, which will be best filled by applying a transitions paradigm. In the mid-20th century, most children and young people in Western Europe grew up in households where the adults were regular supporters of one of the main political parties. The young people's initial political identities were thereby likely to be 'inherited'. During youth they could consolidate or change, but they had foundations from which to develop politically (see Rose and McAllister, 1990). Since the 1950s successive cohorts have been progressively less and less likely to grow up in households where politics is discussed regularly (Chauvel and Smits, 2015). They have become eligible to vote without forming any party political loyalties (Roberts, 2015). Individuals who build long-term political careers as active party members or, in some cases, make politics their profession, have increasingly resembled a class apart – atypical 'wonks'. We know a lot about them individually but little collectively and how their biographies compare with those of their political predecessors and non-political or far less politically engaged contemporaries. It is possible that today's politicians are drawn from what has become a tiny minority of political families.

Their links with voters may thereby have become fragile. Hence the periodic surges in support for alternatives, as in the Anti-Globalisation/Global Justice movement of the late-20th and early 21st centuries, and the upsurges in 2011: the Indignados (mainly in Spain and Portugal) and the Occupy movement (mainly but not confined to North America). Transnational networks are formed and disintegrate just as rapidly. A political careers perspective will illuminate how this current state of Western politics has arisen.

Conclusions

Youth transitions research is not just unfinished business: it has barely started. It has demonstrated its capabilities: the value added to profiling the youth age group. It is compatible with other youth research paradigms, including those which address social change and when the changes meet the conditions (which need to be specified) to justify proclaiming the birth of a new generation. The transitions paradigm is also compatible with and complementary to studies of youth cultures which explore subjective states and meanings, and show how young people themselves can play a part in the construction and main-tenance of youth careers. The transitions paradigm can be used in studies of life domains other than education, training and work careers. It must be extended horizontally (into other domains) and also vertically so as to locate youth within the longer life course.

Social researchers must specialise. Focusing on youth life stage transitions is legitimate sociological practice. So is focusing even more narrowly on youth transitions in just one life domain. However, the big gains in knowledge will be made by whoever looks most widely, across the different youth life domains and the links between them, and extensively over time, into links with adjacent life stages and how the life course has changed historically.

Birth cohort longitudinal studies are the 'crown jewels' for youth transitions and other life course researchers, and these studies need to be conducted sequentially, no more than 20 years and preferably no more than 10 years apart, so as to engage with historical change. Retrospectively narrated biographies are an adequate substitute for some purposes, but information on subjective states must be gathered at the time, and we need this information in order to explore the role and limits of agency in individuals' journeys through life. All other kinds of youth research, including snapshots of just one part of the lives of one sub-section of the age group, have their value enhanced if the subjects can be located within youth transition career groups. Hence the justification for treating transitions as the lead paradigm for sociology as the lead discipline in the study of youth.

References

Arnett, J J (2005), *Emerging Adulthood: The Winding Road from Late Teens through the Twenties*, Oxford University Press, Oxford.

Ashton, D N and Field, D (1976), *Young Workers*, Hutchinson, London.

Banks, M, Bates, I, Breakwell, G, Bynner, J, Emler, N, Jamieson, L and Roberts, K (1992), *Careers and Identities*, Open University Press, Milton Keynes.

Beck, U (1992), *Risk Society: Towards a New Modernity*, Sage, London.

Bell, C (1968), *Middle Class Families*, Routledge, London.

Bennett, A (2006), 'Punk's not dead: the continuing significance of punk rock for an older generation of fans', *Sociology*, 40, 219–235.

Bennett, A and Hodkinson, P, eds (2012), *Ageing and Youth Cultures: Music, Style and Identity*, Berg, London.

Brakenhoff, B, Jang, B, Slesnick, N and Snyder, A (2015), 'Longitudinal predictors of homelessness: findings from the National Longitudinal Survey of Youth-97', *Journal of Youth Studies*, 18, 1015–1034.

Bukodi, E, Goldthorpe, J H, Waller, L and Kuha, J (2014), 'The mobility problem in Britain: new findings from the analysis of birth cohort data', *British Journal of Sociology*, doi:10.1111/1468–4446.12096

Carter, M P (1962), *Home, School and Work*, Pergamon, Oxford.

Chauvel, L and Smits, F (2015), 'The endless baby boomer generation: cohort differences in political participation in nine European countries in the period 1976–2008', *European Societies*, 17, 242–278.

Cohen, P and Ainley, P (2000), 'In the country of the blind? Youth studies and cultural studies in Britain', *Journal of Youth Studies*, 3, 79–95.

Corlett, A, Clarke, S and Tomlinson, D (2017), *The Living Standards Audit 2017*, Resolution Foundation, London.

Cote, J (2000), *Arrested Adulthood: The Changing Nature of Maturity and Identity. What does it Mean to Grow Up?* New York University Press, New York.

Dhillon, N and Yousef, T, eds (2009), *Generation in Waiting: The Unfulfilled Promise of Young People in the Middle East*, Brookings Institute Press, Washington, D.C.

Edgerton, J D, Melnyk, T S and Roberts, L W (2015), 'An exploratory study of multiple distinct gambling trajectories in emerging adults', *Journal of Youth Studies*, 18, 743–762.

Elder, G (1974), *Children of the Great Depression*, University of Chicago Press, Chicago.

Elder Jr, G H, Johnon, M K and Crosnoe, R (2003), 'The emergence and development of life course theory', in Mortimer, J T and Shanahan, M J, *Handbook of the Life Course*, Kluwer, London, 3–22.

Emmett, I (1971), *Youth and Leisure in an Urban Sprawl*, Manchester University Press, Manchester.

Esping-Andersen, G (1990), *The Three Worlds of Welfare Capitalism*, Princeton University Press, Princeton, NJ.

Friedman, S, Laurison, D and Miles, A (2015), 'Breaking the "class" ceiling? Social mobility into Britain's elite occupations', *Sociological Review*, 63, 259–289.

Gangl, M (2001), 'European patterns of labour market entry: a dichotomy of occupationalized and non-occupationalized systems?' *European Societies*, 3, 471–494.

Goodwin, J and O'Connor, H (2006), 'Norbert Elias and the lost Young Worker Project', *Journal of Youth Studies*, 9, 159–173.

Goodwin, J and O'Connor, H (2007), 'Continuity and change in the experience of transition from school to work', *International Journal of Lifelong Education*, 26, 555–572.

Goodwin, J and O'Connor, H (2009), 'Whatever happened to the young workers? Change and transformation in 40 years at work', *Journal of Education and Work*, 22, 417–431.

Green, K, Thurston, M, Vaage, O and Roberts, K (2015), '"(We're on the right track baby), we were born this way"! Exploring sports participation in Norway', *Sport, Education and Society*, 20, 285–303.

Hall, G S (1904), *Adolescence*, Appleton, New York.

Hall, S and Jefferson, T, eds (1976), *Resistance through Rituals*, Hutchinson, London.

Hammer, T, ed (2003), *Youth Unemployment and Social Exclusion in Europe*, Policy Press, Bristol.

Haycock, D and Smith, A (2014), 'A family affair? Exploring the influence of childhood sports socialisation on young adults' leisure sports careers in north-west England', *Leisure Studies*, 33, 285–304.

Heath, S and Kenyon, L (2001), 'Single young professionals and shared household living', *Journal of Youth Studies*, 4, 83–100.

Heinz, W (2009), 'Youth transitions in an age of uncertainty', in Furlong, A, ed, *Handbook of Youth and Young Adulthood*, Routledge, London, 3–13.

Henderson, S, Holland, J, McGrellis, S, Sharpe, S and Thomson, R (2007), *Inventing Adulthoods: A Biographical Approach to Youth Transitions*, Sage, London.

Hodkinson, P (2011), 'Ageing in a spectacular "youth culture": continuity, change and community amongst older goths', *British Journal of Sociology*, 62, 262–282.

Irwin, S (1995), *Rights of Passage: Social Change and the Transition from Youth to Adulthood*, UCL Press, London.

Kelly, P (2006), 'The entrepreneurial self and "youth at risk": exploring the horizons of identity in the twenty-first century', *Journal of Youth Studies*, 9, 17–32.

Kuhn, T (1962), *The Structure of Scientific Revolutions*, University of Chicago Press, Chicago.

Liegregts, N, Pol, P van der, Graaf, R de, Laar, M van, Brink, W van den and Korf, D J (2015), 'Persistence and desistance in heavy cannabis use: the role of identity, agency and life events', *Journal of Youth Studies*, 18, 617–633.

MacDonald, R and Shildrick, T (2007), 'Street corner society: leisure careers, youth (sub)culture and social exclusion', *Leisure Studies*, 26, 339–355.

Maizels, J (1970), *Adolescent Needs and the Transition from School to Work*, Athlone Press, London.

Mays, J B (1954), *Growing Up in the City*, Liverpool University Press, Liverpool.

McGuire, F A, Dottavio, F D and O'Leary, J T (1987), 'The relationship of early life experiences to later life leisure involvement', *Leisure Sciences*, 9, 251–257.

Mead, M (1928, 1961), *Coming of Age in Samoa*, Penguin, Harmondsworth.

Nagel, I (2010), 'Cultural participation between the ages of 14 and 24: intergenerational transmission or cultural mobility', *European Sociological Review*, 26, 541–556.

Nilsen, A and Brannen, J (2014), 'An intergenerational approach to transitions to adulthood: the importance of history and biography', *Sociological Research Online*, www.socresonline.org.uk/19/1/9.html.

Park, A, Phillips, M and Johnson, M (2005), *Young People in Britain: The Attitudes and Experiences of 12–19 Year Olds*, Research Report RR564, Department for Education and Skills, Nottingham.

Parry, W (2015), *Do Active Children Become Active Adults? Investigating Experiences of Sport and Exercise Using the 1970 British Cohort Study*, PhD thesis, University College London, London.

Peters, E (1995), 'The modernisation of the youth phase: educational, professional and family careers of Dutch youth in the nineties', in Bois-Reymond, M, Diekstra, R,

Hurrelman, K and Peters, E, *Childhood and Youth in Germany and the Netherlands*, de Gruyter, Berlin, 3–40.

Raffe, D (2008), 'The concept of transition system', *Journal of Education and Work*, 21, 277–296.

Raffe, D (2014), 'Explaining national differences in education-work transitions: twenty years of research on transition systems', *European Societies*, 16, 175–193.

Roberts, K (1968), 'The entry into employment: an approach towards a general theory', *Sociological Review*, 16, 165–184.

Roberts, K (2015), 'Youth mobilisations and political generations: young activists in political change movements during and since the twentieth century', *Journal of Youth Studies*, 18, 950–966.

Roberts, K, Minten, J H, Chadwick, C, Lamb, K L and Brodie, D A (1991), 'Sporting lives: a case study of leisure careers', *Society and Leisure*, 14, 261–284.

Rose, R and McAllister, I (1990), *The Loyalties of Voters*, Sage, London.

Rugg, J, Ford, J and Burrows, R (2004), 'Housing advantage? The role of student renting in the constitution of housing biographies in the United Kingdom', *Journal of Youth Studies*, 7, 19–34.

Savage, M (2015), 'Introduction to elites: from the "problematic of the proletariat" to class analysis of "wealth elites"', *Sociological Review*, 63, 223–239.

Schoon, I (2006), *Risk and Resilience: Adaptations in Changing Times*, Cambridge University Press, Cambridge.

Scott, D and Willits, F K (1989), 'Adolescent and adult leisure patterns: a 37-year follow-up study', *Leisure Sciences*, 11, 323–335.

Seaman, P and Ikegwuonu, T (2011), '"I don't think old people should go to clubs": how universal is the alcohol transition among young adults in the United Kingdom?' *Journal of Youth Studies*, 14, 745–759.

Shildrick, T, MacDonald, R, Furlong, A, Roden, J and Crow, R (2012), *Poverty and Insecurity: Life in Low-Pay, No-pay Britain*, Policy Press, Bristol.

Smith, L, Gardner, B, Aggio, D and Hamer, M (2015), 'Association between outdoor play and sport at age 10 years old with physical activity in adulthood', *Preventive Medicine*, doi:10.1016/j.ypmed.2015.02.004

Solga, H (2002), '"Stigmatization by negative selection": explaining less-educated people's decreasing employment opportunities', *European Societies*, 18, 159–178.

Tenen, C (1947), 'The adolescent in the factory', *British Journal of Educational Psychology*, 21, 75–81.

Thomson, R, Bell, R, Holland, J, Henderson, S, McGrellis, S and Sharpe, S (2002), 'Critical moments, choice, chance and opportunity in young people's narratives of transition', *Sociology*, 36, 335–354.

Thrasher, F M (1936), *The Gang: A Study of 1,131 Gangs in Chicago*, University of Chicago Press, Chicago.

Tumino, A (2015), *The Scarring Effect of Unemployment from the Early '90s to the Great Recession*, Working Paper 2015–2005, Institute for Social and Economic Research, University of Essex, Colchester.

Veness, T (1962), *School-Leavers*, Methuen, London.

Wakeling, P and Savage, M (2015), 'Entry into elite positions and the stratification of higher education in Britain', *Sociological Review*, 63, 290–320.

Wallace, C and Kovacheva, S (1998), *Youth in Society: The Construction and Deconstruction of Youth in East and West Europe*, Macmillan, London.

Whyte, W F (1943), *Street Corner Society: The Social Structure of an Italian Slum*, University of Chicago Press, Chicago.

Willis, P.(1977), *Learning to Labour*, Saxon House, Farnborough.

Woodman, D and Bennett, A (2015a), 'Cultures, transitions, and generations: the case for a new youth studies', in Woodman, D and Bennett, A, eds, *Youth Cultures, Transitions, and Generations: Bridging the Gap in Youth Research*, Palgrave Macmillan, Basingstoke, 1–15.

Woodman, D and Bennett, A (2015b), 'Transitions, cultures, and the future of youth research' in Woodman, D and Bennett, A, eds, *Youth Cultures, Transitions, and Generations: Bridging the Gap in Youth Research*, Palgrave Macmillan, Basingstoke, 186–191.

Woodman, D and Wyn, J (2015), *Youth and Generation: Rethinking Change and Inequality in the Lives of Young People*, Sage, London.

Worth, S (2005), 'Beating the "churning" trap in the youth labour market', *Work, Employment and Society*, 19, 403–414.

Wyn, J and Woodman, D (2006), 'Generation, youth and social change in Australia', *Journal of Youth Studies*, 9, 495–514.

3 Transitions from school to work in Norway and Britain among three family generations of working-class men

Julia Brannen, Kristoffer Chelsom Vogt, Ann Nilsen and Abigail Knight

Introduction

The financial crisis and its aftermath have affected young people's life course transitions in many European countries, resulting in high rates of youth unemployment (Heinz 2014; Mortimer 2014) and increasing inequality (Stiglitz 2012). Other longer-term changes have also hit young people, especially young working-class men. The lack of low-skilled employment opportunities predates the financial crisis: the move of much manufacturing to the Far East together with cuts to public expenditure, especially notable in Britain from 1979 onwards and throughout the period in all Western countries including Norway. Both Norway and Britain are established democracies with universal welfare states, although the coverage is much more extensive in Norway under the Nordic model (Esping-Andersen 1990). The countries differ in that the UK has a much larger and more diverse population than Norway and the effects of the current economic downturn are much more severe in the UK than in Norway. Yet, despite these differences, there are parallel trends that, as we show, are evident in the lives of the three-generation working-class families to be discussed in this chapter. Moreover, it is valuable to make such comparisons when it is possible to match the research participants to precise historical and demographic criteria. The exercise of comparison is also beneficial in making 'strange' the familiar or taken-for-granted aspects of people's lives.

In this chapter we draw upon material from a qualitative cohort study of three generations (including grandparents, parents and young people) selected according to the birth date of the middle generation, born 1960–65. The aim of the study is to understand and compare transitions to adulthood in different social contexts, Norway and Britain, and across different generations within the same families. The focus upon generation relates both to the influences of historical context as in period, and family context, notably the ways in which young people draw upon parental resources as they move into adulthood: from school, into further/higher education and into work. Drawing on a contextualist life course perspective (Elder et al 2006), we analyse the influence of institutional arrangements and family practices in different historical periods and countries. Resources provided by different generations within families are important at this life course phase. During times of hardship and cuts in public spending, intergenerational relations become particularly salient.

We compare two cases that consist of chains of working-class fathers and sons living in Norway and the UK respectively who are currently entering the labour market. We focus upon young working-class men because the literature has long suggested that this group has experienced increasingly uncertain transitions to adulthood because of drastic labour market transformations (Ashton and Lowe, 1991; Roberts, 1997; Stiglitz 2012). However, Goodwin and O'Connor (2005), Vickerstaffe (2003) and others have concluded that past transitional experiences, for example in the 1960s, were not as linear, smooth or single step as previously suggested. Many transitions were complex, lengthy and non-linear, similar to those of contemporary youth. (Goodwin and O'Connor 2005)

The case-based research design provides a rigorous framework to understand long-term social change in particular families (Bertaux and Thompson 1997; Brannen 2015), and is a prism through which to examine the conditions in which transitions to adulthood are negotiated. Using a biographical interview method, 23 three-generation family chains were interviewed in Norway and nine in the UK.[1] In both studies the chains were selected on the basis of the year of birth of the middle generation (1960–65) and because they had one parent and a son or a daughter aged 18 or over willing to take part in the study.[2] The three-generation Norwegian and British chains discussed in the chapter provide an optimal match; in the middle target generation, both men were in the same working-class occupation at interview and the current generation of sons were the same age and both entering paid work. The other chain members were also working class.

In the discussion of the two cases we pose three research questions:

- How do structural conditions for working-class male transitions from school to work change over the three generations?
- In what ways do these transitions follow similar or different patterns in Norway and the UK?
- How are changing opportunity structures moderated by intergenerational transmission and transfers in families, with particular reference to the youngest generation?

First, we outline a contextualist life course perspective in relation to the transition to adulthood. Next, we consider some of the historical changes in relation to education and employment that span the lives of the three generations (1930–2014). This is followed by a brief discussion of methodological issues before we embark on a comparative analysis between the chains of men and also across the different generations.

A contextualist life course approach and the transition to adulthood

The life course approach is based on age-graded patterns and practices that are embedded in social institutions that vary over historical periods (Elder 1999 [1974]). It thereby links human agency with the historical and institutional features of a society (Thomas and Znaniecki (1958 [1918–20]; Mills 1980 [1959]). When adopted in a comparative study, '[life course studies] tend to deepen our understanding of cross-national differences when we give a convincing explanation of the impact of institutional and social-cultural conditions on the life course in various nations' (Blossfeld 2009, p. 281).

The transition from youth to adulthood is conceptualised as a sequence of age-graded events that includes: completing education; entry into the labour market; financial independence; setting up a separate household; establishing a long-term relationship with a partner; becoming a parent (Hareven 1978; Elder 1985). Evidence suggests that the transition to adulthood has never been a linear sequence (Jones and Wallace 1992; Nilsen et al 2002); some argue that youth as a life course stage is increasingly obsolete since it is being extended into both younger and older age groups[3] (Buchman 1989). Still others maintain that the life course is being destandardised (Beck and Beck-Gernsheim 1995). On the other hand, it is also clear that transition patterns between youth and adulthood vary considerably according to social origin and gender (Jones and Wallace 1992; Irwin 1995) and notably also between countries (Nilsen et al 2002; Billari and Liefbroer 2010).

Two main perspectives on this transition have been identified: the cultural perspective mainly drawing on ethnographic research to explore a variety of local expressions of youth culture in a short time frame, and the transitions perspective focussing on quantitative data to examine education-to-work transitions in structural contexts over longer time spans (Furlong et al 2011). The two approaches have sometimes been viewed in opposition while more recently there is a trend to bridge the divide (MacDonald et al 2001; Furlong et al 2011). A further theoretical trend is to set youth transitions within a family context (Jones and Wallace 1992) and to examine how young people are supported by the different generations in families in different historical periods (Nilsen and Brannen 2014). This perspective is particularly relevant in times of economic downturn. With the retrenchment of public services and high youth unemployment in many European countries, family relations are becoming more rather than less important as sources of material support (Mortimer 2014; Nilsen and Brannen 2014). In this chapter we set youth transitions within family contexts to examine how young people are supported by the different generations in different historical periods and different countries.

Historical changes across the generations: education and employment

Norway and the UK were both badly affected by World War II. Despite the huge cost and damage caused by the war, both countries established welfare states in its immediate aftermath.

A period of continuous economic growth and prosperity was common to all Western European countries in the post-war period. In Hobsbawm's words 'not until the 1960s did Europe come to take its extraordinary prosperity for granted. By then, indeed, sophisticated observers began to assume that, somehow, everything in the economy would go onwards and upwards forever' (Hobsbawm 1994, p. 259). However, by the 1970s, '…observers – mainly, to begin with, economists – began to realise that the world, particularly the world of developed capitalism, had passed through an altogether exceptional phase of its history; perhaps a unique one' (Hobsbawm 1994, pp. 257–258). The period that followed was characterised by 'the battle between Keynesians and neo-liberals' and 'an ever increasing globalisation of the economy' (Hobsbawm 1994, pp, 409–411). The trend towards cuts in public services and growing privatisation spread across Europe and the United States, although with varying strength and force in different countries.

In most OECD countries, social inequality has grown, with the biggest impact of inequality evident in the increasing gap between low income households and the rest of the population so that income inequality is at its highest level in 30 years (www.oecd.org/social/Focus-Inequality-and-Growth-2014.pdf). In Norway the conservative government that was in power in the period 1981 to 1986 deregulated parts of the banking sector, the health sector and the housing market. As the country became more integrated into the European common market,[4] the overall European and global tendency towards increasing social inequality has spread (Telle 2017). However, the country is still one of the most egalitarian societies in Europe (Aaberge 2016). In the UK, Margaret Thatcher's Conservative government that came to power in 1979 broke the post-war consensus on the welfare state. Thereafter, a relentless dismantling of the public sector, increasing privatisation, major constraints on trade union power, and deregulation of the labour market followed. From the mid 1970s social inequality has grown hugely, including under the UK's New Labour government (1997–2010) until the current period.

The post-war period was marked by a global expansion in educational opportunities throughout Europe (Meyer and Schofer 2007), including in Norway and the UK. However, while in Norway education at all levels has been a state matter and free, Britain has a long tradition of independent fee-paying schools, with 7 per cent of children currently in the UK in attendance.[5] In 1998 university tuition fees were introduced, which increased to £9,000 a year per student in 2012. The Educational Maintenance Allowance (EMA), targeted at low income families for those in further education and sixth forms, was removed in the same year.

Compulsory schooling in Norway only lasted for a total of seven years (7–14) until 1969, when it was extended to nine years (7–16), and in 1997 to ten years (6–16). In 1994 young people became entitled to 12 years of schooling. The children of working-class families in the two older generations in the study (born 1930–40 and 1960–65) were expected to leave school as soon as the state permitted and to contribute to family income. Only families of considerable means could afford extending their child's education. Many young Norwegians would have had to leave home to go to secondary schools, especially since the majority lived in rural areas.[6] Up until the 1970s only a tiny minority went to university.[7] The expansion in education, especially from the late 1960s, led to a marked increase in students at university, particularly women students. In 2016 35% of 16–24 year olds were in higher education (SSB 2017). Student loans and grants became available without means testing in the 1970s.[8]

In England and Wales, the minimum school leaving age until 1944 was 14.[9] The education system was stratified until the 1960s, when comprehensive schools became widespread. This system disadvantaged working-class young people in the cohort born 1930–40 who were growing up before or in World War II. Most left school at 14 until the school leaving age was changed.[10] Working-class British parents, especially those with large families, expected their children to work as soon as they could leave school. However, there was an ample supply of low-skilled employment in the post-war period. For the middle generation, born 1960–65, the minimum age for leaving school rose to 16 (in 1972), with a huge expansion in the university population from the 1980s onwards (House of Commons Library 2012). Before that university education was for the select few, rising to around 40 per cent today.[11] However, as Blanden et al (2002) show, while the chances of a child from a working-class family attending university have grown since the 1970s from one in 50 to one in 20, the chances of a middle-class child have grown far more – from one in ten to one in two for children of teachers and middle managers to near universal for upper middle class children. (www.timeshighereducation.com/features/were-still-skipping-working-class/169329.article).

The current generation of young people in Britain (those born around 1995 in our study) must continue in education or training on a full or part time basis until they are 18 (Irwin 2017, p. 14). Given that in 2015 the unemployment rate for those aged 18–24 was 14.3% (Job Centre Plus 2017), the incentive to stay at school or in training is high. Despite a recent increase in apprenticeships,[12] many British working-class young people do not have access to skills for the modern labour market, especially when we compare them with many of their working-class predecessors (Wolf 2011).

The state has reduced its spending on support for young people through the introduction of fees for higher education and has withdrawn the Education Maintenance Allowance that provided some support to young people from low income families to stay on in education. In this context, family resources and family relationships have become more important as sources of support for young people (Irwin and Elley 2013; Mortimer 2014). In the UK the outlook for young people in the housing market is dire. It is anticipated that the number of young people living with parents in owner-occupied accommodation will increase by approximately 550,000 to 3.7 million in 2020 (Clapham et al 2012).

Analysis of the cases

In cross-national comparative analyses of biographical data, contextual changes come to the fore, highlighting important features of the history-biography dynamic (Mills 1980 [1959]). Biographical interviews lasting about two hours were carried out with individuals in the family chain. The interview focussed on the scheduling of the life course, the transmission of aspirations, material resources and care and support during the transition from youth to adulthood.[13] The analysis followed a case-based logic (Gomm et al 2000; Brannen and Nilsen 2011), allowed for what Geertz terms 'thick description' (Geertz 1973) and employed concepts in a sensitising way (Blumer 1954).

As noted, the two chains analysed here are matched by the occupations of the middle generation (the fathers) at the time of interview: both were Post Office workers. Both their fathers (the grandfathers) had little education, were employed in male-dominated working-class jobs and came from large families. The aim here is to compare the school-to-work transition of the youngest generation of working-class men in relation to the transitions of their fathers and grandfathers in the contexts of particular times and places.[14] Below we will compare each generation of men, setting out the timing of the main transitions including school leaving, jobs, marriage and birth of children (Nilsen et al 2012).

Comparing the life course transitions of the grandfathers (1930–40)

Daniel and Jack were born before the expansion of the welfare state in Norway and Britain: Daniel in Norway in 1929 and Jack in London in 1932. Daniel, one of six children, had a rural childhood and came from a farming family that, while poor, owned the land belonging to the family farm. Both men's lives were affected by the war.[15] Daniel grew up on the farm, where from an early age he was expected to help his father. When he reached school leaving age (14 at the time), it was assumed that in such a large family he would get a job and contribute to the family income as long as he lived at home. In the way typical for many working-class young men who depended upon employment opportunities in local labour markets, he drew on informal help to find work, a relative 'having a word in someone's ear'. He managed to get an apprenticeship as a carpenter and, aged 22, he did military service for a year but was able to return to the same firm afterwards to a job as a qualified carpenter. When Daniel married he was given some land by his parents that, while worth little at the time, enabled him to build a house of his own. He used his parents' farm as collateral on a mortgage to provide the building materials.[16]

Jack was the eighth of ten children and grew up in privately rented housing in inner London until the family was rehoused in one of the new council (inner city) housing estates built in the 1960/70s. Jack's father worked for the council in a manual job and unlike Daniel, Jack spent his life in public or

Table 3.1 Grandfathers

b. 1929 Daniel, farm family, rural Norway	b. 1932 Jack, privately rented flat, inner London
• Five siblings	• Nine siblings
• Father: self-employed farmer	• Father: council worker (manual)
• Worked on farm and did odd jobs	• Worked while attending school
• 1943 left school at 14, lived with parents	• 1947 left school at 14 – building and delivery work
• 1946–49 apprenticeship contributed to family income	• 1950 aged 18 did National Service overseas
• 1949, aged 20 conscript to military service abroad	• 1952 variety of unskilled jobs
• 1951, aged 22 employed as a carpenter	• 1954, aged 22 employed at a British utility company (nationalised in 1948)
• 1953, aged 23 got married and lived in privately rented housing	• 1954, aged 22 got married, left home, lived in privately rented housing
• 1954, aged 24 built house on family land	• Five children
• Five children	• 1970s moved to council housing
• 1969–79 Self-employed builder	• 1986 aged 54 redundant from private utility company
• 1979–1997 caretaker, public sector organisation	• 1987 low-skilled jobs
• 1997 aged 68 retired	• 1995 aged 63 retired

privately rented housing; renting was by far the most common form of housing at the time.[17] Jack was evacuated from London aged 7 to 12 and received only basic education. Like many working-class British young men of his class background at the time, Jack was too old to benefit from 1944 changes to the education system which raised the school leaving age; he attended a state elementary school and left with no qualifications at 14.

Like Daniel, Jack's entry into the world of work came before he left school. He too was expected to contribute to household income. He did odd jobs after school. Like Daniel, his parents clearly assumed he would leave school at the earliest opportunity. Jobs were easy to come by in Britain in the 1950s, as in Norway, especially for working-class men. Jack described being able to 'walk into jobs'. A constant theme of Jack's interview was to compare the past with the present. *'It was far far easier to get a job then than it is now. Now it's traumatic. I don't think they ever thought about that in them days.'* Like Daniel, he was obliged at 18 to do two years' National Service overseas. And, also like Daniel, his later work career was marked by long spells with the same (public sector) employer. Jack was made redundant in 1986. The utility he worked for was privatised in the same year.

Both men described childhoods that had very few material resources to go around. Both gave money to their families until they left home. Both found work easily through informal contacts. Unlike Daniel's family, Jack's family had no assets to pass on to him.

Comparing the life course transitions of the fathers (1960–65)

Daniel's son, Dag, was born in 1959, the third of Daniel's five children. Dag grew up in the house built by his father. He left school two years later than his father (compulsory schooling had been extended). While at school Dag worked part time in the local shop. At 16 after he left school he lived at home and worked with his father and brother in the building trade for a short time while he took a course at the local commercial college. Unlike his father at that age, he was not expected to pay for his keep. At 18 he got a job in the national Postal Service through a tip-off from a neighbour. At 25, he built a house on a plot of land given to him by his parents and, a year later, he married and supported his wife while she studied to become a therapist. Like his father, Dag's transition to work came early in the life course and he was proud of this: of being able to provide for himself at an earlier age than his classmates who stayed on in education. At this time (the mid 1970s) less than a third of his birth cohort completed upper secondary school. Unskilled work was still easy to come by and skills in male-dominated trades could be gained through a variety of ways (Vogt 2017). However, from his current vantage point, Dag was ambivalent about his lack of education and regretted that, unlike his father, he had not done an apprenticeship and learned a trade. Looking forward to his sons' futures, he and his wife encouraged them to complete their education. The older son was studying to become a health

Table 3.2 Fathers

b. 1959 Dag, four siblings	b. 1963 Ray, four siblings
• Lived on family farm	• 1970, aged 7 family moved from rented housing to a council flat
• 1973–75 part-time work in local shop	• 1970s part-time work in local shop
• 1975 left school at 16	• 1979 left school at 16
• 1975–76 clerical college	• 1979–93 series of low-skilled jobs
• 1977, aged 18 moved to bedsit in aunt's house	• 1989, aged 26 moved in with fiancée (clerical worker) into her rented flat
• 1977–2014 Post Office worker	• 1991 got mortgage on a flat
• 1984, aged 25 inherited land and built house	• 1993 aged 30 made redundant and got a job as a Post Office worker
• 1985 aged 26 married student nurse	• 1993 aged 30 got married
• Two sons, born 1991, 1993	• One son, born 1995

worker and the parents were trying to persuade the younger one (Didrik, see below) to get an apprenticeship.

The British father, Ray, the son of Jack, was in many respects similar to Dag. However, unlike Dag, he grew up in the inner city and from the age of seven the family lived in rented housing until they were moved into public housing that continued to be built from the end of the war until the advent of Thatcherism. Like Dag, he spent much of his childhood outside the home playing football with his friends and other activities provided in the local youth club. Unlike Dag, he stressed the resources available to young people living in cities at that time that have since, to his regret, disappeared. Like Dag, Ray clearly now regrets his lack of education.

Also like Dag, Ray had a similar part-time job in a local shop before leaving school aged 16. Ray admitted to bunking off school. He left without qualifications. Like Dag, he found one of his first jobs through a relative. He had a succession of jobs that were easy to come by. In 1993 aged 30 and just married, he was made redundant and, like Dag, Ray joined the Post Office, then part of the state sector. This was also shortly after the couple had taken out a mortgage,[18] based on his wife's credit rating. His wife worked full time in clerical work in the private sector. The couple then sold their flat in 1998 for a considerable profit and moved to a distant London suburb where housing was cheaper and in order to be nearer his wife's family. Ray was very proud of his continuous work record and having always 'paid his way', although it was also clear that his wife was the higher earner.

In contrast to Dag, Ray received no material support from his parents and, in order to get on the housing ladder, he was reliant on his wife's full-time employment. Ray, like Dag, acted very differently towards his son than his father had acted towards him. Because of his awareness of the labour market difficulties for young people, Ray said that he tried to encourage his son in his studies while reflecting on his own lack of resources to help him. Because of Ray's inability to help his son educationally, Ray stressed his ability to give him material things. The couple are very proud of their son's considerable success in his GCSE examinations at 16.

Comparing the life course transitions of the sons

Didrik was born in 1993, the second son of Dag. He did not like school and suffered from Attention Deficit Disorder. At upper secondary school he followed his peer group and chose the subjects that they chose. He lacked focus. While Didrik enjoyed ICT, aged 19, because he failed maths he could not formally graduate.[19] Looking back, Didrik is critical of the emphasis on academic qualifications. He tried and failed to get an apprenticeship in ICT that is in high demand but short supply in Norway. He found work in the local shop where he had worked in his last year at upper secondary school. Aged 20, he did a year's (compulsory) military service.

Table 3.3 Sons

b. 1993 Didrik, one brother	*b. 1995 Charlie, only child*
• 2009 finished compulsory schooling aged 16	• 2011 finished compulsory schooling aged16
• 2009–2012 upper secondary vocational eduation, left before taking exams, no apprenticeships available	• 2011–2013 vocational course in further education college, no carpentry apprenticeships, Educational Maintenance Allowance was removed, left college
• 2012 odd jobs	• 2013– part-time work in supermarket followed by a job with a zero-hours contract as a warehouse worker, lives with parents
• 2012–2013 conscript military service	
• 2013– unemployed, lives with parents	

In contrast to his father and grandfather, Didrik subscribed to the notion of 'choosing a career' and was frustrated by his inability to know 'what I want to do'. He did not regret not having been pushed by his parents in a particular direction because he values the 'freedom' to make his own choices and being 'his own man'. *'It's easier to be your own man these days. No one is telling me what to do. They are not forcing me to do anything. They are just supporting my choices'.*

In contrast to his father and grandfather, Didrik insisted on the importance of having responsibility at work and of enjoying the job: *'I feel you should have fun when you're at work.'* Interestingly, Didrik was critical of his father for not seeking promotion in the Post Office, suggesting that he himself would like a career in which he can progress. Didrik was clearly not inspired by his grandfather who worked in a manual trade. His parents were still encouraging him to do an apprenticeship, as Daniel had done and Dag regretted not doing. But Didrik wants to earn money: *'I'm ready to get a job and earn some money.'* His approach to finding a job was to look online rather than mobilise informal networks in the way that his father and grandfather had done. This was despite the fact that he also believed that getting a job nowadays was dependent on 'who you know'. Didrik recounted how he had applied for a job he wanted at an electrical appliances shop and for which there were several hundred applicants.

Apart from unemployment benefit, Didrik relied on his parents for free accommodation and for supplementary money. He was disheartened at not having enough money to rent his own apartment. He considered moving out as an important step towards adulthood, and as the only real way to learn to become independent: *'You learn a lot by living on your own I think. You have to... you don't get dinner on the table. You have bills to pay, right?'* Buying somewhere to live, the norm in Norway, was so far off in the future that Didrik seemed not to have thought much about it.

Charlie, son of Ray, was born in 1995, aged 19 at interview, slightly younger than Didrik. He was in a not too dissimilar position though for different reasons. He did well at school up to 16 when he left; he gained a large number of GCSEs but chose to go to a further education college to do a vocational course. Like Didrik, Charlie worked in a shop while still in education. During the holidays, he found some part-time work in a supermarket, describing in detail the lengthy and difficult process of getting this job. Charlie only worked there briefly before being laid off.

One year to go on the course, the UK Conservative and Liberal-Democrat Coalition Government of 2010–2015 took funding away from further education as well as introducing very high fees in higher education (Lupton et al, 2015).[20] Charlie decided to give up college because, he said, he did not want to be in debt because he could not afford it, *'like if I'd had to pay £1600 for college along with other things'*. When Charlie left college he got a job through the informal route; having failed to get any interviews after sending his CV to employers, his aunt 'spoke for him' (Wilmot and Young 1957) to employers. As Ray commented, his sister-in-law found a job for Charlie in a big garage supplying car parts: *'it was word of mouth, it come from my sister-in-law cos she phoned up for a [car] part, as I said, and she said "Oh but you ain't got no jobs going for my nephew?" She'll walk past a shop and ask ... she'll walk in a shop and say "Is there any jobs going, because my nephew wants a job" and she's always looking out for him.'*

Charlie got the job in the car parts warehouse found by his aunt. He used his own car to get to work (a long distance) that he had bought with his savings. In contrast to Didrik, Charlie was careful with money. Although he said his mechanics training was helpful in his job, he was not using his training. Charlie was working 33 hours per week on a zero-hours contract.[21] He was paid the National Minimum wage for a person under 21 (£5.03 per hour for 18–21 year olds at the time). He said that although the pay was low, he would be getting only just over £2 per hour if he was doing an apprenticeship. Didrik made the same complaints about apprenticeship wages in Norway.

Reflecting the extension of education in the period, both Didrik and Charlie stayed on in education longer than their parents and grandparents. Both have parents who encouraged them in education. In both cases, it was their mothers who, because of their educational or employment experience, were more important in encouraging them, while both their fathers wanted them to get themselves a 'trade'. Charlie welcomed this but Didrik was more focussed on the notion of 'career choice', with clear expectations about what such a desirable career should entail. Nonetheless, despite both young men having been in the education system until the age of 18/19 – and Charlie having a good crop of GCSEs, they had not completed their courses. In Charlie's case this was because of a change in public policy concerning further education support, while in Didrik's case it was because he failed mathematics.

Discussion

Although Norway and the UK are very different countries in many respects, nonetheless it is striking that the conditions in which the two working-class young men are entering work suggest some similarities. The first similarity concerns the elongation of the transition to adulthood in the youngest generation of young people in Norway and Britain, with both Didrik and Charlie spending longer in education than their grandfathers and fathers. There are also similarities that cut across the generations. All three generations are dependent on their families, in particular for accommodation. Didrik at 21 and Charlie at 19 still relied on their parents for housing and Didrik for his keep. This reflects continuing social class differences: the trend towards leaving home following the end of education occurs earlier among young people of middle-class origin who go to university than among their working-class contemporaries. In the UK, between 1996 and 2013 there has been a large increase in the numbers of young people aged 20–34 living at home, with young men much more likely to do so than young women; for every 10 women, 17 men aged 20 to 34 lived with their parents in 2013 (ONS 2014).

Norway has the same pattern on gender and social class (Dommermuth 2009). In the case of the two grandfathers and the two fathers, they did not leave home until marriage. By contrast, Didrik and Charlie, like a lot of young people today, would prefer to live independently. However, because of the high costs of housing, both to purchase and to rent, they are unlikely to do so. Like Didrik, Charlie is mainly focussed on the here and now. Currently, as a 'not-yet-independent young adult' he talks a lot about learning how to manage his money, *'learning now like how to spend your money. Like I say a couple of years' time, say I do get to move out and that, this could be a lot harder than just what it is now.'*

Thirdly, demonstrating further the importance of other generational transfers during the transition phase, Didrik and Charlie similarly mention their grandparents' financial help in learning to drive. This is an important qualification for those entering particular types of male working-class jobs. Both were encouraged by their parents to save. Charlie was keen on saving, unlike Didrik; he had an account started by his grandmother who had saved a small sum each month for him, and with which Charlie bought a car.

Fourthly, both young men were cautious about taking out loans. Charlie said: *'If I didn't have to pay I would have probably gone back for the third year, cos then that's all the levels done then.'* Neither had any realistic ambition of buying a flat in the near future in the expensive housing markets of Britain and Norway.

Lastly, both fathers, Dag and Ray, were more aspirational for their sons' education than their fathers had been for them, which echoes Irwin and

Elley's (2011) study in which working-class parents stressed the increased importance of education in their children's lives relative to their own. Didrik has a brother who was more academic and was studying at college at the time of the interview. Ray wanted his son to do well at school but was conscious of his own lack of resources to help him. Instead, Ray stressed his ability to give him material 'things'. Like Didrik, an important factor in encouraging Charlie at school was the fact that his mother worked in a non-manual occupation and was numerate. Both mothers were said to nag their sons about homework more than the fathers.

Both Didrik and Charlie also confirmed that their parents had aspirations for their future. Like Didrik's parents, Charlie's parents wanted him to get a trade, something he was in agreement with: *'Like I said they wanted me to stay in education as long as I could. And if I chose some sort of work they wanted me to try and choose a trade. Like the trades – you would always need people in the trade... like they'll probably never die out.'* Charlie did not say this but assumed his parents could not afford, or were not prepared, to pay for him to complete his training. Like Didrik, Charlie did not believe in debt and did not want to get a loan. Didrik articulated a tension between the discourse of 'choice' and the reality of his situation, while Charlie was more realistic, wrestling with the consequences of regressive government policies towards young people and the deregulation of employment conditions.

The differences between the two chains include the more substantial material transfers provided by the Norwegian grandfather (a farmer) to his son, Dag, in the form of a plot of land to build a house. Daniel was also given land by his parents. The value of the land had increased substantially because of the proximity to the city and rising housing prices. The British grandfather, by contrast, lived in an inner part of a large capital city in public housing and had no assets.

In all generations in each country, the notion of a one-step transition into work is not borne out. Both Jack and Ray changed jobs many times in the early part of their careers and Charlie is likely to do the same. Daniel and Dag had also changed occupations over the life course, while Didrik has yet to find work. For the youngest generations the current poor labour market opportunities for young people was a major obstacle against finding a job. Charlie had a fear of debt. Didrik was finding it hard to get into his chosen field (ICT, which is very competitive in Norway). Didrik was sceptical about academic qualifications in general and he did not consider seeking an apprenticeship in a manual trade and would prefer a job that he 'really wanted to do'. He did not want to take out a study loan.[22]

Charlie reflected on how labour market conditions had changed for the worse compared with those of his parents when they were young:

> *...cos like my dad... left school cos he didn't like school and that, and he hadn't any qualifications, but he said he walked straight into a [shop work] and started working there. And then his friend got him a job at a*

window cleaning place and... So like how easy – he just jumped from job to job. My mum walked straight into a job, she didn't have any qualifications, she just did it, and she's been there for 30 odd years.

Conclusions

By adopting a contextualist life course approach, we have analysed the impact of changing period-specific conditions on the school-to-work transition of working-class men in three family generations in the UK and Norway. The comparative analysis of these cases shows the importance of time and place in creating opportunities and constraints for particular individuals according to their gender, class and family circumstances. We will end by returning to questions posed at the beginning of the chapter and draw some conclusions from this case analysis.

We have analysed the changes in the structural conditions of labour markets, systems of education and gender relations as they impact on the life course of each generation of working-class men in the transition from school to work in both countries. Although the Norwegian grandfather was apprenticed as a carpenter, neither he nor the British grandfather were expected to progress beyond compulsory schooling. For financial reasons young men were expected to get a job as soon as they could in order to contribute to the family income. Moreover, job opportunities for low-skilled work were plentiful in part because of the post-war Golden Age of the expanding public sector that offered secure employment (Hobsbawm 1994). The British grandfather found work following redundancy in a public utility nationalised after the war. The Norwegian grandfather who had been a self-employed carpenter for the first part of his working life spent the last 16 years of it in the public sector.

Although the system of education had expanded in both countries by the time the next generation was at school, both fathers left at the minimum school leaving age and went into low-skilled work. At that time job opportunities were also plentiful and lack of skills did not stop young people from finding gainful employment. The two fathers found work in the countries' postal services. Like the grandfathers, over the course of their employment careers, the two fathers shifted between the public sector where jobs were unionised and secure and the private sector. Watching their sons grow up in the 2000s in which the transition from school to work is more protracted than in their day, because of increased emphasis on education and credentialism in both Norway and Britain (Williamson 2002), the two fathers regretted their own lack of education and training. Compared with their own fathers who lived through wartime scarcity followed by growing prosperity which they thought would go on forever, the 1960–65 generation was ambitious for their sons. Yet at the same time the fathers were concerned about the lack of predictability and fragmentation of the labour market and the high cost of housing.

In Britain, the public sector is undergoing severe retrenchment, labour markets have been deregulated and jobs with prospects and security are hard to come by. In addition, the economy has been hit by austerity policies following the economic crisis from 2008 although deregulation in Britain long predates this. In Norway, although there has been a decline in world oil prices with consequences for Norway's dependence on oil production,[23] the impact of the crisis has been much less severe compared with the rest of Europe. However, in both countries, manufacturing and services have largely been moved to countries where labour is cheap and regulation virtually non-existent. In addition, the influx of EU labour to both Norway and the UK has lowered wages, especially in low-skilled male employment. The youngest generation is the first of the three to make the school-to-work transition in the context of these changes. This makes the transition into work even harder for them than it was for their fathers and grandfathers, especially given the rise in credentialism and higher expectations in terms of consumption. The result is that the transition from school to work for the two working-class young men described here is, thus far, less than smooth.

As we have also demonstrated, changing opportunity structures are moderated by intergenerational transmission and transfers in families. Parents' aspirations and expectations for their children's lives are an important aspect of this. Our analysis points to a break in parents' educational expectations, with the two older generations having (been) expected to leave school without qualifications. By contrast, the middle generation whose children were growing up in the 2000s explicitly encouraged their sons to stay on at school. At the same time, the ambition to gain an apprenticeship in a trade remains a constant theme across the older male generations, reflecting continuity with the past.[24]

A further important change that should not be overlooked occurs in the middle generation, again reflecting wider structural changes across historical periods. This involves the increase of mothers in education and the labour market in both countries from the 1970s. Mothers have thereby increased their influence on their children's educational performance. Both the fathers (Dag and Ray) had wives in higher-status occupations than their own. The mothers in both cases were reported to be important in inspiring their children in education.

In terms of family transfers and reflecting the increasing inequality in assets between generations, there is little evidence of *inter vivos* wealth being passed on in these families, with the exception of the older Norwegian rural generations who were given land to build houses by their parents. However, the youngest generation receives free board from their parents. We have also noted the significance of small financial gifts from grandparents that enable the current generation to drive or buy a car, possessions and skills that may make entry into particular types of male working-class jobs possible.

Another, but equally important, aspect of intergenerational transfers is the importance of the decline in family size over the generations. The implication of this trend for family support, both vertical and horizontal, is often overlooked (Thompson 1997). For example, we noted parental support for building housing in rural Norway among the older generations and the young generation's receipt of support from relatives in finding work and a cheap room to rent. The decline in family size means fewer children to make financial transfers to. This has major implications when housing becomes unaffordable, as in the case of the youngest generation.

In examining the three generations, we have mapped the social contexts in which adulthood is achieved and thereby pointed to the changing meanings of adulthood. The young men considered here have barely embarked on adulthood in terms of establishing themselves in the labour market, let alone live independently. They therefore focussed on the 'here and now' and on the idea of learning to be independent as a prerequisite for completing the transition to adulthood. By contrast, the older generations, looking back on their lives, were cogniscent of life course phases already achieved and viewed adulthood in terms of taking responsibility for their families.

Notes

1　The study *Intergenerational Transmission in the Transition to Adulthood: a mixed methods life course approach* is funded by the Norwegian Research Council (2013–2018).
2　The sample was selected both on purposive grounds, i.e. to include chains – male, female and a mix of genders, and different social classes. Recruitment included participants found via workplaces and wider social networks of the project researchers.
3　Hareven (1978) states that particular age groups are problematised and become an issue depending on wider social and economic changes. Hall's book *Adolescence* (1904) is the first instance where the concept of youth as distinct from other phases is discussed (Jordan 1978). Adulthood marks the 'mature individual' (Hareven 1978) and is associated with autonomy and independence from the family of origin. Markers of adulthood change over time, with the life course only becoming clearly structured as a sequence of phases in the West in the 20th century (Hareven 1978, Kohli 2009).
4　Norway joined the European Economic Area (EEA) Agreement in 1994.
5　The number is now higher than at any time since 1974 when figures were first collected (The Independent Schools Council 2015).
6　A large part of Norway's small population lived in rural communities during the time the grandparent generation grew up. The percentage of people employed in the primary sector of the economy – agriculture and fisheries – was very high. In 1949 there were 213,000 farms in the country and in 2002 61,500. There were 100,000 fishermen in 1950 and only 19,000 in 2001 (Norway 2003: SSB)
7　The percentage of the birth cohorts completing upper secondary school with academic subjects was as follows: In 1951 8.8% of 19 year olds took university entrance exams. In 1974 the equivalent percentage was 28.4% and in 2013 83%. The differences are due to both structural changes in the system of education as well as other factors, notably the high increase in women in higher education (Aamodt 1982).
8　The Norwegian State Education Loan Fund (Lånekassen) was established in 1947. It gave means-tested loans to students in higher education. From 1972 the means testing of loans stopped. The number of loan recipients was 2,173 in 1947–48 and 159,922 in 1996–97.
9　Under the 1944 Education Act the school leaving age was raised to 15 but was not enforced until 1947.

10 In the UK children have typically started school at five years of age in the post-war period.

11 In England and Wales only 3.4% went to university in 1950; 8.4% in 1970; and 33.3% in 2000 (House of Commons Library 2012)

12 Modern Apprenticeships were introduced in the UK in 1994 for 16 to 24 year olds in 14 industrial sectors and later expanded to cover 80 different occupational areas. Following numerous reviews and reforms and increased investment, numbers doubled from 1997 to 2009 from approximately 75,000 to around 180,000; at present more ambitious targets have been set to further increase participation. In 2001 only 24% finished the full programme whilst in 2009 63% completed – although questions still remain about the quality of the programmes.

13 Some informants in the British chain were interviewed four years previously for another study.

14 The UK informants live in the London area while the Norwegian informants come from different parts of southern Norway due to geographical mobility across the generations.

15 Norway was occupied by Nazi Germany and Britain was heavily bombarded in the war. This period left a lasting impression in both men's lives, which is evident in their accounts.

16 Housing was very scarce for more than a decade after the war. Urbanisation took hold and in the bigger cities blocks of flats were built in suburban areas. In the period 1945–65 the state intervened and started public housing programmes to build rented accommodation with guaranteed conditions for tenants. A special 'housing bank' (Husbanken) was established to help people who lived in small towns and villages who lacked collateral to get mortgages.

17 Most of the cohort born in 1946 lived in rented housing; only 1 million council houses were available accounting for 10% of households. For the cohort born in 1958 council housing was growing, reaching its peak in 1981. For the 2000s' birth cohort, home ownership had become the norm. *Growing up in social housing in Britain*: a profile of four generations to the present day 2009. www.jrf.org.uk/sites/default/files/jrf/migrated/files/social-housing-britain-FULL.pdf.

18 Home ownership began to rise from the 1960s. In 1979 when Thatcher came to power there was considerable encouragement for people to buy; those in public housing were permitted to buy their homes.

19 In order to graduate from upper secondary school in Norway, exams in key subjects such as Norwegian, maths and English have to be passed.

20 Up until 2013/14, 16 to 19 funding was relatively protected and from August 2014, funding for 18 year olds in further education colleges was cut by 17.5%. The Coalition Government shifted funding from workplace learning to adult apprenticeships. This government abolished the Education Maintenance Allowance and replaced it with a 16–19 Bursary Fund that did not cover Charlie.

21 Employees on zero-hours contracts are not guaranteed a set number of hours a week and have no sick pay or maternity leave entitlement. The percentage of UK workers on these contracts has risen from 0.8% in 2000 to 2.4% in 2015 (ONS 2015).

22 He would have had access to courses for the unemployed but did not mention this in the interview.

23 At the time of writing, June 2017, the impact of the declining oil prices has hit the country hard with increasing unemployment in the oil sector and occupations in associated branches.

24 Apprenticeships have strong roots in the British working class but became less common after the mid-1970s (Vickerstaffe 2003). Currently 3 million apprenticeships are being promised by the UK government between 2015 and 2020 (Mirza-Davies 2015). Similar policy measures to improve the situation for apprentices in Norway are also promised.

References

Aaberge, R (2016) Inntekstulikhet i Norge i lys av Piketty-debatten [Income inequality in light of the Piketty-debate], *Samfunnsspeilet* 1, 3–9

Aamodt, P. O.(1982) *Education and Social Background*. Oslo: Central Bureau of Statistics Norway

Ashton, D. and Lowe, G. (1991) *Making Their Way: Education, Training and the Labour Market in Canada and Britain*. Milton Keynes: Open University Press

Beck, U. and Beck-Gernsheim, E. (1995) *The Normal Chaos of Love*. Cambridge: Polity Press

Bertaux, D. and Thompson, P. (1997) Introduction, in Bertaux, D. and Thompson, P. (Eds.) *Pathways to Social Class: A Qualitative Approach to Social Mobility*. Oxford: Clarendon Press, pp. 1–31

Billari, F. C. and Liefbroer, A. C. (2010) Towards a new pattern of transition to adulthood? *Advances in Life Course Research* 15, 59–75

Blanden, J., Goodman, A., Gregg, P. and Machin, S. (2002) *Changes in Intergenerational Mobility in Britain*. London: Centre for the Economics of Education, LSE

Blossfeld, H-P (2009) Comparative life course research: A cross-national and long-itudinal perspective, in Elder, G. and GieleJ. (eds) *The Craft of Life Course Research*, New York: Guilford Press, pp. 280–306

Blumer, H. (1954) What is wrong with social theory? *American Sociological Review* 18, 3–10

Brannen, J. (2015) *Fathers and Sons: Families, Fatherhood and Migration*. Basingstoke: Palgrave

Brannen, J., and Nilsen, A. (2011) Comparative biographies in case-based cross-national research: Methodological considerations, *Sociology* 45(4), 603–618

Buchman, M. (1989) *The Script of Life in Modern Society: Entry into Adulthood in a Changing World*. Chicago: University of Chicago Press

Central Bureau of Statistics Norway (2003). *Demography*

Clapham, D., Mackie, P., Orford, S., Buckley, S. and Thomas, I. with Atherton, I. and McAnulty, U. (2012) *Housing Options and Solutions for Young People in 2020*. York: The Joseph Rowntree Foundation

Dommermuth, L. (2009) Når flytter de unge hjemmefra? [When do young people leave home?] *Samfunnsspeilet* 1

House of Commons Library (2012). *Education: Historical Statistics*. London: House of Commons Library

Elder, G. (1985) *Life Course Dynamics: Trajectories and Transitions, 1968–1980*. Cornell: Cornell University Press

Elder, G. (1999 [1974]) *Children of the Great Depression: Social Change in Life Experience*. Oxford: Westview Press

Elder, G., Johnson, M. K. and Crosnoe, R. (2006) The emergence and development of life course theory, in Mortimer, J. and Shanahan, M. J. (eds) *Handbook of the Life Course*. New York: Springer, pp. 3–19

Esping-Andersen (1990) *Three Worlds of Welfare Capitalism*. Princeton NJ: Princeton University Press

Furlong, A., Woodman, D. and Wyn, J. (2011) Changing times, changing perspectives: Reconciling 'transition' and 'cultural' perspectives on youth and young adulthood. *Journal of Sociology* 47(4), 355–370

Geertz, C. (1973) *The Interpretation of Cultures: Selected Essays*. New York: Basic Books

Goodwin, J. and O'Connor, H. (2005) Exploring complex transitions: Looking back at the 'Golden Age' of from school to work. *Sociology* 39(2), 201–220

Gomm, R., Hammersley, M. and Foster, P. (eds) (2000) *Case Study Method.* London: Sage

Hall, G. S. (1904) *Adolescence.* Englewood Cliffs, NJ: Prentice Hall

Hareven, T. (1978) The last stage: Historical adulthood and old age, in Erikson, E. (ed) *Adulthood.* New York: Norton & Co, pp. 201–215

Heinz, W. R. (2014) Did the Great Recession affect young people's aspirations and reinforce social inequality? *Longitudinal and Life Course Studies* 5(2), 189–198

Hobsbawm, E. (1994) *Age of Extremes: The Short 20th Century.* London: Michael Joseph

Irwin, S. (1995) *Rights of Passage: Social Change and the Transition from Youth to Adulthood.* London: UCL Press

Irwin, S. and Elley, S. (2011) Concerted cultivation? Parenting values, education and class diversity. *Sociology* 45(3), 480–495

Irwin, S. and Elley, S. (2013) Parents' hopes and expectations for their children's future occupations. *The Sociological Review* 61, 111–130

Irwin, S. (2017) Parenting teenagers as they grow up: Values, practices and young people's pathways beyond school in England. *The Sociological Review.* doi:10.1177/0038026117691718

Job Centre Plus (2017). *Briefing Paper 5871.* London: House of Commons Library, 18 October 2017

Jones, G. and Wallace, C. (1992). *Youth, Family and Citizenship.* Buckingham: Open University Press

Jordan, W.(1978) Searching for adulthood in America, in Erikson, E. (ed) *Adulthood.* New York: Norton & Co, pp. 189–199

Kohli, M. (2009) The world we forgot: A historical review of the life course, in Heinz, W., Huinink, J., Swader, C. S. & Weyman, A. (eds.) *The Life Course Reader.* Frankfurt/Main: Campus Verlag, pp. 64–90

Lupton, R., Unwin, L. and Thomson, S. (2015) The coalition's record on further education, skills and access to higher education, 2010–2015. *Social Policy in a Cold Climate.* CASE, LSE and University of Manchester

Macdonald, R., P., Mason, T. Shildrick, C. Webster, L. Johnston and L. Ridley (2001) Snakes and ladders: In defense of studies of youth transitions. *Sociological Research Online* 5(4)

Meyer, J. and Schofer, E. (2007) The university in Europe: 20th century expansion, in Krucken, G., Kosmut, A. and Torka, M. (eds) *Towards a Multi diversity: Universities between Global Trends and National Traditions.* Bielefeld: Die Deutsche Bibliothek

Mills, C. W. 1980 [1959] *The Sociological Imagination.* London: Penguin

Mirza-Davies, J. (2015) *Apprenticeships Policy, England.* Briefing Paper Number 03052, 2 September 2015. London: House of Commons Library

Mortimer, J. T. (2014). Familial transmission, support, and youth unemployment in hard economic times. *Longitudinal and Life Course Studies* 5(2), 97–104

Nilsen, A. and Brannen, J. (2014) An intergenerational approach to transitions to adulthood: The importance of history and biography. *Sociological Research Online* 19(2)

Nilsen, A., Brannen, J. and Lewis, S. (eds) (2012) *Transitions to Parenthood in Europe: A Comparative Life Course Perspective.* Bristol: Policy Press

Nilsen, A.das Dores Guerreira, M. and Brannen, J. (2002). 'Most choices involve money': Different pathways to adulthood, in Brannen, J., Lewis, S., Nilsen, A. and Smithson, J. (eds) *Young Europeans, Work and Family: Futures in Transition.* London: Routledge, pp. 162–184

Office of National Statistics (ONS) (2015) *Contracts with No Guaranteed Hours 2015*London: Office of National Statistics

Office of National Statistics (ONS) (2014) *Young Adults Living with Parents 2013 Release.* London: Office of National Statistics. Released 21 January 2014, http://webarchive.nationalarchives.gov.uk/20160105160709/http://www.ons.gov.uk/ons/rel/family-demography/young-adults-living-with-parents/2013/sty-young-adults.html.

Roberts, K. (1997) Structure and agency : The new youth research agenda, in Bynner, J., Chisholm, L. and Furlong, A. (eds) *Youth, Citizenship and Social Change in a European Context.* Aldershot: Gower, pp. 56–66

Stiglitz, J. (2012) *The Price of Inequality.* London: Penguin

Telle, K. (2017) Perspektiver, i *Økonomiske analyser* [Perspectives, in *Economic Analyses*]. Oslo: SSB, Norway

The Independent Schools Council (2015) London: The Independent Schools Council. www.isc.co.uk/research/

Thomas, W. I and Znaniecki, F. (1958) [1918–1920]. *The Polish Peasant in Europe and America.* Vol 1–2. New York: Dover

Thompson, P. (1997) Women, men, and transgenerational family influences in social mobility, in Bertaux, D. & Thompson, P. (Eds.) *Pathways to Social Class: A Qualitative Approach to Social Mobility.* Oxford: Clarendon Press, pp. 32–61

Vickerstaffe, S. (2003) Apprenticeship in a 'golden age': Were youth transitions really smooth and unproblematic back then? *Work, Employment and Society* 17(2), 269–287

Vogt, K. C. (2017) *Men in Manual Occupations: Changing Lives in Times of Change.* Oslo: Cappelen Damm Akademisk.

Wilmot, P. and Young, M. (1957) *Family and Kinship in East London.* London: Penguin Books

Williamson, H. (2002*)* *Supporting Young People in Europe. Principles, Policy and Practice.* Strasbourg: Council of Europe Publishing

Wolf, A. (2011) *Review of Further Education: The Wolf Report.* London: Department for Education

4 How parents see their children's future

Education, work and social change in England

Sarah Irwin

Introduction

Social and economic change is reconfiguring transitions from youth to adulthood and relationships across generations. How are young people and their families positioned in this changing context and how is change experienced and negotiated across diverse class circumstances? This chapter focuses on England. It explores parents' perspectives on their teenage children's experiences and prospects for securing a decent living and in so doing it illuminates commonalities and differences in the experiences, orientations and practices of parents supporting their children growing up.

Recent decades have seen significant developments in educational, training and labour market arrangements for young people in England. Post-compulsory secondary educational participation has grown over recent decades, most notably in the 1980s and again from 2000 to 2015 with an increase from 57% to 71% of 16–18 year olds in full-time education (Bolton 2015). There has been a significant growth in the necessity of qualifications for securing employment in the youth labour market (George et al 2015) and school leavers with few or no qualifications are altogether less likely to find employment (Allmendinger and von den Driesch 2014; Wilson and Bivand 2014). Academic middle attainers and those seeking vocational routes to the labour market are confronted with an incoherent 'system' with low-quality training opportunities and pathways with uncertain outcomes (eg. Keep 2015). Those pursuing a university education enter a higher education sector characterised by a marked growth in participation rates and a remarkable rise in the level of the loan-based student tuition fee. These changes have been accompanied by concerns over the sustainability of levels of professional graduate employment and of earnings premia attached to graduate status (Brown 2013). Despite cohorts of young adults being more qualified than ever before, they face an increasingly difficult job market, with shrinking levels of full-time employment and worsening relative earnings across the spectrum as compared to their predecessors (Hills et al 2015). How are families differently positioned in these changing times and how do parents respond and seek to support their young adult children?

Family background remains crucial in predicting and influencing young people's educational and wider life chances. A long tradition of research explores the reproduction of inequalities across generations and parents' role and positioning here (see Irwin 2009 for a review). This chapter builds on research designed to explore the reproduction of inequalities across generations and how parents perceive and orient to childrearing and to their children's futures. The research design took as a starting point a puzzle relating to the disparate conclusions of quantitative and qualitative research regarding the inheritance of inequalities across generations (see Irwin 2009). Widely influenced by Bourdieu, researchers have operationalised his concepts in differing ways and arrived at rather different conclusions (e.g. Reay 1998; de Graaf et al 2000; Lareau 2003, 2011; Barone 2006). Quantitative researchers have shed light on patterns of reproducing inequalities and have often been circumspect in making claims about the existence of distinctive class cultural groupings, and the precise mechanisms which 'translate' family background into future educational and occupational success. Qualitative researchers have provided especially rich insights into everyday classed experiences and interactions and through these presumed to pinpoint the enactment of cross-generational transmission of inequalities. They have tended to make relatively strong claims regarding both causal process and the distinctiveness of class groupings. The empirical evidence explored in this chapter stems from research designed to investigate diversity within as well as across social class groupings. I have previously explored parents' relationships with their children, their orientations to their children's education and their hopes and expectations regarding their children's occupational futures (Irwin and Elley 2011, 2013). In that work, with Elley, I foregrounded the importance of current circumstances and of parents' backgrounds, biographies and own experiences of being parented in influencing their values and how they engage with their children. I also examined classed inequalities in the transmission of resources across generations and how these play out in biographical time (Irwin and Elley 2013; Irwin 2017). In this chapter I shift the analytic focus more explicitly onto parents' evaluations of educational pathways in contexts of change and their perceptions of economic recession and longer-run trends in opportunities facing their young adult children. I explore diversity in parents' perceptions of changes confronting young people today, and their beliefs about how their children can best navigate these. Perceptions of extensive risks and challenges confronting young people are widespread, yet the families were very differently situated in respect of such risks. Their accounts illuminate some ways in which contemporary social changes reinforce the stratification of life chances, and offer insight into parents' diverse subjective experiences and orientations in the current context.

The restructuring of youth opportunity and constraint

The UK, with its residual welfare state and weakly regulated training pathways and employment relationships, is characterised by its neo-liberal mediation of long-run socio-economic change and globalisation processes (Buchholz et al 2011). It is said that the post-war decades of inclusive growth gave way to widening inequalities from the 1970s onwards (Taylor-Gooby 2013). Longer-run trends to inequality have been particularly marked by the significant increase in elite fortunes (Dorling 2014), and evidence suggests that middle as well as working classes are being squeezed in this new world, particularly since upward mobility chances are less certain than in the post-war growth decades (Brown 2013; Devine and Sensier 2017). The recession of 2008 and subsequent austerity measures implemented by the Coalition government were layered on top of longer-run trends which have undermined youth independence and pathways to secure employment (eg Irwin 1995a,b; Purcell et al 2011; Stone et al 2011). The recession engendered falls in living standards across the population (Gordon 2015) but evidence shows that young adults were particularly vulnerable (Bell and Blanchflower 2011). Recently there has been extensive interest in predictions that, in their adult lives, today's young people will fare less well than their parents (Pew Center 2014). In this evolving context we can sketch some key developments in education, training and youth labour market opportunities and wider prospects for young people. I consider briefly some of the changes as they impacted upon young people from diverse family backgrounds, across a spectrum from graduate middle class to the under-acknowledged 'middle' to low-qualified and marginalised working-class youth.

In England, higher education young participation rates increased from 30% in the mid-1990s to 38% by 2012 (Hefce 2013). Loan-based student fees were increased from just over £3000 pa to approximately £9000 pa in 2012. Some commentators question the conventional wisdom of young people pursuing higher education in a context which has seen increasing young participation rates, uncertainty over whether graduate-level employment demand and earnings premia can be sustained, and the massive hike in tuition fees to be paid by students themselves via a loan system. For example, Brown and colleagues identify a pattern of social congestion in which insufficent employment demand leads to graduate under-employment and frustrated expectations (Brown et al 2011). Others have provided an alternative analysis in which graduate salaries have been maintained (as an outcome of organisational restructuring) but they also question the sustainability of this pattern (Blundell et al 2016). Meanwhile, the demand for higher education has been sustained since the 2012 fees increase.[1] We will see that despite doubts, for graduate families expecting their children to access research-intensive universities, there is little question over the ongoing value, and necessity, of graduate-level education. Interestingly, amongst families without any university background but with children seriously contemplating applying for university, there is a much more explicit cost-benefit account of the value of such an education vis-à-vis vocational pathways. This contrast shines light on the different positioning of such families in respect of changing educational options for their children.

Recently, we have seen more academic and policy interest directed at 'middle' pathways from education to the labour market. This middle group has been relatively overlooked by an emphasis on higher education and on those 'not in employment, education or training' (NEET) amongst both academic researchers and by policy makers (Roberts 2011; Hodgson and Spours 2015). The group confronts a confusing array of options in a system which under-serves their needs. In her review, Wolf noted that '*the staple offer for between a quarter and a third of the post-16 cohort is a diet of low-level vocational qualifications, most of which have little to no labour market value*' and '*at least 350000 get little to no benefit from the post-16 education system*' (Wolf 2011, p. 105). The long-run pattern of labour market restructuring has meant fewer opportunities for young adults entering work, and vocational education and training has become increasingly problematic, with a host of different players involved (Purcell et al 2011; Keep 2015). This is partly due to the neo-liberalisation and opening up of training 'markets', with key players and institutions often pulling in different directions, leading Keep (2015) to characterise vocational education and training (VET) provision as a fractured 'system', 'a set of related but fragmented and. partially overlapping sub-systems or streams of activity' (Keep 2015, p. 464). Currently the government is moving to implement recommendations for a much more streamlined and coherent set of 16+ pathways (DfE 2016; Sainsbury 2016). There is some scepticism in the sector that the resources allocated to this task will engender meaningful change, a scepticism which we will see is echoed by some study participants when describing the decline in valued training opportunities for their (male) children.

Amongst those with fewest resources, prospects appear bleak as widening inequalities leave a group of disadvantaged and low-qualified youth at risk of marginalisation, not just in their young adult years but throughout their working lifetimes (eg. Macdonald and Shildrick, this volume). George and colleagues document how young people without qualifications are more dis-advantaged than their peers 20 years ago, and how the penalties for having no qualifications have increased for young people (George et al 2015). They also document the declining chances of securing qualifications through working-class employment, so qualifications gained at the end of school become more crucial to lifetime chances (see also Allmendinger and von den Driesch 2014). In general, young people participate in education for longer and face increased competition for accessing work, particularly work with prospects for progression (Keep and Mayhew 2014). The absence of qualifications is increasingly an obstacle to subsequent success in a society with fewer work-based ladders for the less advantaged.

Differentiated change is also evident in the distribution of income across the population. Gregg et al (2014) demonstrate that real wage growth stag-nated in the early 2000s across the UK population, and became negative after 2009. From 1979 until the early 2000s there was a secular growth in real weekly earnings for the upper deciles. Median real wages effectively flatlined through the 2000s and then fell in 2009, whilst a more irregular trend characterised the lowest decile. Overall, the lowest earners were hardest hit and inequalities widened (Gregg et al 2014; see also Finch and Rose 2017). This wider pattern of an end of real wage growth in the early 2000s for median earners, and decline for low earners, appears to be integral to the situation of less advantaged participants in the study, some of whom described their experiences of relative decline in wages whilst their children were growing up. The study data exemplifies parents' experiences associated with these and the wider trends described above. We will see how young adult childrens' futures are perceived and mediated by parents across diverse socio-economic circumstances.

Research design

The project 'Family contexts, class and parenting values'[2] was originally designed to explore parents' values, perceptions and practical commitments to their children, their views on if and how things have changed across generations, and their expectations for their children's education and for their wider futures. It was designed to investigate the situated experiences and values of parents with reference to debates on class, parenting and the reproduction of inequalities across generations (Bourdieu 1986; Reay 1998; Lareau 2003; Vincent and Ball 2007). In 2008 I ran a self-completion questionnaire survey of parents with children involved in organised activities in towns across Yorkshire (and included venues such as leisure centres, community-based activities and various clubs). 564 questionnaires were completed. The survey was designed to ensure coverage of socio-economic diversity. The focus around organised activities means that the sample was weighted towards middle-class parents, and excluded severely disadvantaged people, or those who were less engaged with their children. However, it accessed a range of circumstances *within* as well as *across* middle, intermediate and working classes.[3] Respondents were invited to provide contact details with a view to running qualitative interviews with a sub-sample, and 250 did so. 34 semi-structured interviews were undertaken with individuals identified strategically from the survey sample.

Within the survey questionnaire, respondents were asked a series of questions relating to how important different characteristics are for a child to do well in life. The questions were adapted from the British Social Attitudes Youth Survey (Park et al 2004). Parents were also asked: 'Have these characteristics changed in their importance since you were a child?' and were asked to say if each characteristic had become more important, less important, or stayed about the same. Almost uniformly, respondents thought that a good education was important for a child to do well in life (and 80% thought it *very* important). They were more evenly divided over whether the value of a good education has increased or stayed about the same. The results, disaggregated by social class, reveal that approximately half of the professional/managerial and of the intermediate-class parents thought that a good education had become more important than in the past, compared to three-quarters of routine/manual-class respondents. This higher percentage amongst routine/manual-class respondents is consistent with the secular increase in the importance of formal qualifications for accessing paid work, and the decline in work-based routes to a secure job with prospects (cf. Barham et al 2009).

In deciding who to approach for qualitative interview, a sample of parents was chosen with reference to the age of their children (upper primary school age, or just starting secondary school so about 10–12 years old), to social class and to parents' responses regarding whether or not education holds the same, or more, importance than in past. This latter index succeeded in opening up a range of experiences *within* classes including diverse current circumstances, differing backgrounds (of class stability and mobility) and different kinds of orientation to children's futures. There was a high rate of agreement to interview, and interviews were undertaken across 34 households (with 24 mothers and 12 fathers). The interviews were fairly evenly spread across class groupings. In 2011 a second round of interviews was run with 30 of the original participants, and in 2014 a third round of interviews with 21 of them. This qualitative longitudinal stretch meant that parents were interviewed across the period in which their children were growing up through their teenage years and approaching young adulthood, as well as through the economic recession and austerity. In prior analyses I have explored participants' accounts of parenting, their values and their perspectives as their children were growing up, and sought to understand the contextual shaping of values and practices. In the following account I particularly focus on parental perspectives on their children's futures as mediated by the social and economic changes outlined earlier in this chapter. Their diverse subjective experiences offer a revealing picture of classed experiences of educational, social and economic changes.

Orientations and values relating to young adult children's education and training in contexts of change

It has been well documented that graduate families tend to normalise higher education and their children commonly perceive university as a natural or obvious route to take (Ball et al 2002; Power et al 2003; Devine 2004). This was very clearly the case too amongst parents in the study who were themselves graduates. Participants interviewed in the first round described their expectations for their children who were then commonly aged 11 and under:

> *I expect him to, I personally I think he'll, a child of that calibre he ought to be getting four A grades at A level and thinking about Oxford University, you know, or Cambridge because I have that belief in his abilities.*
>
> (middle-class mother)

> *I suspect coming from the family we come from, it'd be difficult not to do a degree; they'll feel a degree of pressure even if we don't say it, that they ought to be going to university.*
>
> (middle-class father)

> *Erm, and she'll say, like, "When I go to university..." And my nieces are all at university now as well... she's got that thing buzzing around her that that's where they're all at.*
>
> (middle-class mother, graduated as mature student)

For these parents, pursuing higher education had been part of their own experience and was an obvious route for their children. When children diverged at all in their thinking, parents encouraged their children to remain on a path to higher education (HE). They drew on resources of various kinds in so doing and the longitudinal data indicates that these children fell back in line with their parents' expectations (Irwin 2017). Over recent decades UK higher education participation has expanded significantly and is the baseline expectation for professional occupations and careers. In the course of the study, higher education fees were very significantly increased, to be paid for by a loan repayable through future earnings. In 2012 fees increased from just over £3000 to a maximum of £9000 per annum although in practice most universities charged this amount. Parents were interviewed in 2011, when the new fees arrangements were being decided upon by government, and in 2014 when the new fees regime was in place. At this point many parents had children who were actively applying for university, and older children who were presently at university. Middle-class parents were typically angry about the fees increases, but this did not deflect their very clear belief that university was the proper route for their children to pursue, a *rite de passage* and a gateway to securing a professional job and career:

> *I think [fees] that's a terrible state of affairs. But it won't affect us providing, it doesn't affect our opinions or desires for them to go away in any way, shape or form.*
>
> (middle-class father, self-employed)

> *Oh its crap. [My son] has been really lucky cos he's caught the end of the cheaper fees yeah... he also got a bursary... [My daughter] is just a bit sort of phlegmatic about it, well she'll just pay that loan back really slowly. I think it's criminal, that we are not investing in talent.*
>
> (middle-class mother, professional)

There has been a significant expansion of higher education participation, especially since the early 1990s, and an accompanying momentum towards sharpening institutional differentiation and hierarchy. Graduate parents are very familiar with fine-grained status differences across universities (Power et al 2003), as well as to the kudos deemed to be attached to different degree subjects. This differentiation invited some commentary, as did their child's choice of degree with reference to its future economic value in light of the recession. Middle-class parents' engagement with hierarchies of university status is not new. However, HE 'massification' and concerns about children's future economic and social success may further sharpen the perceived importance of related judgements. More broadly, academic qualifications to degree level remained both highly valued and unassailable regardless of the fees increase even though the fees and linked future debt caused extensive anger. University education is valued for a range of reasons, having intrinsic value both as a path to independence and for furthering academic pursuit, often valued as an end in itself and as a route to a decent future.

Amongst parents in intermediate-class circumstances[4] there was a much more contingent commitment to higher education than for graduate middle-class parents. The increase in university fees and prospective debt may well have influenced, or been a lightening rod for, the cost-benefit reckoning these parents described in their accounts. Such appraisals appear to be associated with the non-normative nature of higher education in these intermediate-class family contexts and its more marginal value. This mother's son had accepted a place to study at university but changed his mind soon before starting:

> *There was no point coming out of University... fifty seven thousand pounds of debt to do a job he really doesn't want to do... I said you've got to live the life you want to live.*
>
> (intermediate-class mother)

For another:

> *And if they start earning money and then they've got that loan... looming over them. It's only a minimum payment that they have to pay back per month isn't it? But it's for a long time. It can be slightly offputting.*
>
> (intermediate-class mother)

Such contingency sometimes led young people towards higher education rather than away from it. One mother described how she had told her 17-year-old daughter: *'I'm not going to say you can't go to university but I don't think it's the right thing for you'* yet three years later she explained that her daughter had gone to university and was flourishing there. Intermediate-class parents were also much more likely to tailor their advice in line with the evolving preferences of their young adult children than were graduate middle-class parents (a pattern intermediate-class parents held in common with those from trades and working-class backgrounds). Nevertheless, they firmly believed their children needed to secure reasonable qualifications in order to be a step ahead in the search for opportunities, especially in the context of recession and extensive competition for jobs:

> *I think the best way to go, and I keep telling them this, is to try and just educate yourself as best as possible so that you will have the best chances.*
> (intermediate-class mother)

> *You have to teach your kids even more that if you get a better education you might be that one step more [ahead], the tick in the box [compared to] the person who's in front of you trying for the same job.*
> (intermediate-class mother)

An overlapping and shared view across many of the intermediate and working-class participants was seeing their children's success in education not in terms of pursuing education as far as they could, but in terms of doing well in the qualifications they took. A good education has become more important than in the past to many, especially working-class, families.[5] This does not necessarily mean pursuing education ever further but is calibrated against understandings of education and decent qualifications as a platform for a promising future:

> *I said [joining the army] "it's, it's your decision I said it's up to you". I said "If you are going to do something like that you know you still want to get your qualifications... and you want to go in and go for a good career... rather than just go in with no qualifications and think 'no I'm goin' into the Army anyway it doesn't matter'".*
> (working-class mother)

> *So I think, you know, with him, if the right job came up at sixteen, seventeen that could give him a career, a future, then I'd be just as happy for him to do that than to stay on at University... What he needs to be able to do is to have options. You know, if you get a good education now you've then got options of what you want to do. It's taking control of your own life rather than your life taking control of you.*
> (working-class father)

In short, whilst many maintained a keen sense of the importance of educational qualifications, this was often about doing well so far as you chose to go. However, some, especially with trades backgrounds, were sceptical or even scathing about the declining ability to secure work even with paper qualifications. Doing well in the qualifications you take is of obvious value, but pursuing academic qualifications might, in the current context, be counterproductive, especially if there are other routes available. The concern that a university education might lead nowhere helpful is echoed in the following comment (by a plasterer) on the current value of academic qualifications and his son's prospects:

> *To be honest with you and I, I don't, even if he's got eh, fifteen A levels I don't think it'd help, help him at this particular moment in time... he could be brainiest kid in world to be honest wi' you it doesn't count for a job for you now.*
>
> (working-class father)

Alongside this concern with the value of academic qualifications some fathers also expressed dismay at a decline in manual skill:

> *In this country, unfortunately in this last twenty years there's too many people getting certificates and getting things. But what can they really do [laughs], you know? The days of manual work, of skills and things are going. And, and the country suffers for that because, you know, we have to import everything that we, we don't build any more or make.*
>
> (working-class father)

> *And like it's what I said before is never mind bringin' people up from abroad, get us own working. Get 'em into apprenticeships, get them from, comin' from school... Start training your own when they're young.*
>
> (working-class father)

Prior research has shown contingent decision-making where parents are 'weak framers', allowing their children more autonomy around their educational futures (Ball et al 2002). Lareau (2003) identified a cleavage in her sample between middle-class parents whose childrearing ethos and practices were described as concerted cultivation and working-class parents whose childrearing enabled an accomplishment of natural growth. The latter supported their children extensively but accorded them significantly more autonomy. In my research, intermediate and working-class parents allowed their children a significant degree of latitude in arriving at decisions around education and training. Nevertheless, they were deeply engaged with their children's decisions, seeking to steer and guide them. Whilst the children appeared to hold greater autonomy, if they made an unanticipated decision then parents were often 'alongside' in seeking to ensure such decisions were well thought through.This probably reflects the sample composition in which intermediate and working-class parents possessed and sought to mobilise cultural knowledge and resources. It may also be indicative of a growth in the perceived importance by parents of intervening in support of their children's future success.

Recent decades have seen significant changes in educational opportunities and costs and greater uncertainty over outcomes. How are parents and their young adult children positioned in respect of such changes? Despite its very significant growth, the labour market value of (research-intensive university and elite) higher education is being sustained, and what professional middle-class parents do here, compared with their own parents, has changed little. Intermediate-class parents engaged with the idea of higher education for their children, and cost-benefit calculus reveals its less normative standing here and the linked contingency of young people from these backgrounds pursuing higher education. Amongst working-class parents there were mixed attitudes to academic qualifications, and the value of educational qualifications (including training) was contingent on their granting a good foothold in the labour market. At interview these parents revealed how they tailored their advice to children in line with the latter's evolving interests and ambitions. In the survey, working-class parents 'correctly' identified that educational qualifications have become more important for children to do well in life than they were in the past, but they held a much more contingent evaluation of academic qualifications than did graduate parents. They are also under-served by (and recognised) shrinking opportunities for valued training and employment pathways for school leavers. Across the social-class spectrum experiences of changing educational arrangements, costs and the perceived value of qualifications are all deeply important yet play out very differently. These differing classed experiences of social change are also put into sharp relief when parents describe their children's prospects in the long view, explored next.

Orientations and values relating to young adult children's future life chances in contexts of change

I reflect here on parents' wider perceptions of their children's route to a decent future, and of social and generational change. In the second round of interviews in 2011, parents were asked *'Has the economic recession made you think any differently about your child(ren)'s future work?'* In the third interview in 2014, one of the general questions about the future was asked as follows: *'A lot has changed in the economy over the last few years, so in that context would you say that you're concerned or hopeful about the future, for yourself and for your children?'* Many common concerns were articulated but there were also some distinct differences across social-class groupings. In their accounts of the future, the issue of children struggling to do as well as their parents resonated for middle-class and working-class participants. For the former, this seemed to tap into a familiar contemporary vernacular about change and living standards as well as concerns about prospects for house purchase, whilst for the latter it was an expression of frustration about the loss of job opportunities for young people (*'there is nothing there for them'*) and of immediate constraint.

Middle-class graduate parents reflected on different aspects of change, particularly the ability to secure improved living standards across generations, and linked issues relating to income, careers and housing. For example:

> *I think, long term, there's quite a concern, and I think that might impact our children's, my children's generation, because, obviously, every genera-tion has been better off, you know, I've been better off than my parents, but my parents were better off than my grandparents and so on. Erm... you know, my granddad did the same job as me, so you think, well, you know,*

we should be absolutely identical, and we're not, you know [I am better off]. So I think the expectation of our children is they're going to be better off than I am, and I think there's quite a concern, long term, that we may not be able to achieve that.

(middle-class father)

His vision of how to succeed in this context squared with his ethos of drive on behalf of his children and neatly echoes the arguments of Vincent and Ball (2007) about middle-class investments against children's risk of downward mobility:

I'm not sure that we're going to be as successful in the future, so the only way to do better than your parents is actually to move up your grade, through either brains, luck or hard work erm... you know, which goes back to the ethos that you're trying to get your kids to understand, that, actually, bone idleness will probably slip you down.

(middle-class father)

Other parents shared the concern about their children faring as well as they had anticipated:

My young adult life has been a lot more comfortable than my parents' young adult life, I think they struggled at their early stages erm... and yet we... did quite well early on. We got jobs... got on the housing ladder... we had a few good comfortable years before we had kids and we seemed, we were quite stable when we started having kids and would be in a position to set them up quite well. And actually that's not how it worked, who would have thought over the last four or five years we would have been saving towards University? I think things are going to be harder for them and certainly a lot harder than we expected them to be.

(middle-class mother)

I do worry that they're going to find some things really difficult, like buying a house, because I think that sort of thing is going to be increasingly difficult. And I think... I'm sure they will struggle to find jobs... there seems to be greater competition. Looking at what kids have to do to get into university these days, it was very different, different game to the one I had to play, you know, where you basically just had to turn up and smile sweetly, and you would get some decent grades and you were in. Getting decent grades isn't good enough these days, because everybody seems to get reasonable grades. So I do worry about that.

(middle-class father)

Many middle and intermediate-class parents foregrounded housing issues. For example:

I don't see, for the vast majority, how they're ever going to be home owners. And if you define success as owning your own home... they are not going to have the same opportunities and things aren't going to be necessarily as good unless they've got parents who can pass on wealth.

(middle-class father)

Housing was an area of concern also routinely identified by intermediate-class parents. Home ownership has become much more difficult to achieve from young ages than in the recent past. For example, in the UK amongst those aged 25 to 34, 62% were home owners in 1981, rising to 66.5% in 1991; this declined a few percentage points to 2001 and then fell sharply, to 36% by 2014 (ONS 2016). One mother aired a widely held concern as follows:

I just... I worry about from the housing point of view when I think how little even in... how little I paid for my first house in my lifetime, that worries me that how they are ever going to get on the housing ladder?

(intermediate-class mother)

It is of course difficult to make a clear judgement about the extent to which people tap into contemporary discourse about squeezed middle classes and the extent to which this really captures their values and feelings. Middle-class participants highlighted issues relating especially to university fees, to housing and employment opportunities. Many did identify with the suggestion that children will struggle to do as well as their parents, yet so too they immediately pointed to resources, capacities and agency (their own and that of their children) which will support their children into the future.

Questioned about the impact of the recession and prospects for the future, working-class parents also recounted general future constraints for their children, particularly the lack of employment opportunity but, importantly, current experiences of constraint and retrenchment also characterised responses. A significant theme here was experiences of declining wages. Parents' accounts echo the wider evidence that working-class wages have fallen in their real value (Gregg et al 2014). For example, asked about whether recession had made her think differently about her son's future work options one mother said:

I'm, well I suppose we're hoping that he will go into something that, that's of a higher level that'll need educatin' to, he'll, he does need to get a better job, better quality job. Because now the, the ordinary jobs are gettin' lower and lower paid they're, they're actually...going down, aren't they, in value?

(working-class mother)

Her partner was currently non-employed due to ill health, but reflected on his recent experience of work:

> *when I w'[was] workin' I w' getting less than I w' twenty-five years ago.*
> (working-class father)

For a semi-skilled factory operative (who himself first became a father in his teens):

> *I was earning more money ten or fifteen years ago than I'm earning now. My wage is 10 or 15% down on what I wo' earning ten or fifteen years ago. I couldn't imagine having a kid now, like seven or eight year old, and bringing them up now. I just couldn't do it on the wages I'm on now*
> (working-class father)

He reflected further on how opportunities for modest progression have, in his view, been undermined:

> *Life's a roller coaster. You get your ups and downs. But work shouldn't be like that, work shouldn't be a rollercoaster. You should start at the bottom and work your way to the top. But it doesn't work like that any-more, you work at the bottom and you stay at the bottom.* (working-class father)

Many working-class participants made links between the shortage of jobs, low pay, and immigration. For example, the above father felt that his son's prospects are influenced by *'how many immigrants there are here as well. They work for less money, so we're not earning what we think we should be earning and someone else is doing that job for less'.*

In sum, asking these parents about their children's futures turned out to be less of a prompt to general speculation and more of a prompt to reflect on social changes felt to hold a direct and present impact. This itself tells of the immediacy of social change for those more exposed to economic retrenchment. This pattern was amplified amongst several less advantaged participants reflecting on social change confronted by their children:

> *There's no jobs out there. There's literally young men walking round the streets with no jobs and no money. The crime rate's gonna go up. They are gonna be bored. What's the government providing for them? Nothing.*
> (working-class mother)

> *To be honest wi' you, if I were, at this time, starting out right now with (the kids), they wouldn't be 'ere. They would not be in this world... There's nothing for 'em. And I can't see it changing in t' near future neither. And I feel so sorry for young families now. Or lasses that are pregnant now. And I think to myself, if [my granddaughter] has kids, if [my son] has kids, nowt is there? Nothing. There's no jobs about.*
> (working-class father)

Well, there's nowt out there for em, is there?... We were talking about it (at work) today, actually, you know, we were on about, you know, people bringing kids into this world, what is there for em? [My partner's nephew], he's been wanting to get an apprenticeship job since he left school, since he was sixteen, and he's nineteen now, and he hasn't worked for three year... And he's just sat at home on dole.

(working-class mother)

It is widely argued that as economic growth has stalled in western economies, both middle and working classes face new constraints, and aspirational parents can no longer assume that their children will do better than they did. Such futures cannot be predicted. What is notable however, and manifests in the evidence shown here, is that what graduate middle-class parents seek to do is very consistent with their past experience, despite the new costs and challenges associated with both fee levels and competition. Working-class parents clearly seek to support their children into routes which will secure their futures, but they confront a disparate and fragmented youth training and labour market landscape (Keep 2015), and fewer opportunities than they had experienced. They described their children's futures in ways which reflected extensive uncertainty, and keenly sought to support their children secure a promising foothold in the labour market. Through the evidence on subjective experience we see parallels as well as marked differences across parents' orientations to their young adult children's futures, closely linked to diverse contexts of relative privilege and constraint.

Finally, it is important to note that whilst parents are very keenly concerned about competition and the need for their children to succeed through education, hard work and drive, they simultaneously identify social structural change and constraints as these shape their children's opportunities. They may advocate individualised response to contemporary changes but this does not mean that they are naïve in respect of the social nature of the demands confronting their children. Such situated knowledge could be a force for progressive political and policy change if it were to be more effectively harnessed.

Conclusion

The current context of social and economic change heralds extensive uncertainties which impact across the population. Important changes in the education system in England which occurred through the study period included the very significant increase in university fees paid by students through a student loan system, alongside continuing structural difficulties within vocational education and training. Such developments are layered upon longer-standing trends which put young people in a more precarious situation than their forebears, whether it is because of credential inflation, intense competition and concerns about debt for middle-class children or a weak youth labour market and declining opportunities for good quality training and jobs with prospects for many working-class young people. These developments point to important aspects of change across generations. The long-term picture is one in which inequalities have been increasing since the 1980s, and post-war generations which benefitted from growth and full (male) employment have been superseded by generations raising children facing a faltering economy, austerity and reduced expectations of lifetime upward mobility.

It has been argued that concerns about uncertain futures are held both by middle and working-class families whose children's prospects seem less assured than in the past, and which are increasingly contingent on personal and family resources and on academic qualifications (Buchholz et al 2011). As explored in this chapter, insecurities and uncertainties about the future are tempered by diverse current circumstances and great unevenness in parents' perceived agency in intervening on behalf of their children. Across the sample, parents described their considered engagements with their children in helping them towards a hoped-for future, interactions which were profoundly important and meaningful to them. Across different backgrounds, parents varied greatly in their accounts of their children's chances both now and in the future. Through seeing aspects of educational, economic and social change through these diverse accounts, I hope to have shown some of the ways such changes are experienced as well as how they position families, allowing them different prospects and different degrees of influence in helping their children forge decent futures.

Notes

1 Recent evidence points to a decline in university applications (UCAS 2017). This has been linked in media commentary to the sharp rise in interest repayable on student loans.
2 This was originally run as an extension project of Real Life Methods (part of the ESRC National Centre for Research Methods; ESRC grant 576255017). Interviews conducted in 2009 and in 2011 and 2014 were transcribed with support from the School of Sociology and Social Policy, University of Leeds.
3 Social class here is defined in relation to parents' socio-economic circumstance in turn assessed with reference to the occupations of both partners, educational background and wider living circumstances. The three broad class groupings will be defined more precisely through the analysis section.
4 The intermediate grouping was identified as such through participants' occupations, educational background and wider living circumstances. Here parents had not themselves been to university (or in one case had started an arts degree but dropped out early on), and were in intermediate-class positions as defined by reference to ONS classification (for example, a homemaker married to a police officer, a pre-school teacher married to a mechanic).
5 I consider as working class those parents who were employed in manual roles and /or (men) who had a background in occupational trades, or mothers in junior positions married to such men, or living as single parents in circumstances of extensive constraint.

References

Allmendinger, J. and von den Driesch, E. (2014) *Social inequalities in Europe: Facing the challenges*, Discussion Paper P2014–2005, Berlin: Berlin Social Science Center (WZB).

Ball, S., Reay, D. and David, M. (2002) 'Ethnic choosing': minority ethnic students, social class and higher education choice', *Race, Ethnicity and Education* 5(4): 333–357.

Barham, C., Walling, A., Clancy, G., Hicks, S. and Conn, S. (2009) 'Young people and the labour market', *Economic and Labour Market Review* 3(4): 17–29.

Barone, C. (2006) 'Cultural capital, ambition and the explanation of inequalities in learning outcomes: a comparative analysis', *Sociology* 40(6): 1039–1058.

Bell, D.N.F. and Blanchflower, D.G. (2011) 'Young people and the Great Recession', *Oxford Review of Economic Policy* 27(2): 241–267.

Blundell, R., Green, D. and Jin, W. (2016) *The puzzle of graduate wages*, Institute for Fiscal Studies Briefing Note BN 185, London: IFS.

Bolton, P. (2015) *Participation in education and training: 16–18 year olds*, House of Commons Library, standard note, UK Parliament. http://dera.ioe.ac.uk/22733/

Bourdieu, P. (1986) 'The forms of capital', in J. Samson (Ed.) *Handbook of theory and research for the sociology of education*, 241–258, New York: Greenwood.

Brown, P. (2013), 'Education, opportunity and the prospects for social mobility', *British Journal of Sociology of Education* 34(5–6): 678–700.

Brown, P., Lauder, H. and Ashton, D. (2011) *The global auction: The broken promises of education, jobs and incomes*, Oxford: Oxford University Press.

Buchholz, S., Kolb, K., Hofacker, D. and Blossfeld, H-P. (2011) 'Globalized labour markets and social inequality in Europe: theoretical frameworks', in H-P. Blossfeld, S. Buchholz, D. Hofacker and K. Kolb, (eds) *Globalized labour markets and social inequality in Europe*, 3–24, Basingstoke: Palgrave Macmillan.

de Graaf, N.D., de Graaf, P.M. and Kraaykamp, G. (2000) 'Parental cultural capital and educational attainment in the Netherlands: a refinement of the cultural capital perspective', *Sociology of Education* 73: 92–111.

Department for Education (DfE) (2016) *Post-16 skills plan*, CM 9280, London: HMSO. www.gov.uk/government/uploads/system/uploads/attachment_data/file/536043/Post-16_Skills_Plan.pdf

Devine, F. (2004) *Class practices: How parents help their children get good jobs*, Cambridge: Cambridge University Press.

Devine, F. and Sensier, M. (2017) 'Class, politics and the progressive dilemma', *The Political Quarterly* 88(1): 30–38.

Dorling, D. (2014) *Inequality and the one percent*, London: Verso.

Finch, D. and Rose, H. (2017) *A mid-life less ordinary? Characteristics and income of low-to-middle income households age 50 to state pension age*, Resolution Foundation Briefing Paper, www.resolutionfoundation.org/app/uploads/2017/05/A-mid-life-less-ordinary.pdf

George, A., Metcalf, H., Tufekci, L. and Wilkinson, D. (2015, July) *Understanding age and the labour market*, York: Joseph Rowntree Foundation.

Gordon, D. (2015) *UK living standards election brief*, Poverty and Social Exclusion, UK, www.poverty.ac.uk/sites/default/files/attachments/UK_Living_Standards_%20Election_Brief_PSE_%20May_2015.pdf

Gregg, P., Machin, S. and Fernandez-Salgado, M. (2014) 'Real wages and unemployment in the big squeeze', *The Economic Journal* 124: 408–432.

Hefce (2013) *Trends in young participation in higher education*, issues paper, www.hefce.ac.uk/media/hefce/content/pubs/2013/201328/HEFCE_2013_28.pdf

Hills, J., Cunliffe, J., Obolenskaya, P. and Karagiannaki, E. (2015) *Falling behind, getting ahead: the changing structure of inequality in the UK, 2007–2013*, Research Report 5, London: LSE/Centre for Analysis of Social Exclusion, Social Policy in a Cold Climate.

Hodgson, A. and Spours, K. (2015) *The missing middle: how middle attaining students in 14–19 education are being overlooked and squeezed by policy*. Briefing paper to House of Lords Select Committee 120, London: UCL Institute of Education, http://kenspours.org/uploads/3/6/0/5/3605791/missing_middle_hol_2015.pdf

Irwin, S. (2017) 'Parenting teenagers as they grow up: values, practices and young people's pathways beyond school in England', *The Sociological Review*, doi:10.1177/0038026117691718

Irwin, S. (2009), 'Locating where the action is: quantitative and qualitative lenses on families, schooling and structures of social inequality', *Sociology* 43(6): 1123–1140.

Irwin, S. (1995a) *Rights of passage: Social change and the transition from youth to adulthood*, London: UCL Press.

Irwin, S. (1995b) 'Social reproduction and change in the transition from youth to adulthood', *Sociology* 29(2): 293–315.

Irwin, S. and Elley, S. (2013) 'Parents' hopes and expectations for their children's future occupations', *The Sociological Review* 61(1): 111–130.

Irwin, S. and Elley, S. (2011) 'Concerted cultivation? Parenting values, education and class diversity', *Sociology* 45(3): 480–495.

Keep, E., (2015) 'Governance in English VET: on the functioning of a fractured "system"', *Comparative and International Education* 10(4): 464–475, Published online: doi:10.1177/1745499915612185

Keep, E. and Mayhew, K. (2014) 'Inequality – 'wicked problems', labour market outcomes and the search for silver bullets', *Oxford Review of Education* 40(6): 764–781.

Lareau, A. (2011) *Unequal childhoods: Class, race and family life*. Second edition, Berkeley, CA: University of California Press.

Lareau, A. (2003) *Unequal childhoods: Class, race and family life*. First edition, Berkeley, CA: University of California Press.

Office for National Statistics (ONS) (2016) UK perspectives 2016: housing and home ownership in the UK, http://visual.ons.gov.uk/uk-perspectives-2016-housing-and-home-ownership-in-the-uk/

Park, A., Phillips, M. and Johnson, M. (2004) *Young people in Britain: The attitudes and experiences of 12 to 19 year olds*, RR564, London: Department for Education and Skills.

Pew Research Center (2014) Emerging and developing economies much more optimistic than rich countries about the future, www.pewglobal.org/2014/10/09/emerging-and-developing-economies-much-more-optimistic-than-rich-countries-about-the-future/

Power, S., Edwards, T., Whitty, G. and Wigfall, V. (2003) *Education and the middle class*, Buckingham: Open University Press.

Purcell, C., Flynn, M. and Na Ayudhya, U.C. (2011) 'The effects of flexibilization on social divisions and career trajectories in the UK labour market', in H-P. Blossfled, S. Buchholz, D. Hofäcker and K. Kolb (eds) *Globalized labour markets and social inequality in Europe*, 261–292, New York: Palgrave Macmillan.

Reay, D. (1998) *Class work: Mothers' involvement in their children's primary schooling*. London: UCL Press.

Roberts, S. (2011) 'Beyond 'NEET' and 'tidy' pathways: considering the 'missing middle' of youth transition studies', *Journal of Youth Studies* 14(1): 21–39.

Sainsbury, D. et al (2016) Report of the Independent Panel on Technical Education, www.gov.uk/government/uploads/system/uploads/attachment_data/file/536046/Report_of_the_Independent_Panel_on_Technical_Education.pdf

Stone, J., Berrington, A. and Falkingham, J. (2011) 'The changing determinants of UK young adults' living arrangements', *Demographic Research* 25(20): 629–666. doi:10.4054/DemRes.2011.25.20

Vincent, C. and Ball, S. (2007) 'Making up' the middle-class child: families, activities and class dispositions', *Sociology* 41(6): 1061–1078.

Taylor-Gooby, P. (2013) 'Why do people stigmatise the poor at a time of rapidly increasing inequality, and what can be done about it?', *The Political Quarterly* 84(1): 31–42.

UCAS (2017) Applicants for UK higher education down: 5% for UK students and 7% for EU students, www.ucas.com/corporate/news-and-key-documents/news/applicants-uk-higher-education-down-5-uk-students-and-7-eu-students

Wilson, T. and Bivand, P. (2014) *Equitable full employment: A jobs recovery for all*, TUC, Touchstone Extra, London: TUC, www.tuc.org.uk/research-analysis/reports/equitable-full-employment-jobs-recovery-all-touchstone-extras-pamphlet

Wolf, A. (2011) *Review of vocational education – the Wolf Report*, London: Department for Education, www.gov.uk/government/publications/review-of-vocational-education-the-wolf-report

5 Biography, history and place

Understanding youth transitions in Teesside

Robert MacDonald and Tracy Shildrick

Introduction: *Transitions*

This chapter is about young people's transitions to adulthood. During the 1990s and 2000s, the concept of 'transition' took some buffeting in Youth Studies. It was alleged to be overly normative and policy-driven, dominated by dry, quantitative approaches that failed to engage with the agency and cultures of the young and to be obsolete because of the blurring of the boundaries between youth and adulthood (Cohen and Ainley, 2000; Miles, 2000; Jeffs and Smith, 1998). We have argued, however, that there remains value in a concept that captures the *inherently* transitional nature of youth as a life phase, without prejudging what the nature, content, direction, form or length of what that transition might be (see MacDonald et al, 2001). 'Transition' has survived these earlier skirmishes. It remains one of the most important concepts in Youth Studies; by examining transitions in the youth phase, we gain a particularly privileged vantage point from which to discern wider processes of social change and continuity (Furlong and Cartmel, 2007; MacDonald, 2011).

The research material that underpins the chapter has been gathered in a town, Middlesbrough (at the centre of Teesside in North East England), which itself has undergone remarkable transitions: from a rural hamlet in the early 19th century, to smoky industrial boom town within 50 years, to a place world-famous for its industrial prowess and output by the mid-twentieth century, to one of the poorest and most deindustrialised parts of the country in the early twenty-first century. Teesside is a fascinating place; the rapidity and sheer scale of change in its fortunes allow for close investigation of the sociological consequences of economic collapse. Dave Byrne (1999: 93) has described Teesside 'as one of the most deindustrialised locales' in the UK and, in fact, it is hard to think of anywhere else, including amongst the rust belt cities of the USA and Europe, that has undergone such a dramatic turnaround. It is in this place that we have undertaken a series of research projects first begun in the late 1990s – *the Teesside Studies of Youth Transitions and Social Exclusion.*

The focus of the chapter, then, will be on the way that young people make transitions to adulthood in times of socio-economic change, under inauspicious conditions (of rising rates of poverty for young adults; of declining opportunities for standard, rewarding employment; a policy context that reduces social security for young adults; austerity cuts to youth services) and in a place (Teesside, North East England) that has high levels of multiple deprivation.

The first aim of the chapter is to describe these studies. The original contribution and the difference with our previous publications comes with the second and third aims. The second aim is to provide an overall, composite summary of the main, thematic findings from *all* of these studies *in toto*. The third aim of the chapter is to make sense of the twists and turns of economically marginal youth transitions by setting them in a developed discussion of the social, economic, geographic, historic and political context in which these biographies have played out. Emphasis is given here to the active processes and decisions that result in the economic marginality of places and populations. Our argument is that we cannot hope to make sense of the complexities of individual biographies or answer the pressing policy problems that relate to 'socially excluded youth' without this deeper and wider sociological analysis.

Researching youth transitions and social exclusion: *the Teesside Studies*

These are a set of five main, connected studies funded by the Joseph Rowntree Foundation and the Economic and Social Research Council, undertaken by the authors and colleagues, that have sought to describe and theorise the transitions to adulthood made by young people who were growing up in Middlesbrough, the main town of the conurbation of Teesside in North East England. At the time of the research, i.e. from the late 1990s onwards, the research neighbourhoods (in East Middlesbrough) were amongst the most extremely deprived in the town – and the country (DETR, 2000).

Each of the studies had its own particular aims but, in general, the research has been motivated by a desire to critically engage with powerful but controversial theories and novel but abstract concepts via a qualitative, critical case study approach that puts ideas to the empirical test. An abiding aim has been to test different forms of underclass theory. The idea of a cultural underclass of the undeserving poor has a very long history, with variants appearing under different names and guises, in successive historical periods (MacDonald, 1997; Welshman, 2013). There has been considerable academic critique as well (e.g. Bagguley and Mann, 1992; Morris, 1994). In the 1990s, Charles Murray and others argued that in the UK, like the USA, there had emerged below the working class a new, welfare-dependent, anti-social and morally reprehensible 'underclass' (Murray, 1990, 1994). MacDonald (1997) argued that many of the extant studies that wished to contest these theories were methodologically unlikely to be able empirically to locate the alleged underclass (even if it existed). Thus, we have developed critical case study methods that have allowed the best possible chance to uncover a new 'underclass' and, more recently, 'cultures of worklessness' and 'families where no-one has worked over three generations' (a current phrasing of very old underclass ideas).

Each study published a main report or book, and associated journal articles and chapters in edited collections. The first two studies – *Snakes and Ladders* (Johnston et al, 2000) and *Disconnected Youth?* (MacDonald and Marsh, 2005) – each carried out biographical interviews (Chamberlayne et al, 2002) with 15 to 25 year olds. The combined sample totalled 186 young people (82 females and 104 males), from the predominantly white working-class population resident in Middlesbrough's social housing estates. These were purposive, theoretical samples rather than statistically randomised ones. People were recruited (via different agencies and 'gatekeepers' in the research sites, and via snowballing from initial interviews) in order for us to be able to generate convincing analyses of different aspects of youth transition and to be able to answer our theoretical questions. Both studies also used episodes of participation observation and together interviewed around 50 welfare practitioners who worked in some capacity with young people.

The third study – *Poor Transitions* (Webster et al, 2004) – followed up a proportion of the 186 interviewees (34 in total; 18 females and 16 males) to see where earlier transitions had led these individuals in their mid to late twenties (aged 23 to 29 years), including in respect of their labour market progress (or lack of progress, as was the case for most). A fourth study, *Poverty and Insecurity* (Shildrick et al, 2012a), had a primary interest in longer-term experiences of the 'low-pay, no-pay cycle' – that is, of churning between insecure, low-paid jobs and time unemployed and on benefits. The sample included 30 people who had participated in the earlier Teesside studies and who were, at the time, now aged over 30 years (in addition, we talked to 30 new interviewees, aged over 40 years). The fifth study – *Are Cultures of Worklessness Passed Down the Generations?* (Shildrick et al, 2012b) – was different from its predecessors in that it also included comparative research in a deprived neighbourhood of Glasgow (Scotland), as well as in Middlesbrough, and in that it included none of the original research interviewees. Rather, this project sought to investigate the value of the idea of 'intergenerational cultures of worklessness' – a variant of underclass theory – in explaining concentrations of poverty and unemployment in the UK. This involved a new sample of 47 interviewees from across two generations in 20 families (in Middlesbrough and Glasgow).

The first four Teesside studies incorporated elements of qualitative longitudinal youth research. This is quite rare and Gunter and Watt (2009: 516) have described the 'Teesside School' as providing the 'most intensive example of youth transitions research in the UK'. Because youth transitions typically have become extended and more complex (Furlong and Cartmel, 2007), studying them requires a longer time frame. Just looking at the immediate post-school years, or even the early twenties, provides an age span that is insufficient to the task of gauging their twists, turns and outcomes. As we will note, answering important theoretical and policy questions has only been possible because our research has followed youth transitions as they play out over a longer period (until their thirties, for some interviewees). As noted in the introduction, one of the criticisms of youth research has been an overly narrow focus on 'school to work careers'. As well as a long view, the Teesside studies took a broad view of 'youth transition' and investigated how six facets of young people's lives interrelated to form the overall shape and nature of their transitions to adulthood. In addition to 'school to work careers', these were: 'housing careers' (including the movement to independent living); 'family careers' (including the movement from 'family of origin' to 'family of destination'); what we coined 'leisure careers' (changing patterns of free-time association and activity); 'criminal careers' (patterns of offending, non-offending and desistance) and 'drug-using careers' (engagement with illicit drug use). A final characteristic of the Teesside studies that is worth mentioning here is that they have managed to gain first-hand, detailed and lengthy biographical accounts from the sorts of young people and young adults who are often described as 'hard to reach' and upon whom a variety of inaccurate labels are sometimes pinned and whom, it is often claimed, need to be 'given a voice' (e.g. Barry, 2005). They are variously described as 'disengaged', 'disconnected', 'socially excluded', 'disaffected' and so on (MacDonald, 2008), labels which proved to be unhelpful to the job of describing their dispositions and conditions of life.

Growing up in Britain's 'poor neighbourhoods': Research findings

In sum, we have gathered a substantial amount of research material from young people about transitions to adulthood under adverse conditions of multiple deprivation. We have published widely but we have not previously gathered together all of the most significant findings from these separate studies in summary form. This is what we do in the following section under five sub-headings.

Conventional aspirations

A sensible starting point is to report the sorts of values, goals and aspirations expressed by the young people we interviewed. These were stubbornly normal and conventional, even if the circumstances in which they were growing up were abnormal and unusually difficult. An abiding motivation of social scientists (sociologists interested in the underclass, criminologists interested in deviant subcultures; e.g. Cohen, 1955) has been to pin down alien, subterranean values amongst those 'at the bottom'. Rarely if ever are these found. 'They' tend to want the same sorts of things that 'we' do. This was the case with our research participants. They aspired to 'settling down' with someone they loved – and having children 'when the time was right'.

They wanted in due course to have their own homes (which they owned, preferably) 'somewhere quiet'; this is a throw-away phrase loaded with meaning. They meant they wanted to live somewhere that was not as troubled with crime, anti-social behaviour, street disturbances and the ill-effects of the local heroin economy as were the neighbourhoods in which they had grown up. They did not, however, want to move far away from the neighbourhoods they knew and where their extended families and friends all tended to live.

Even though dominant media stereotypes might regard these as 'welfare-dependent' groups, participants predominantly imagined their futures in jobs. The work ethic expressed by interviewees was strong and typical of industrial working-class communities in the UK (Jackson, 1972). This was one aspect of their intergenerational inheritance; parents passed on norms and values about work and welfare even if the conditions of the local labour market had altered radically over the last decades of the twentieth century. There was a strong moral opposition to being 'welfare dependent'. Stigma pervaded interviewees' discussions of 'being on benefits', reflecting not only the public disgust about 'scroungers' that has been fomented by politicians and the media so vigorously in the last few years in the UK (Jensen, 2014) but longer-standing working-class beliefs about being, and being perceived as, 'respectable' rather than 'rough' and part of the 'undeserving poor' (Roberts, 1971; Roberts, 2001). Thus, even being labelled as 'poor' was a source of shame (Shildrick and MacDonald, 2013).

The sorts of jobs that people aspired to were the sorts of jobs that were typically done by working-class people like them. Gender norms, too, influenced choices about training schemes and possible jobs (MacDonald and Marsh, 2005). Rarely did we come across individuals expressing employment aspirations that seemed incredible or absurdly ambitious. Interestingly, given the speedy transformation in the nature of available employment, neither did we find interviewees expressing antiquated job preferences that harked back to the realities of previous decades. On this same theme, nor did there seem to be much of a 'crisis of masculinity' going on (McDowell, 2000). Some young men still could find jobs that enabled the expression of what are regarded as traditional forms of 'hard' working-class masculinity (e.g. as labourers, trainee mechanics, security guards, factory workers). Others did not baulk at what are described as more feminised forms of service-sector employment (e.g. working in bars, fast food restaurants, shops).

In sum, then, in terms of what are regarded as the three core aspects of transition to adulthood (employment, family and housing careers), young people expressed highly conventional views and aspirations. This was even true of our fifth study (Shildrick et al, 2012b) where we interviewed a sample of young adults who came from families that were highly unusual in the extremity and multiplicity of troubles they faced (and caused) (Shildrick et al, 2016). Indeed, the strength of this finding was such that it was a key part of our overall rejection of the validity of the 'cultures of worklessness' thesis (MacDonald et al, 2014);

young people did not 'inherit' from their long-term unemployed parents values and aspirations that were different from the mainstream.

'Poor work' and the 'low pay, no pay cycle'

If there was no obvious disconnection between mainstream social values and those of our research participants, there was a disjuncture between what they aspired to and what they achieved. For reasons of space, we will mainly concentrate on their school to labour market experiences.

They had low qualifications – and attended schools where low qualifications were the norm. Interviewees' recollections of their school days ranged across descriptions of disappointment, dismay, disaffection and disengagement (MacDonald and Marsh, 2005). Oppositional working-class attitudes to school were only part of the story (Willis, 1977; Brown, 1987) and not set in stone where they existed; re-engagement with college courses in later years was quite common but the pay-offs in terms of improved labour market fortunes were patchy (Webster et al, 2004). Thus, these underqualified working-class young people tended to enter the labour market relatively early, making 'fast-track' transitions to jobs, training schemes and unemployment (Jones, 2002). Unsurprisingly, all the young people we interviewed had some experience of being unemployed. These experiences were reminiscent of accounts gathered in previous decades, in the UK and elsewhere (Jahoda, 1982). The vocational courses that they undertook tended to be of poor quality and provided little obvious enhancement to their labour market fortunes. Again, this is in line with what we know about the long-standing stratification of youth training schemes (Roberts and Parsell, 1992) and the muddled and parlous state of post-16 vocational education in the UK (Wolf, 2011).

One of the 'headline' findings of the Teesside studies is this: even in this depressed labour market young adults were able to access low-skilled, low-quality, low-paid jobs; they were able to do this repeatedly; this work tended to be insecure (it was offered on temporary contracts or was otherwise short-lived, with employees leaving jobs most often not through their own choice); and this 'poor work' (Byrne, 1999) was central to and constitutive of a 'low-pay, no-pay' cycle wherein interviewees churned between insecure jobs and unemployment over months and years. Because of the hassles and stigma of claiming benefits, many of those in the low-pay, no-pay cycle would avoid registering as unemployed during what they hoped would be shorter periods of unemployment. Not only did they miss out on rightful benefits, they were missed from the unemployment count. For this reason, we coined the phrase 'the missing workless' (Shildrick et al, 2012a). Critically, against the policy and research orthodoxy (MacDonald, 2017), the research showed that this was *not* a 'natural' facet of the youth labour market, i.e. that new labour market participants would eventually settle down into steady, lasting employment (Quintini et al, 2007), nor was it a feature of an experimental phase of 'Emerging Adulthood' (Arnett, 2006). Rather, this was a lasting experience.

Following research participants over time showed that this was the pattern of working life for people at 17, at 27 and at 37 years. This low-pay, no-pay cycle was also a typical experience for older workers in Teesside and elsewhere (Shildrick et al, 2012a).

What effect did these forms of faltering, difficult employment career have on family and housing careers? Perhaps surprisingly, many of the research participants were able to make relatively successful housing transitions and transitions to becoming parents themselves. Indeed, we found that in later rounds of interviewing, developments in these spheres of people's lives imbued a sense of personal change and progress (even where they were still stuck in cycles of unemployment and low-paid jobs) (Webster et al, 2004). It should be noted that our participants were making these transitions in the 2000s, prior to the effects of the Great Recession and subsequent austerity programmes, and in a local context where, at the time, affordable and reasonable quality, rented social housing was relatively easily available.

'Welfare to work', austerity 'reforms' and what employers want

The policy orthodoxy in the UK, as with the EU more generally, is that unemployment can be tackled by Active Labour Market Programmes (ALMPs), increasing conditionality tests on, and reductions in, welfare benefits, and potentially, by upskilling the workforce to meet the skills needs of employers (MacDonald, 2016). None of these policy planks was supported by evidence from our research. The unemployed were active job-seekers regardless of ALMPs[1]; and the interventions of the latter had apparently little positive effect on chances of employment. In fact, official employment service practices sometimes *inhibited* informal ones that seemed to work better (MacDonald and Marsh, 2005). Young unemployed people in our studies collectively spent thousands of hours engaged in them but very rarely, if ever, did they get jobs through Job Clubs, Job Centre advertised vacancies, youth training schemes and New Deal programmes.

The full force of increased conditionality tests and welfare benefit sanctions regimes had not hit our research participants at the time of our first four studies. This came later with the advent of the Coalition Government in 2010 and Conservative Government in 2015. We know these have had a very adverse effect on already disadvantaged and vulnerable populations, with young people hit particularly hard (Beatty and Fothergill, 2013; Watts, 2014; Unison, 2016). Dramas like the film *I, Daniel Blake* (dir. Ken Loach, 2016) have made more visible the cruel machinations of the UK's degraded benefit system. The perversity of these 'reforms' is that there is no evidence that unemployed people require more motivation to seek work; in this sense, they appear to be 'punishing the poor' (Wacquant, 2009) and are a way of disciplining populations to the requirements of a late capitalist economy for workers ready to accept casualised 'poor work' (Byrne, 1999). Thus, we have argued that there is, in fact, *already* a close fit between what at least some local employers *really* want (which is *not* qualifications and skills but 'the right attitude') and what underqualified job-seekers can offer, i.e. this 'right attitude', which means being ready and willing to take on irregular, insecure, low-paid, work, repeatedly over months and years (Shildrick et al, 2012a).

'Social exclusion'? Social capital and deprived neighbourhoods

'Social exclusion', we conclude, is a label readily applied to people and places that experience social and economic inequalities and disadvantage but which does not capture the conditions of life of our participants in a literal sense (MacDonald et al, 2005). Instead, their strong ties to family and friends in these neighbourhoods (places where these families had tended to live over decades) was at the root of a sense of social *inclusion*. Social networks of friends and family enabled a sense of 'knowing' (other people, local cultural mores and rules) and of 'being known' (to other people, of 'fitting in'). This 'bonding social capital' (Putnam, 1995) it is often reported as facet of working-class neighbourhoods (Forrest and Kearns, 2001). Thus, rather than lacking in social capital, these neighbourhoods had a sort of supportive, bonding social capital that is perhaps lacking from middle-class suburbia. It was drawn upon in numerous ways, for example in providing emotional support in times of distress; for informal care (e.g. of children); for loans of money; in protection against criminal victimisation and so on.

A final example is one of the most significant. A traditional aspect of life in working-class communities in the UK (Marsden and Duff, 1975), this is still maintained in these parts of Teesside: local networks of information and recommendation were the principle source of employment. People got jobs through 'who they knew, not what they knew'. In thinking about patterns of continuity and exchange in intergenerational relationships, this was one of the most substantial ways in which parents could assist young people. Being connected into these community networks was essential for 'getting by' and getting jobs. The value of these informal networks was far in excess of the value of formal employment services and 'work readiness' schemes. They still 'worked' in a locality of high unemployment and in a context of a shift from the dominance of heavy industry to the dominance of service-sector work. As time went on, however, and as older workers in the parent generation spent longer periods out of work or in only insecure 'poor work', there were indications that this social capital depleted and their power to assist their children in the search for jobs slowly waned (Shildrick et al, 2012a). The fact of this was evidenced by our fifth study. The middle generation we sampled had been out of the labour market for several years and they had unusually limited experience of jobs. Low on financial and cultural capital, they also lacked the sort of social capital that elsewhere can be valuable for young working-class job-seekers.

A paradox was uncovered by our investigation of 'social exclusion'. Although the networks of social support made life liveable and helped people to get by in arduous circumstances, there was also a sense in which they tied people into place, socially and geographically. Leaving – giving up the security of knowing and being known and abandoning the trusted networks that worked – was difficult to do but *not* leaving them meant facing the continued restrictions and inequalities of some of the most deprived and poorest wards in England.

Anti-social youth?

This was a locality that at the time of the research had higher than average rates of youth offending, was said to be plagued by 'anti-social behaviour' (the UK in the 1990s and 2000s had a national obsession with targeting and punishing 'anti-social behaviour', which usually meant disciplining the informal, public socialising of gatherings of young working-class men and women) and was badly affected by 'problematic drug use' (see Simpson et al, 2007 for definitions of drug-using behaviour). Thus, to reiterate, as well as the standard aspects of youth transition now researched by youth sociologists, we also investigated the leisure, drug-using and criminal careers of our participants (see MacDonald and Marsh, 2002).

The value of our long-term view of youth transitions and the longitudinal element to the research was well demonstrated by the detailed picture we gained of the typical criminal careers that were evident for a minority of interviewees. In short, disaffection from school hardened into disengagement and persistent truancy, with time spent with others in the 'street corner society' of their estates (MacDonald and Shildrick, 2007). 'Leisure-time crime' – petty thieving and vandalism – spiced up the monotony of truanting days. For some, and before long, illicit but 'normal' patterns of *recreational* alcohol and drug use (of cannabis, ecstasy, speed) morphed into more destructive, addictive *problematic* drug use (of heroin, and later, crack cocaine). The intertwining of drug and criminal careers, with addiction to heroin driving chaotic, acquisitive offending and subsequent repeated imprisonment, led to some of the saddest narratives that we gathered, with participants describing their sense of shame, regret and loss at the crimes and damage they had done. Desistance from crime and drug use was possible, however, and attempts at this were reported commonly in our later studies (Webster et al, 2004); new partnerships, parenthood, employment, decent drug treatment, separation from criminogenic peer groups and other factors were important in this process (if difficult to achieve for already and otherwise disadvantaged young adults).

Our account is one that seriously questions both underclass theories of crime (Murray, 1990) and risk factor approaches (see MacDonald, 2006) (e.g. these populations were awash with all the 'worst' risk factors but only a minority offended). More contingent, biographic-level explanations – including the unpredictable impact of unpredictable 'critical moments' (MacDonald and Shildrick, 2013) – were helpful in explaining why some offended and some did not and why and when some desisted from crime. Above this, however, was a key meso-level factor that framed the sets of circumstances in which these biographies were made. This was the impact of what became known as a '*second wave*' heroin outbreak on Teesside (Parker et al, 1998), in the mid-1990s – prior to which there was no discernible heroin market in the area. The arrival of heroin onto the streets of Middlesbrough at this time in history meant that our participants were faced with the threat of a particularly destructive drug as they were passing through their teenage years. For a minority, this had dramatic consequences for their lives. The long-term impact of the early effect of heroin drug careers was demonstrated by our interviews in Glasgow with a sample of middle-aged and long-term unemployed parents. In all these cases heroin addiction in young adulthood (resultant from the UK's '*first* wave' heroin outbreak, in Glasgow in the 1980s) was heavily implicated in the later troubles of these individuals and their families.

Explaining youth transitions in Teesside: biography, history and place

In summary, the young people we talked to were united in an experience of long-term economic marginality and poverty, which lasted into adulthood. It is *not* possible to explain this in relation to deviant values or non-conventional aspirations, by outlandish expectations for the future, in relation to widespread anti-social or criminal dispositions, by negative attitudes towards employment or by 'welfare dependency', by 'social exclusion' or a lack of social capital, or by a mismatch between what they offer and the needs of local employers.

Voodoo sociology

Too often accounts of the social exclusion, unemployment or transitions of young adults rely on one-sided stories of their characteristics – which are usually painted as a series of lacks. Indeed, in the UK for politicians, policy makers, think-tanks, social welfare agencies and even some academics, 'lack of aspiration' has now become one of the most common and taken-for-granted 'explanations' (e.g. Chapman et al, 2011). MacDonald (2016) describes this as *voodoo sociology*: an insistence, against the weight of substantial available evidence, that problems of youth unemployment can be magically resolved by recanting the mantra of 'raise aspirations'. This available evidence includes a long tradition of UK sociological research that documents how young people's transitions are socially structured and not the simple outcome of agency or aspiration (e.g. Ashton et al, 1982; Bynner et al, 1997; Ball et al, 2000).

Some basic labour market statistics can confound this voodoo sociology. For instance, in Middlesbrough, Teesside, in March 2015 there were 3.3 unemployed claimants for every notified vacancy. Experts agree that not all vacancies are 'notified'; there are more jobs on offer than this. Experts also agree, however, that there are more people looking for jobs than are registered to claim unemployment benefits. That in Teesside typically 28 young adults apply for every *single* manufacturing and engineering apprenticeship would seem to confirm this point (TVU, 2014). The same pattern can be seen on a bigger canvas. In the US in 2011, the McDonald's fast food chain held a hiring day. They were looking to recruit 50,000 new staff. They had 1 million applications! (eventually taking on 62,000 new workers[2]). Similarly, 'welfare to work programmes' falter when there are limited numbers of decent jobs to which the unemployed can be moved. For instance, the government's flagship 'Work Programme' for the long-term unemployed has a success rate in Middlesbrough of 8% (i.e. it could help fewer than one in ten participants into lasting employment) (Northern Echo, 2013).

If we are accurately to make sense of youth transitions we need to lift our gaze, from the characteristics of young people and the minutiae of the twists and turns of their transitions, and 'look up' to the opportunity structures that prevail for them and the social, economic and political forces that shape these conditions. In doing this we can seek to rise to the challenge laid down by C Wright Mills (1959) and develop a sociological imagination that connects the 'private troubles' of individuals with the 'public issues of social structure', to connect biography and history. This also necessitates close attention to place – and to the biography of Teesside. This is a place that allows us to see this connection, between private troubles and public issues, between biography and social structure, in sharp focus. It is a microcosm of wider social and economic change, showing general patterns in dramatic relief.

A story of Teesside

Arguably, nowhere else in the developed economies of the Global North has witnessed such rapid and deep changes in its economic fortunes; from 'boom to bust in quick time' as one report described it (Foord, 1995). What has happened here has happened elsewhere but it has happened here more dramatically and more quickly.

As recently as the 1960s Teesside had full employment, was one of England's most prosperous and successful local economies, and was world renowned for its industrial prowess and productivity. It boasted the world's largest single chemical plant (ICI Billingham) at one point, and from here came the iron and steel that built many of 'the wonders of the industrial world' – e.g. the Golden Gate Bridge, Sydney Harbour Bridge, the Indian railway system. Reflecting traditional class and gender patterns, Teesside was a place 'that worked'. From a rural hamlet, it was brought into life in the nineteenth century to be a centre for heavy industry and the well-paid, high-skilled ('male') jobs that the economy eventually provided during the boom years of the mid-twentieth century were the basis of the social and cultural life of Teesside. In the post-war decades, industry brought relative prosperity. Gross Value Added (GVA) statistics measure the contribution of regions and sub-regions to the national economy (usually taking average income as a measure) (ONS, 2016b). Chiefly owing to its low levels of unemployment, the success of its core industries and the relatively high wages paid to the skilled workforce, in the early 1970s Teesside was one of the most prosperous parts of the country, having a GVA figure that was 'above the national average and third highest in the country, after London and Aberdeen' (TVU, 2011: 4).

Teesside's economic collapse was sudden and not typical of wider, British industrial malaise (see Hudson, 1986: 13). For instance, industrial relations on Teesside tended to be relatively harmonious and there had been significant capital investment and support from national government. Following the global economic crises of the early 1970s, increased international competition in Teesside's main chemical, steel and engineering industries, shifting national policy in respect of support for steel, came together to presage massive restructuring and redundancy (Hudson, 1989). Production was shifted overseas to benefit from cheaper labour costs. The limit to the state's capacity to manage a national economy under conditions of intense international competition was cruelly exposed on Teesside. In 1965 the unemployment rate in Middlesbrough stood at less than 2%. By 1987 it reached over 21% and, overall, close to 100,000 manufacturing jobs were lost in Teesside between 1971 and 2008. The scale of this is staggering and the shock and damage caused can probably be likened to a community undergoing severe trauma (from which it struggles to recover) (Walkerdine, 2010).

These manufacturing jobs were gradually replaced by ones in the service sector (92,000 were created in this same period), mainly in local government, health and education, call centres and leisure services. Consequently, jobs became less 'masculine' and less likely to be full time and permanent. A collective emphasis on industrial modernisation and technological investment in the 1960s was replaced by a government-led emphasis on employment 'flexibility' during the 1980s. High local unemployment, weakened trade unions and Conservative government legislation to deregulate the labour market enabled employers to adopt a much more flexible approach to the hiring and firing of workers. Thus, during the 1980s and 1990s Teesside's economy was transformed from one of comparatively high-skilled, high-waged and secure jobs, to a predominantly low-waged, 'flexible' labour market (Beynon et al, 1994).

Even with this new service-sector employment Middlesbrough has typically had significantly higher unemployment rates than the national average (usually at least double the rate) since the 1980s. Many millions of pounds have been spent on 'area-based regeneration' schemes and 'action zones' for health, employment, enterprise and so on, rolled out successively through the 1980s, 1990s and 2000s but at the time of writing, in 2017, rates of youth and adult unemployment remain amongst the highest in the country (Elledge 2016; House of Commons Library, 2016). The long decline since the 1980s has meant that in some cases what once were popular estates of working-class council housing have become 'difficult-to-let' and, in others, derelict and abandoned zones of entrenched poverty and multiple social problems (Lupton and Power, 2002). Teesside's 'new' service-sector economy has not been immune to cuts and closure. In the 2000s, big call centres have closed as work has been outsourced to lower-wage economies (Shildrick et al, 2012a). The new big employers –

the public sector of health, education and local government – have themselves shed jobs, particularly since the recession of 2008 and the subsequent austerity programmes pursued by UK central government. One study from 2010 made particularly gloomy predictions for Middlesbrough. Because of its heavy reliance on the public sector for local employment – 42% of the workforce in 2010 – it was identified as the town that was 'least resilient' to planned government cut-backs, from 324 surveyed (BBC, 2010). In the subsequent five years, the local council shed hundreds of jobs, reducing its workforce by over 40% (Brown, 2015).

In brief, this is the story of the deindustrialisation of Teesside. Once one of the most prosperous localities in the UK, Middlesbrough now has high rates of unemployment, of poor health, of educational under-achievement and all the other objective indicators of multiple deprivation. Middlesbrough in the 2000s was the 'poorest town' in England (i.e. it had the greatest proportion of heavily deprived wards of any town in the country); it still features in the list of ten 'poorest towns' (ONS, 2016a). It was described on a popular TV programme as 'the worst place to live' in England (Thornton, 2007). 'Worst' awards come with depressing regularity; most recently the town was described as 'the worst place for a girl to grow up' (because of high rates of child poverty, teenage conception, young people not in education, employment or training, etc; see BBC, 2016).

Hard(er) times for youth

It is against this backdrop that our research participants made their transitions to adulthood, during the 1990 and 2000s. Our direct research with them has not (so far) allowed for full investigation of the impact of the Great Recession and later austerity. What might the consequences have been for young people and youth transitions on Teesside? Given that this is a place that some label as being in 'permanent recession' since the 1980s, how much worse could things become?

The return of (inter)national recession added to deeper on-going changes in the UK labour market, wherein middle-range, intermediate jobs were 'hollowed out' of the economy (Sissons, 2011). The mass shedding of jobs in local authorities since 2010 is a good example of this process in action on Teesside. Redundant white-collar workers 'bump down' increasing pressure on lower quality jobs (of the sort typically undertaken by our research participants). It becomes harder to get even insecure 'poor work'. This is one likely consequence for the sort of working-class young adults we interviewed. National research also points to the very difficult context young people have faced since the Great Recession, and earlier. For instance, Fahmy and colleagues (2015) demonstrate how in the UK young adults (aged 18 to 29 years) are now the age group most likely to experience material deprivation, with an alarming upward trend since 1999. Across every different measure of poverty, young people are especially disadvantaged compared to other age groups.

The UK government's austerity programme from 2010 onwards heavily forefronted 'welfare reform' and young people have been particularly hard hit by this more punitive regime for the provision of what used to be called 'social security' (Watts, 2014). Not only are they now denied support to which previous generations were entitled (e.g. student grants, housing benefit) compared with other age groups, they are now more likely to face punitive sanctions (i.e. denial of benefit payments for infringement of tightened rules and tests) (ibid.). Some already deprived groups of young people, such as homeless young people, face an even greater risk of sanction, often leading to even worse and less secure housing situations, food poverty, anxiety and depression, and disengagement from welfare and employment services (North East Homelessness Think Tank, 2016). This report implies that the latter outcome is an *unintended* consequence of 'welfare reform'; it is, of course, quite plausible that this is an *intended* consequence of these changes. Services for young people have also faced heavy austerity cuts. Between April 2010 and April 2016, £387m was cut from youth service spending across the UK. This meant that 603 youth centres closed, 3,652 youth work jobs were lost, and 138,898 places for young people in youth projects were cut (Unison, 2016). Locally, on Teesside's social housing estates, many of the youth centres, sports clubs and libraries in which we used to meet and interview young people during the 1990s and 2000s have now been closed because of cuts to local authority spending. These are hard times to be young, in the UK. Recently, the author of one of the most authoritative studies of the English riots of 2011 suggested that the underlying conditions that sparked those disorders have now become more severe.[3] Of course, there is a generational dimension to some of these issues. A 2014 policy briefing from the *European Youth Forum* points to a wider context of rising rates of youth unemployment, increased levels of poverty and social exclusion and a growing inequality between older and younger generations. Related to this, the UK's decision to leave the EU has been seen as betraying the aspirations of the younger generation (over 70% of whom voted to 'remain'; Cresci, 2016).[4]

In summary, it is likely that the processes that marginalised and impoverished working-class young people as they made transitions to adulthood in the 1990s and 2000s are likely to have become more intense over the past decade, particularly since the Great Recession of 2008 and the subsequent austerity programmes set in train by the UK government.

Rise and fall: or, 'it didn't have to be like this'!

Stepping back, and returning to our main discussion, the story we have told of Teesside didn't have to be *the* story of Teesside. The biography of Middlesbrough could have been different. The fact of Teesside's industrial decline was not predestined. Limits of space mean we can only give a few examples.

Following Veit-Wilson (1998) and Byrne (1999), we prefer a 'strong' to a 'weak' conceptualisation of social exclusion; one which highlights questions of power and asks 'who or what is doing the excluding?' The urban sociologist Alice Mah studies 'industrial ruination' (2012); the processes that create and destroy industrial centres, and the long decay and class memories of once thriving communities. Inspired by driving through 'the Rust Belt of the United States and Canada – through Detroit, Michigan, Hamilton, Ontario and Buffalo, New York – and seeing vast abandoned factories; old car plants, steelworks, chemical factories', she asks the same question that we ask of Teesside, 'what happened to produce this scale of abandonment?' (Mah, 2013). The title of Ray Hudson's important book about the North East of England – *Wrecking a Region* (1989) – also indicates a powerful line of thinking which accentuates the *active* processes that underlie the decline of once-great industrial centres like Teesside (and the North East more widely). This is a Marxian economic geography that explains how places – regions – are *necessarily* hit with successive waves of capitalist investment and disinvestment; this is the uneven regional development that is a chronic and integral feature of capitalist economy. Since the 1970s, 'processes of neo-liberal globalisation have deepened' (Hudson, 2006: 8) and the mobility of capital has intensified, in the constant search for profitability, new markets and reduced production and wage costs. These are strong and deep economic currents but their force can be limited or diverted (or, indeed, added to) by the policies of governments (regionally, nationally or supra-nationally, as with the EU's active regional policy). These can play a part in defending (or not) the economic viability of regions and influencing which of them experience 'growth, decline and revival' (Hudson, 2006: 6).

Following this line of argument, whilst their power should not be over-stated, important social actors in the offices of government and boardrooms of multi-nationals made decisions and took courses of action which were of enormous consequence for Teesside's dramatic socio-economic collapse (and limiting its chances of recovery). We point to three examples.

Firstly, we can point to how the *laissez-faire* economics of Conservative (Thatcher) governments in the 1980s involved the choice *not* to protect the important industries of the North of England from the vicissitudes of a globalising economy (a trend evident still, with the final closure in 2015 of the last steel plant in Teesside, at Redcar, again under a Conservative government). From the 1980s, rather than acting as a buffer against globalisation, central government chose to define its industrial policy as *actively embracing* the pressures of international competition 'as *the* mechanism through which to restructure the UK's productive base' (Beynon et al, 1994: 99), particularly to reduce labour costs by shedding jobs and by increasing workforce 'flexibility'.

Secondly, we can point to how, in the boom years, employment was deliberately and highly concentrated in nationally important industries. Neither government (national or local) nor captains of industry wanted to diversify the local economy, either through the encouragement of a small and medium enterprise sector (which remains very underdeveloped to this day) or through the expansion of alternative industries. Plans to develop car production were opposed by central government and local employers because of the fear that this would threaten the supply of skilled labour to the chemical and steel industry (Hudson, 1989). Hindsight shows how catastrophic this was for Teesside's fortunes. The over-concentration of local employment in such a narrow set of traditional industries, the political choices of national government and the globalising search for profit of big business combined with calamitous effects for the economic and social life of Teesside.

Thirdly, we can point to how the social and economic regeneration policies pursued by local and national government have, at best, served to limit and contain some of the harshest consequences of capital disinvestment and, at worst, have added to Teesside's problems. Since the 1980s, many millions of pounds have been spent on schemes, zones and programmes to deal with the fall-out of economic collapse. Private development corporations and training agencies have made substantial profits (sometimes fraudulently; BBC, 2015), which is part of the reason why very similar schemes are rolled out again and again, over decades, with an awful 'waste' of public money, little sense of lessons learned and with a strong whiff of 'policy amnesia' (Robinson, 2005). In prime place in this cabinet of remedies have been measures to tackle unemployment by 'raising aspirations' and making people more 'work ready'. In understanding the real nature and causes of unemployment on Teesside (as described in this section), we understand that such policy approaches *cannot* have significant impact on the *overall* levels of unemployment locally (albeit that the circumstances of some *individuals* may change as a consequence). Given this, it might be better to understand the motivations of such approaches in terms of their effects in: temporarily 'warehousing' the unemployed (and circulating them on and off unemployment benefits and reducing the unemployment count); disciplining benefit claimants (through ramped-up conditionality and job availability tests) *and* low paid workers (with the fear of falling into the degradations and impoverishment of unemployment) – see Wacquant (2009); providing employment and profits for private businesses in the social welfare sector; and in setting in place 'welfare to work' processes which provide a steady stream of 'flexible', unpaid/low-paid workers for the low-quality employment that now constitutes much of the Teesside labour market (Byrne, 1999; Shildrick et al, 2012a).

The logic of uneven regional capitalist development is that deindustrialisation and collapse can be followed by reinvestment and recovery. This in part, as indicated, depends on active regional policy to defend and promote the interests of a place. However, as Mah (2013) puts it, for many dispossessed regions, revival seems a distant prospect; 'the "post-industrial" has yet to take hold... [and] not every old industrial city can have a Tate'. Thus, there are many 'old industrial regions' like the North of England (and Teesside within it) – Hudson (2006: 6) lists the Ruhrgebiet (Germany), Wallonia (Belgium), Nord-Pas-de-Calais (France), the industrial mid-west of the USA and Nova Scotia (Canada) as examples – that were once centres of capital accumulation and growth but which 'flipped and became regions of decline, characterised by capital flight, devalorisation and disinvestment'. The future of these places – places like Tees-side – remains uncertain: 'some places are developed or redeveloped while others are left behind' (Mah, 2013). Mah was writing in 2013 and this motif – 'the left behind' – has gained enormous political resonance since, in the US presidential elections and the UK EU Referendum of 2016, referring to the people and places that have lost out in processes of globalisation and socio-economic change. Indeed, the resentment of 'the left behind' seems to have played a large part in both. A small but striking example vis-à-vis 'Brexit' stands out from our own research. East Middlesbrough, our research locality in Teesside, is reported to have had the highest proportion of 'leave' voters of anywhere in the country, at 82.5% (BBC, 2017). On the other side of the Atlantic, the election of Donald Trump to US President seems to have reflected the popularity of his plans, via tax, the pressure of public opinion and other measures, to limit globalisation in favour of protecting US industry and jobs. One immediate outcome of this was the speedy *volte-face* by Ford Motors regarding a planned car plant in Mexico, choosing to expand a factory in Michigan, USA instead (Agren, 2017). After decades of politicians extolling the virtues and inevitability of globalisation, it seems that alternatives were possible after all.

Conclusion

With our research, we have tried to give a picture of youth transitions to adulthood as they play out over the long term, that captures a breadth of experiences and which, through detailed biographical interviews, forefronts the accounts of the sorts of 'socially excluded' young people who are typically the target of policy interventions. They are often talked about but less often asked to speak about their lives. After years of research, and the summary of findings we present here, one or two conclusions stand out.

Firstly, it is really quite astounding that, despite the collapse of the local economy and the time-honoured routes to respectable working-class adulthood, the impoverishment of their communities and the opportunities available to them, and the multiplicity and depth of social problems that make Teesside 'worst' and 'poorest' –after decades of this, young people here still retain such straightforwardly conventional, 'respectable', normal values and aspirations. It would be far less surprising to have discovered 'underclass cultures' of worklessness and 'welfare dependency'. There is a longevity and resilience to working-class culture, even when the economic base that once supported it has become so shrunken and degraded.

Secondly, even in one of the most deindustrialised locales in the UK there are still jobs; unlike W.J. Wilson's portrait of the US urban ghetto, work 'has *not* disappeared' (Wilson, 1996). This is a very important finding. We are not describing UK versions of zones of *complete* abandonment (Wacquant, 2008), or a redundant underclass surplus to economic requirements. This is part of the reason for our rejection of 'social *exclusion*' as an adequate descriptive term, even though it is far superior to the falsehoods of underclass theory

(MacDonald and Marsh, 2005). Rather, economic *marginality* better captures what is going on here – for the place and its people. This economic marginality is demonstrated most clearly in long-term labour market careers marked by persistent insecurity and recurrent poverty (Shildrick et al, 2012a). The combined legacies of the persistence of structurally caused high unemployment and more flexible, insecure employment left in the wake of de-industrialisation mean that the biographies of many working-class people are now characterised not by complete worklessness, nor by a life in steady work, but by the insecurities of churning between unemployment and low-paid and low-skilled jobs.

In the final part of the chapter we have shown how the voodoo sociology and weak versions of 'social exclusion' that infect much policy thinking would have it that this pattern is an outcome of individual choices or other facets of supply-side characteristics (recent versions stress young adults' alleged preference for the fragmented work of 'the gig economy'). It is not. It is an outcome of the fundamental restructuring of the local economy of Teesside, itself resulting from the heightened globalising tendencies of late capitalism. The poverty and insecurity of the lives of our informants were not 'personal troubles' of individual biographies but 'public issues' of social structure (Mills, 1959). Thus, to understand youth transitions in this place we need, firstly, to grapple qualitatively with the twists and turns of individual biographies but, secondly, to lift our eyes so as to appreciate properly the conditions which frame the making of those lives. In doing so we are then able to comprehend how young men and women make their own histories but do so not as they please or would freely choose but under existing conditions that constrain their choice, agency and possibilities (Marx, 1852).

Notes

1 This was not wholly true of middle-generation interviewees in our fifth study. They had unusually lengthy unemployment and, often, a host of contributory factors had led to a more fatalistic withdrawal from the labour market.
2 This acceptance rate of 6.2% meant it was harder to get a job at McDonalds than a place at Yale University, as one commentator noted at the time www.motherjones. com/politics/2011/05/mcdonalds-national-hiring-day.
3 Tim Newburn, quoted in the *Guardian* 5 August 2016, www.theguardian.com/ uk-news/2016/aug/05/conditions-that-caused-english-riots-even-worse-now-says-lea ding-expert
4 The relationships between age, class, education and place in the shaping of views and voting about EU membership are highly complex and warrant much greater space than can be given here (Antonucci et al, 2017).

References

Agren, D. (2017) 'Mexico afraid that Trump's policy making by tweet will put car industry into reverse', *The Guardian*, 7 January 2017.

Antonucci, L., Horvath, L., Kutiyski, Y., and Krouwel, A. (2017, forthcoming) 'The malaise of the squeezed middle: challenging the narrative of the left behind Brexiteer', *Competition and Change*, 21, 3: 211–229.

Arnett, J.J. (2006) 'The case for emerging adulthood in Europe: a response to Bynner', *Journal of Youth Studies*, 9: 111–123.

Ashton, D., Maguire, M., and Garland, V. (1982) *Youth in the Labour Market*, Research Paper 34, London: Department of Employment.

Bagguley, P., and Mann, K. (1992) 'Idle, thieving bastards: scholarly representations of the "underclass"', *Work, Employment and Society*, 6, 1: 113–126.

Ball, S., Maguire, M., and Macrae, S. (2000) *Choice, Pathways and Transitions Post-16: New Youth, New Economies in the Global City*, London: Routledge/Falmer.

Barry, M. (ed.) (2005) *Youth Policy and Social Inclusion*, London: Routledge.

Beynon, H., Hudson, R., and Sadler, D. (1994) *A Place Called Teesside*, Edinburgh: Edinburgh University Press.

BBC (2010) 'Spending cuts to hit north harder', *BBC News*, www.bbc.co.uk/news/uk-england-11141264

BBC (2015) 'A4e staff jailed for DWP back-to-work training fraud', *BBC News*, 31 March, www.bbc.co.uk/news/uk-england-32139244

BBC (2016) 'Girls face huge quality of life difference across England', *BBC News*, 12 September, www.bbc.co.uk/news/uk-england-37337893

BBC (2017) 'Local voting figures shed new light on EU referendum', *BBC News*, February 7, www.bbc.co.uk/news/uk-politics-38762034

Beatty, C. and Fothergill, S. (2013) *Hitting the Poorest Places Hardest: The Local and Regional Impact of Welfare Reform*, Sheffield: CRESC.

Beynon, H., Hudson, R., and Sadler, D. (1994) *A Place Called Teesside*, Edinburgh: Edinburgh University Press.

Brown, M. (2015) 'Middlesbrough Council spends £17m in six years on making staff redundant', *Middlesbrough Evening Gazette*, 14 June, www.gazettelive.co.uk/news/teesside-news/middlesbrough-council-17m-redundancy-staff-9451808

Brown, P. (1987) *Schooling Ordinary Kids*, London: Tavistock.

Bynner, J., Chisholm, L., and Furlong, A. (eds.) (1997) *Youth, Citizenship and Social Change in a European Context*, Aldershot: Ashgate.

Byrne, D. (1999) *Social Exclusion*, Milton Keynes: Open University Press.

Chamberlayne, P., Rustin, M., and Wengraf, T. (eds.) (2002) *Biography and Social Exclusion in Europe*, Bristol: Policy Press.

Chapman, T., Van der Graaf, P., and Bell, V. (2011) *Raising Aspirations, Recognising Achievements and Realising Potential: Providing Non-formal Learning to Excluded Young People: Final Evaluation Report of the YSDF Youth Achievement Foundation Pathfinder*, Middlesbrough: Social Futures Institute, Teesside University.

Cohen, A. K. (1955) *Delinquent Boys*, Glencoe: The Free Press.

Cohen, P., and Ainley, P. (2000) 'In the country of the blind? Youth studies and cultural studies in Britain', *Journal of Youth Studies*, 3, 1: 79–95.

Cresci, E. (2016) 'Meet the 75%: the young people who voted to remain in the EU', *The Guardian*, 24 June, www.theguardian.com/politics/2016/jun/24/meet-the-75-young-people-who-voted-to-remain-in-eu

DETR (2000) *Index of Multiple Deprivation*, London: Department of the Environment, Transport and the Regions.

Elledge, J. (2016) 'The north-south divide in England's youth unemployment rate is still the size of a chasm', *City Metric*, www.citymetric.com/business/north-south-divide-englands-youth-unemployment-rate-still-size-chasm-1913

European Youth Forum (2014) *Policy Paper on Youth Employment*, www.youthforum.org/assets/2014/06/0166-13_PP_Employment_Final1.pdf

Fahmy, E. (2015) 'On the frontline: the growth of youth deprivation in Britain, 1990–2012', *Discover Society*, 20, http://discoversociety.org/2015/05/05/on-the-frontline-the-growth-of-youth-deprivation-in-britain-1990-2012/

Foord, J. (1985) *The Quiet Revolution: Social and Economic Change on Teesside 1965 to 1985*, a Special Report for BBC North-East, Newcastle: BBC.

Forrest, R., and Kearns, A. (2001) 'Social cohesion, social capital and the neighbourhood', *Urban Studies*, 38, 12: 2125–2143.

Furlong, A. and Cartmel, F. (2007) *Young People and Social Change: New Perspectives*, Milton Keynes: Open University Press.

Gunter, A., and Watt, P. (2009) 'Goin' college, goin' work and goin' road: youth cultures and transitions in East London', *Journal of Youth Studies*, 12, 5: 515–529.

House of Commons Library (2016) *Youth Unemployment Statistics*, August 17 2016, http://researchbriefings.parliament.uk/ResearchBriefing/Summary/SN05871

Hudson, R. (1986) 'Sunset over the Tees', *New Socialist*, September, p. 13.

Hudson, R. (1989) *Wrecking a Region: State Polic[i]es, Party Politics, and Regional Change in North East England*, London: Pion.

Hudson, R. (2006) *The EU's Ultra-peripheral Regions: Developmental Considerations and Reflections*, paper prepared for the Conference on the Macroeconomic Situation of the European Ultra-periphery, Brussels, 15/12/2006, www.azores.gov.pt/NR/rdonlyres/5269CA5D-562B-4B43-B9DE-1839F2BEDF7F/118203/RayHudson.pdf

Jackson, B. (1972) *Working Class Community*, London: Pelican.

Jahoda, M. (1982) *Employment and Unemployment: A Social Psychological Analysis*, Cambridge: Cambridge University Press.

Jeffs, T., and Smith, M. (1998) 'The problem of "youth" for youth work', *Youth and Policy*, 62: 45–66.

Jensen, T. (2014) 'Welfare common-sense, poverty porn and doxosophy', *Sociological Research Online*, 19(3), 3.

Johnston, L., MacDonald, R.Mason, P.Ridley, L., and Webster, C. (2000) *Snakes and Ladders*, York: JRF.

Jones, G. (2002) *The Youth Divide*, York: Joseph Rowntree Foundation/York Publishing Services.

Lupton, R., and Power, A. (2002) 'Social exclusion and neighbourhoods', in Hills, J., Le Grand, J., and Piachaud, D. (eds.) *Understanding Social Exclusion*, Oxford: Oxford University Press.

MacDonald, R. (1997) 'Dangerous youth and the dangerous class' in MacDonald, R. (ed.) *Youth, the 'Underclass' and Social Exclusion*, London: Routledge.

MacDonald, R. (2006) 'Social exclusion, youth transitions and criminal careers: five critical reflections on risk', *Australian and New Zealand Journal of Criminology*, 39, 3: 371–383.

MacDonald, R. (2008) 'Disconnected youth? Social exclusion, the underclass and economic marginality' *Social Work & Society*, 6, 2, special issue on 'Marginalized Youth': 236–248.

MacDonald, R. (2011) 'Youth, transitions and un(der)employment: plus ça change, plus c'est la même chose?', *Journal of Sociology*, 47: 427–444.

MacDonald, R. (2016) *Voodoo Sociology, Unemployment and the Low-pay, No-pay Cycle*, Blog for SARF, http://www.the-sarf.org.uk/voodoo-sociology/

MacDonald, R. (2017,) 'Precarious work: the growing precarité of youth' in Furlong, A. (ed.) *The International Handbook of Youth and Young Adulthood* (second edition), London: Routledge.

MacDonald, R., and J. Marsh (2002) 'Crossing the rubicon: youth transitions, poverty drugs and social exclusion', *International Journal of Drug Policy*, 13: 27–38.

MacDonald, R., and J. Marsh (2005) *Disconnected Youth? Growing up in Britain's Poor Neighbourhoods*, Basingstoke: Palgrave

MacDonald, R., and Shildrick, T. (2007) 'Street corner society', *Leisure Studies*, 26, 3: 339–335.

MacDonald, R., and Shildrick, T. (2013) 'Youth and wellbeing: experiencing bereavement and ill health in marginalised young people's transitions', *Sociology of Health and Illness*, 35, 1: 147–161.

MacDonald, R., Mason, P., Shildrick, T., Webster, C., Johnston, L., and Ridley, L. (2001) 'Snakes & ladders: in defence of studies of youth transition', *Sociological Research Online*, 5, http://socresonline.org.uk/5/4/macdonald.html

MacDonald, R., Shildrick, T., Webster, C., and Simpson, D. (2005) 'Growing up in poor neighbourhoods: the significance of class and place in the extended transitions of "socially excluded" young adults', *Sociology*, 39, 5: 873–891

MacDonald, R., Shildrick, T., and Furlong, A. (2014) 'In search of "intergenerational cultures of worklessness": hunting yetis and shooting zombies', *Critical Social Policy*, 34, 2, 199–220.

Mah, A. (2012) *Industrial Ruination, Community, and Place*, Toronto: University of Toronto Press.

Mah, A. (2013) 'Living with industrial ruination', *Discover Society*, October 1, http://discoversociety.org/2013/10/01/living-with-industrial-ruination/

Marsden, D., and Duff, E. (1975) *Workless*, Harmondsworth: Pelican.

Marx, K. (1852/1963) *The Eighteenth Brumaire of Louis Bonaparte*, New York: International Publishers.

McDowell, L. (2000) 'The trouble with men? Young people, gender transformations and the crisis of masculinity', *International Journal of Urban and Regional Research*, 24, 1: 201–209.

Miles, S. (2000) *Youth Lifestyles in a Changing World*, Buckingham: Open University Press.

Mills, C. W. (1959) *The Sociological Imagination*, New York: Pelican.

Morris, L. (1994) *Dangerous Classes*, London: Routledge.

Murray, C. (1990) *The Emerging British Underclass*, London: Institute of Economic Affairs.

Murray, C. (1994) *Underclass: The Crisis Deepens*, London: Institute of Economic Affairs.

North East Homelessness Think Tank (2016) *Benefit Sanctions and Homelessness*, http://youthhomelessnortheast.org.uk/wp-content/uploads/NEHTT-final-rep ort-2015.pdf

Northern Echo (2013) 'Results of government's work programme in the north-east "appalling" – Labour', *Northern Echo*, 27 June, www.thenorthernecho.co.uk/news/local/teesvalley/middlesbrough/10513443.Results_of_Government_s_Work_Programme_in_the_North_East__appalling____Labour/?action=complain&cid=11750335

ONS (2016a) *Towns and Cities Analysis, England and Wales, March 2016*, www.ons. gov.uk/peoplepopulationandcommunity/housing/articles/townsandcitiesanalysi senglandandwalesmarch2016/2016-03-18

ONS (2016b) *Regional Gross Value Added (Income Approach), UK: 1997 to 2015*, www.ons.gov.uk/economy/grossvalueaddedgva/bulletins/regionalgrossvalueadde dincomeapproach/december2016.

Parker, H., Bury, C., and Eggington, R. (1998) *New Heroin Outbreaks Amongst Young People in England and Wales*, Police Research Group, Paper 92, London: Home Office.

Putnam, D. (1995) 'Bowling alone: America's declining social capital', *Journal of Democracy*, 6, 1: 65–78.

Quintini, G., Martin, P., and Martin, S. (2007) *The Changing Nature of the School to Work Transition Process in OECD Countries*, Discussion paper 2582, Bonn: Institute for the Study of Labor.

Roberts, K. (2001) *Class in Modern Britain*, London: Palgrave.

Roberts, K., and G. Parsell (1992) 'The stratification of youth training', *British Journal of Education and Work*, 5: 65–83.

Roberts, R. (1971) *The Classic Slum*, London: Penguin.

Robinson, F. (2005). 'Regenerating the west end of Newcastle: what went wrong?', *Northern Economic Review*, 36, 15–42.

Shildrick, T., MacDonald, R., Webster, C., and Garthwaite, K. (2012a) *Poverty and Insecurity: Life in Low Pay, No Pay Britain*, Bristol: Policy Press.

Shildrick, T., MacDonald, R., Furlong, A., Roden, J., and Crow, R., (2012b) *Are Cultures of Worklessness Passed Down the Generations?* York: Joseph Rowntree Foundation.

Shildrick, T., and MacDonald, R. (2013) 'Poverty talk: how people experiencing poverty deny their poverty and why they blame "the poor"' *The Sociological Review*, 61, 2: 285–303.

Shildrick, T., MacDonald, R., and Furlong, A. (2016) 'Not single spies, but in battalions: a critical, sociological engagement with so called "Troubled Families"', *Sociological Review*, 64, 4: 821–836.

Simpson, M., Shildrick, T., and MacDonald, R. (eds.) (2007) *Drugs in Britain: Supply, Consumption and Control*, Basingstoke: Palgrave.

Sissons, P. (2011) *The Hourglass and the Escalator: Labour Market Change and Mobility*, London: The Work Foundation.

Tees Valley Unlimited (TVU) (2011) *Interim Work and Skills Plan 2010–11*, Middlesbrough, http://s3.amazonaws.com/zanran_storage/www.teesvalleyunlimited. gov.uk/ContentPages/2478634462.pdf

Tees Valley Unlimited (TVU) (2014) *Tees Valley Skills Strategy 2014–20*, www.lep network.net/modules/downloads/download.php?file_name=37

Thornton, L. (2007) 'Middlesbrough worst place in UK', *Daily Mirror*, www.mirror. co.uk/news/uk-news/middlesbrough-worst-place-in-uk-513534

Unison (2016) *A Future at Risk: Cuts in Youth Services*, London: Unison, www. unison.org.uk/content/uploads/2016/08/23996.pdf

Veit-Wilson, J. (1998) *Setting Adequacy Standards*, Bristol: Policy Press.

Wacquant, L. (2008) *Urban Outcasts*, London: Polity.

Wacquant, L. (2009) *Punishing the Poor: The Neoliberal Government of Social Insecurity*, Durham and London: Duke Press.

Walkerdine, V. (2010). 'Communal beingness and affect: an exploration of trauma in an ex-industrial community'. *Body and Society*, 16(1): 91–116.

Watts, B. (2014) 'Benefits sanctions are adding to bleak prospects for young people', York: JRF, www.jrf.org.uk/blog/benefits-sanctions-are-adding-bleak-prospects-young-people

Webster, C., Simpson, D., MacDonald, R., Abbas, A., Cieslik, M., and Shildrick, T. (2004) *Poor Transitions: Young Adults and Social Exclusion*, Bristol: Policy Press/JRF.

Welshman, J. (2013) *Underclass: A History of the Excluded since 1880*, London: Bloomsbury Press.

Willis, P. (1977) *Learning to Labour: How Working-class Kids Get Working-class Jobs*, London: Saxon House.

Wilson, W.J. (1996) *When Work Disappears*, New York: Knopf.

Wolf, A. (2011) *Review of Vocational Education: The Wolf Report*, London: Department for Education, www.gov.uk/government/uploads/system/uploads/attachment_data/file/180504/DFE-00031-2011.pdf

6 Social inequality and the transition to education and training

The significance of family background in Germany

Birgit Jentsch and Herwig Reiter

Introduction

Over the last few decades, it has been recognised that public pillars of welfare provision – the state, the market and civil society – have not diminished the influence and impact of intergenerational family support. Rather, such solidarity with its relational and emotional dimensions has been understood to compensate for the retrenchment of the welfare state (Kohli and Albertini, 2008; Kohli et al, 2010). Thus, family solidarity, that is the lifelong emotional and material support of family members across generations, represents a positive value in society. At the same time welfare provisions by families also have an unintended and undesirable side-effect: while levelling out inequalities between generations within individual families, they tend to exacerbate social inequalities between different strata in society. Intergenerational family support can thus undermine equality of opportunity.

International comparisons have demonstrated that in Germany the tie between family background and social and economic achievements is particularly strong (Stompe, 2005; Mayer et al., 2007; Schnitzlein, 2013). For instance, the results of the OECD's Programme for International Student Assessment (PISA) 2000 generated extensive commentary in the media and political concern.[1] Not only did the performance of pupils in Germany prove to be relatively poor, but in addition, the study revealed a particularly strong link between social background and educational outcomes in the country. As a consequence, this international study put the 'social background – educational success' topic back on the public and political agenda (Stompe, 2005; Waldow, 2009). Despite some subsequent improvements (OECD, 2016a), the German education system still stands out for its unequal opportunities, highlighting the importance of parents' financial and other resources (Schnitzlein, 2013; Debuschewitz and Bujard, 2014; OECD, 2016a). While general educational inequalities have been well documented in international and national studies, there is less theoretical debate and empirical evidence with regard to its causes (Debuschewitz and Bujard, 2014). Two central theoretical approaches often referenced in attempts to explain the reproduction of inequalities in the education system consist of Boudon's (1974) theory of educational choice and

Bourdieu's (1983) theory of cultural reproduction. In particular, Boudon's (1974) distinction between primary and secondary effects of social origin, in which educational pathways are the result of rational decision-making and parental aspirations, is still frequently employed as a theoretical framework for empirical studies in Germany (Schneider, 2004; Dumont et al., 2014; Fend, 2014; Hillmert, 2014). According to Boudon:

> [p]rimary effects are all those, whether of a genetic or socio-cultural kind, that are expressed via the association between children's class backgrounds and their actual levels of academic performance. Secondary effects are those that are expressed via the educational choices that children from differing class backgrounds make within the range of choice that their previous performance allows them.
>
> (Jackson et al., 2007, 211).

While Boudon's theory remains largely at the micro-level, Bourdieu's (1983) interest lies in the interplay between micro and macro perspectives. He relates cultural capital to a person's familiarity with and ability to fit into the dominant culture of a society (Debuschewitz and Bujard, 2014). In the education system, some forms of cultural capital are more valued than others, so that success here is shaped by the cultural tools a person has acquired (Sullivan, 2002). Bourdieu's concept of *habitus* represents the embodiment of the cultural capital which has been accrued due to life experiences (Wacquant, 2016). We will not engage with these theories in detail but through the chapter we seek to highlight points at which the German context provides interesting questions for theory and for further research.

More specifically, this chapter explores patterns of the reproduction of social inequality at crucial transition points in the German education and training contexts, and discusses factors and processes that may underlie them. For this purpose, the key facets of the German education and training systems are described in some detail. While gender and migratory history are important socio-structural characteristics which clearly influence the education experiences and outcomes in Germany (see, for example, Mayer et al., 2007; Beicht et al., 2011; Debuschewitz and Bujard, 2014; Minello and Blossfeld, 2016), the focus of this chapter is on the significance of social origin in young people's transition to education and training. Moreover, the consequences of particular educational or training pathways for subsequent labour market opportunities are considered in the context of continuities and change: despite the favourable employment statistics for young people in Germany, even across the Great Recession, those youths with low educational credentials have experienced increasing difficulties with accessing high quality training and, as a consequence, are bearing the brunt of a growing segmentation of labour market risks. The conclusion reflects on the key issues discussed, including ways in which the above-mentioned theoretical approaches can enhance our understanding of the social inequalities experienced by young people at crucial transition points in their lives.

Primary and secondary education in Germany[2]

Germany is one of the few EU countries in which the transition from primary to secondary education holds particular significance: at the age of ten children are selected to enter one of three main types of secondary schools. While there are a number of differences in the education system amongst the *Länder*, who are in charge of educational policies, some basic systemic structures are common across Germany. Three school types are available: *Hauptschule* (lower-secondary schools), *Realschule* (intermediate-secondary schools) and *Gymnasium* (upper-secondary schools). In each school type the curriculum is aimed at a particular set of educational qualifications associated with specific employment opportunities.[3] Pupils at *Hauptschule*, which covers grades five to nine or ten (depending on the *Land*) receive basic general education and attend pre-vocational courses. On successful completion of the final grade and examination, they graduate at age 15 or 16 with a *Hauptschulabschluss* – a leaving certificate which typically leads them to dual vocational and education training, provided that they can secure a training place (as discussed in more detail below) (Edelstein, 2013). The certificate also allows for access to some full-time vocational schools (*Berufsschulen*), or to institutions offering secondary education for adults – the pathway of second-chance education (*Zweiter Bildungsweg*) (Lohmar and Eckhardt, 2015). Pupils who attend *Realschule*, which covers grades five to ten, receive a more general education. After the successful completion of grade ten and having passed the final exam, the *Realschulabschluss* certificate is awarded. It allows the *Realschule* graduate, who in most cases will be 16 years old, to access *Berufsschulen* and the more advanced *Berufsfachschulen*. In addition to these opportunities, which are similar to those that graduate from *Hauptschule* enjoy, *Realschule* graduates can continue their education at advanced *Fachoberschulen*, which cover grades eleven and twelve (Lohmar and Eckhardt, 2015). Moreover, *Realschulabschluss* equips graduates with better chances for securing a training place in the dual system of vocational education and training than their *Hauptschule* counterparts.

Only a small minority of graduates from *Hauptschule* and *Realschule* with outstanding results can switch to the third, most prestigious as well as most challenging, type of secondary school, the *Gymnasium*, which provides an academic education track and runs in most *Länder* until grade 12, in others until grade 13. As a general rule, the final degree of this track, the general *Abitur* or subject-specific *Fachabitur* (a higher education entry certificate), which is generally obtained at the age of 18 or 19, is a requirement for admission to tertiary education.[4] The percentage of higher education students without Abitur, so-called 'non-traditional students', amounts to only around 1% (Powell and Solga, 2012, 78) Hence, this upper-secondary track allows for the pursuit of university qualifications and the achievement of the most desirable occupational positions. However, as will been seen below, there are also graduates from *Gymnasium* who embark on training courses in the dual vocational education and training system (Lohmar and Eckhardt, 2015). As an indicator of educational inflation in Germany, these graduates are the most wanted candidates for employers offering training places. Concerning the distribution of pupils at secondary education first stage, in the school year 2014/2015, 12% attended *Hauptschule*, 23% *Realschule*, and 34% *Gymnasium* (Statistisches Bundesamt, 2016a, 12). Of the remaining school types, the *Integrierte Gesamtschule* and *Schularten mit mehreren Bildungsgängen* (school types with various educational programmes) were the most significant, attracting 16% and 12% of the pupils, respectively (Statistisches Bundesamt, 2016a, 13). The relative large significance of these two school types reflects the trend over the last decade in most *Länders* to gradually or actually abolish *Hauptschule*. [5] However, it is important to note that even where *Hauptschule* has been abolished as an autonomous school type, it continues its existence in the form of *Hauptschule* degrees, which the two school types mentioned above must also have on offer (Braun and Lex, 2007).

Given the fact that secondary schools are rigidly segmented and set children on very different courses of education and associated labour market prospects, it is not surprising that much research studying the impact of intergenerational support in Germany has focused on the transition from primary to secondary education. This significant educational decision occurs after only four years at primary school when teachers recommend what type of secondary school pupils ought to go to. In some *Länder*, these recommendations are based on grades and are binding (Bavaria, Brandenburg, Saxony, Saxony-Anhalt, Thuringia and Bremen). Here, an admission exam can be taken when the desired *Gymnasium* or *Realschule* recommendation has not been given. In other *Länder*, the recommendations are neither linked to grades nor are they binding (Baden-Württemberg, Hamburg, Hessen, Lower Saxony, Saarland, Mecklenburg-Western Pomerania, Northrhine-Westfalia, Rhineland-Palatinate, and Schleswig-Holstein). Berlin does not fit in either of these two groups as recommendations here are based on grades but are not binding (Helbig and Nikolai, 2015).

There is extensive evidence that parents' level of education significantly influences intergenerational mobility and children's pathways into these different school types (Mayer et al., 2007; Schneider, 2008; Keller and Neidhöfer, 2014). For example, in 2015, 61% of children whose parents had higher educational qualification went to *Gymnasium*. This percentage was reduced to 30% where parents had medium educational qualifications, and to 17% where parents had low educational levels.[6] Looking at the development of these proportions between 2010 and 2015, there have hardly been any changes (Statistisches Bundesamt, 2016b). Explanations that may account for these inequalities include institutional and structural factors such as the fact that compulsory education consists of half-day teaching only, thereby exacerbating the effects of social inequality in familial resources. The high proportion of time spent at home and differences in how families with varying amounts of cultural capital spend that time results in unequal levels of competence amongst children. For example, confirming the relevance of Boudon's primary effects, PISA 2006 demonstrated that in Germany, the extent of children's extra-curricular activities related to the natural sciences varied according to social origin. In addition, the study found the same tendencies in assessments of the vocational relevance of the natural sciences for occupations. These two factors turn out to crucially shape children's motivation for competence acquisition in this field (Solga and Dombrowski, 2009, 21). Inequalities that pervade the everyday life of families are thus poorly addressed by the German education system (Solga and Dombrowski, 2009, 21). Moreover, the early branching point of the education system, in which children are on average ten years old when they are selected for different secondary school tracks, is seen as strengthening the influence of family background: the earlier such selection takes place, the more important is the social context of the family home (Mayer et al., 2007; Schneider, 2008; Keller and Neidhöfer, 2014). In addition, as each school track entails particular curricula, school requirements, and learning conditions, pupils accumulate different cognitive developments and academic knowledge, and so experience different opportunities for further educational progression (Mayer et al., 2007).

The focus of much research on the reproduction of inequality in education has tended to be on the micro-level, especially on Boudon's (1974) primary and secondary effects (e.g. Maaz and Nagy, 2009; Neugebauer, 2010; Hillmert, 2014). Empirically, such research has employed statistical procedures to decompose primary effects (i.e. the association between social origin and academic performance) and secondary effects (i.e. the transition propensities of families of different social origin). Concerning primary effects, differences in children's competences by social class are well documented already at primary-school level. As shown by the Progress in International Reading Literacy Study (PIRLS), in Germany, the extent of that difference is above the international average (Solga and Dombrowski, 2009, 13).

Similarly, secondary effects appear to be particularly prominent in the German context. Studies conducted cross-nationally in Europe demonstrate that compared to other countries, in Germany, secondary effects play a relatively large role, accounting for at least 50% of educational inequality at this educational branching point[7] (Neugebauer, 2010). Not surprisingly, these effects are weaker for children who have either very low or very high grades (thus fulfilling clearly the formal access criteria associated with a certain school type), and strong for children with medium grades, where parents have more discretion in choosing a particular school type. Parents' preferences thus appear to play a crucial role. Even where children's reading and basic competences are the same, parents in the higher grade professionals are 3.7 times more likely to prefer *Gymnasium* for their children than parents who are skilled workers, and 5.7 times more likely than low-skilled workers (Solga and Dombrowski, 2009, 14).

Moreover, the relative importance of secondary effects tends to be higher in those federal states where parents can decide on the secondary school track (61%), and lower where teachers' recommendations are binding (54%). (Neugebauer, 2010). This seems to apply in spite of teachers having been found to support stratification rather than reducing it: children from lower social backgrounds need to perform better to secure a recommendation to *Gymnasium* than their counterparts whose parents hold higher social positions (Debuschewitz and Bujard, 2014; Schneider, 2008). Even where reading and basic competence are the same, children with parents in the higher grade professional ranks were shown to be 2.6 times more likely than children from skilled workers, and 4.5 times more likely than those from unskilled workers, to attain a *Gymnasium* recommendation from their teachers (Solga and Dombrowski, 2009, 14).

> As a paradox of the German educational system, lower-status pupils face a dual barrier on the road to the highest track (*Gymnasium*): they need higher achievements in order to get the same school-track recommendation from their primary-school teachers; and they have to 'convince' their parents by their higher achievements that they should be launched on the academic trajectory.
>
> (Keller and Neidhöfer, 2014, 4)

In line with Bourdieu's (1984) findings, teachers contribute to a dominant culture in the education system which reflects the shared *habitus* of the higher classes and then reward those students who possess the same cultural capital (Dumais, 2002, 46). Independent of teachers' role, in circumstances where parents' sphere of influence is reduced, decision processes are more meritocratic, and parental values, preferences and resources are less likely to influence children's educational pathways (Neugebauer, 2010, 208).

Where parents do have a choice, it is less the family income than parents' educational background that plays a role in the secondary school opted for. Indeed, differences in educational preferences can largely be attributed to this factor. Parents who themselves have a *Gymnasium* education can assess the extent to which they can support their children academically and financially (for example, when outsourcing academic support) and are thus more inclined to send them to that same school type. Other parents are likely to choose other school types even if they see *Gymnasium* education as a worthwhile aspiration (Paulus and Blossfeld, 2007). Peer pressure may explain these education-dependent parental choices to some extent. Parents' preference for a vocational route (as a positive choice) for their children has been linked to professional traditions, which are particularly strong in the craft sector in Germany. As such, the parents' own education and occupation can impact on their preferences for their child's educational and occupational future, so that the lower educational track and an early labour market entry may be regarded as the best way forward. Moreover, especially for the craft sector, knowledge transmission is likely to contribute to occupational continuity across generations (Dustman, 2004). It is noteworthy that these explanations have remained at a rather speculative level, not least due to a lack of qualitative research into these areas, which could explore the more subtle processes behind education-dependent parental choices. However, these educational pathways and processes need to be distinguished from the final educational outcome, since many children deviate from an ideal-typical sequence of educational transition. After all, there are institutionalised opportunities to 'correct' initial educational decisions and obtain qualifications through a 'second chance'. Research data demonstrate that these opportunities tend to strengthen inequalities since it is mainly children from well-educated families who climb up the educational ladder from lower to higher secondary educational streams (Hillmert and Jacob, 2008). For those who stay at *Realschule* or *Hauptschule*, their competences fall further and further behind their peers at *Gymnasium*. These inequalities are attributed to different learning milieux and curricula in the three school types (Solga and Dombrowski, 2009).

Following secondary schooling, *Gymnasium* graduates can either directly enter the labour market – an option which is rarely pursued; or, together with all other secondary school leavers, they continue education and training in a non-tertiary or tertiary institution. The subsequent sections examine first of all the role of parental background in tertiary education before turning to non-tertiary pathways.

Tertiary and non-tertiary education

Since unification, tertiary attainment of young adults (25–34 year olds) has increased from 22% in 2005 to 30% in 2015. Yet, it still remains well below the OECD average of 32% in 2005 and 42% in 2015 (OECD, 2016c, 5). Apart from universities, higher education is offered in *Fachhochschulen* (universities of applied sciences) as well as art colleges, divinity schools and business schools (Mayer et al., 2007). While research on parents' influence on their children's school education is extensive, transitions following secondary school are less often investigated (Keller and Neidhöfer, 2014). The *Abitur* acts as an almost exclusive bottleneck for accessing tertiary education: combined with the inequality in educational results at secondary school level outlined above, it is not surprising that young people's transitions to higher education are also shaped by parents' educational backgrounds. For example, in 2009, 77% of children of parents with a tertiary degree entered tertiary education themselves. This percentage is more than three times higher than that of children from parents with qualifications below that level, which amounts to 23% (BMBF, 2016, 58–59).

Recent research has stressed the relevance of families' ambition to advance or maintain their social position, as well as students' desire for self-realisation (Marginson, 2016). The tertiary education sector is horizontally stratified: i.e. with the expansion of higher education, institutions have become hierarchically classified, for instance on the basis of their academic prestige and quality (Triventi, 2013). 'Knowledgeable' families try to navigate these structures by controlling those pathways which are associated with the greatest value and advantage: "Educational differentiation allows the elite status of those 'born into privilege' to be protected" (Marginson, 2016, 422).

Hence, in contrast to the factors relevant at the level of compulsory schooling for the reproduction of inequalities, in the tertiary sector opportunity costs appear to constitute a major secondary effect with regard to the type of tertiary institution chosen. Again, while we have insights into the relationship between social class and educational differentiation, the processes underpinning this relationship are still poorly understood. The extent and nature of parents' influence on their children's tertiary education choices is therefore unclear. Similarly, we do not know whether there are less tangible factors which shape the interaction between families and educational structures. It is possible that perceived norms associated with an institution encourage potential students to choose their place of learning on the basis of where they may better 'fit in'.

VET – the non-tertiary vocational education and training pathway – consists of three pillars. First, firm-based programmes (i.e. apprenticeships) in the dual system; second, fully qualifying vocational schooling; and third the 'transition scheme' (*Übergangssystem*), that is, pre-vocational, school-based training (Ahrens, 2014; Powell and Solga, 2014). The 'transition scheme' does not lead to any recognised vocational qualification, but rather provides a stopgap measure for those youths who were unable to secure a place in the other two systems. Its purpose is to strengthen individual competencies and thus to prepare young people for 'proper' VET places. For youths with *Realschule* or *Hauptschule* degrees, VET is the only possible route to skilled employment. For *Gymnasium* graduates, the well-developed dual VET programme can be regarded as a reasonable alternative to tertiary education, also due to promising labour market prospects after completion. In 2016, more than half (51%) of the 25–34 year olds completed the programme (OECD, 2016c), which involves concurrent school-based and work-based education and training.

About a third of *Gymnasium* graduates choose the vocational education and training (VET) pathway instead of tertiary education. The option is particularly attractive to youths with a working-class background, even if they are qualified to enter university, in part perhaps due to the ideological and normative commitments to vocationalism in Germany (Powell and Solga, 2012, 81). In addition, parents' transmission of knowledge, which inevitably is widest in areas in which a person has experiences, is also likely to contribute to occupational inheritance (Dustman, 2004). An additional pull factor may be the promise of a smooth transition into the labour market. Evidence shows that following the completion of such programmes, young people enjoy higher employment rates than those whose highest level of qualification is an upper-secondary general programme (OECD, 2016b). This certainly applies to Germany where the unemployment rate of adults with secondary or post-secondary non-tertiary vocational qualification is only 4.2%, compared to 7.7% across the OECD; and where the employment rate of individuals with upper-secondary or post-secondary non-tertiary qualification (86%) nearly equates the rate for those with tertiary education (88%) – percentages which in both cases are 5% above the OECD average (OECD, 2016c). Internationally and in Germany, dual VET is seen as being able to deliver, not least due to the labour market results it achieves. However, since the 1990s, the system has become increasingly stratified. Disadvantages for young people with lower education levels have increased due to "a dramatic devaluation of lower school leaving certificates" (Protsch and Dieckhoff, 2011, 72), a result of a decrease in demand for lower-skilled work at the same time as the proportion of those with higher levels of education has expanded (Protsch and Dieckhoff, 2011, 72). Despite the absence of formal criteria defining access to VET, educational credentials have clearly been shown to shape recruitment decisions and training opportunities, tending to exclude youngsters with lower school degrees (Protsch and Dieckhoff, 2011, 72–73). Where *Haupt-schule* graduates do access the dual system, they can primarily be found in vocational training for the crafts, agriculture and domestic jobs – the less attractive occupational segments with few career prospects.[8] By contrast, concerning industry, commerce, public service and free professions, trainees are recruited from the intermediate (*Realschule*) track, and increasingly more from upper-secondary (*Gymnasium*) graduates (Ebner and Uhly, 2016; Powell and Solga 2012).

The lack of non-standardised selection processes in the dual system also confers an undue relevance to 'personal impressions', which have an inherent bias (Granato and Unrich, 2014). Firm-specific selection criteria include 'visible' social markers, such as personal appearance and clothing, which are taken as indicators of the extent to which the person 'fits in' (Granato and Ulrich 2014, 215). Inequalities by social origin have been observed, which could not immediately be linked with performance indicators. Granato and Ulrich (2014) conclude that employers' autonomy over the recruitment process coupled with a lack of training opportunities place youths who come from socially poorer backgrounds at a further disadvantage. Similarly, Solga and Dombrowski (2009) show that young people from disadvantaged families and with lower qualifications are less likely to access VET: young people with qualifications from *Hauptschule* are in particularly vulnerable positions as they are disadvantaged in terms of the competence levels they managed to achieve in their educational pathway. Moreover, they may find themselves stigmatised due to the low esteem in which their secondary school is held (Solga and Dombrowski, 2009). Hardly any of those young people are able to secure the training place of their choice, as two-thirds of the places offered by the Chamber of Industry and Trade require at least a degree from *Realschule* (BMBF, 2017). The hurdles these youths have to overcome in order to succeed in the labour market are significant. Their family background may in part have compromised their educational attainment and disadvantaged them in their educational pathways. The structure of the education system has reinforced these disadvantages in both concrete terms (i.e. inferior competence levels) and in abstract ways (i.e. they are unlikely to 'be suitable').

Continuities and change in the position of young people in Germany

Germany has been regarded as a country which has largely remained unaffected by the Great Recession. Although the country's GDP dropped by 4.7% in 2009 compared to 2008, employment figures still remained at record level, reaching new heights in May 2011, when the working population exceeded 41 million (Rinne and Zimmermann, 2012). The main labour market adjustment in response to the crisis comprised a reduction in working hours, and the expansion of short-time work (*Kurzarbeit*) – a labour market instrument with which the government aims to support companies at times of recession. Compared to other major OECD countries, average working hours decreased particularly strongly in Germany in the wake of the crisis (Brenke et al., 2011; Rinne and Zimmermann, 2012). The number of short-time work contracts rose between 2008 and 2009 by more than 1,000%. On average in 2009, there were 1.1 million short-time workers registered with the Federal Employment Agency (Bundesagentur für Arbeit) – an agency which provides some compensation for the loss of income experienced by these underemployed workers (Brenke et al., 2011; Statistika, 2017).[9] Short-time work programmes were implemented mainly in the export-oriented industrial sector and the service sectors which were closely linked to industrial production. For example, at the height of the crisis in the second quarter of 2009, over 30% of metal workers subject to social security contributions were employed on reduced hours. In the car industry, the percentage was around 25% (Brenke et al., 2011, 1–2).

One of the key advantages of short-time work programmes highlighted in the international literature is the presumed 'burden sharing' at times of economic recession: instead of making some employees redundant, all employees can mitigate the downturn by reducing their working hours. Hence, it is argued, the costs of the crisis are not disproportionately borne by those most at risk of unemployment – such as youths and migrants – but are spread across all employees (Will, 2010, 10). This is certainly true to some extent. However, evidence shows that the risks of the crisis are not distributed evenly amongst core workers. For example, while working-time accounts and large credit hours can be used to compensate for the impact of short-time work, these provisions are only available in certain branches, occupations and qualifications – predominantly those relating to master craftsmen, foremen, and highly skilled workers. The poorly qualified are less likely to benefit from such provisions (Giesecke and Wotschack, 2009). The situation is worse for peripheral workers with temporary and short-time contracts – mainly young people and the poorly qualified. These workers tend to be excluded from short-time work provisions and as such function as a buffer for economic fluctuations and can easily be made redundant. A representative survey of companies in 2005 (so before the Great Recession) showed that around 30% of all these businesses had responded to slumps in orders by increasing redundancies amongst workers who were temporary and amongst those with short-time contracts (Giesecke and Wotschack, 2009, 3).

Indeed, the notion that young people's employment rates have hardly been affected by the Great Recession seems to distract from another development that long preceded the recession regarding the types of employment available. Eurostat Labour Force data indicates that although there has been an increase in employment rates between 1996 and 2011, this has been accompanied by a growth in atypical employment (Allmendinger and von den Driesch, 2014, 37). In Germany, only 19% of low-skilled workers enjoy standard employment; the rate for mid- and high-level workers is around 50% – a gap which has increased over the past two decades (Allmendinger and von den Driesch, 2014, 40), reflecting a growing segmentation of labour market risks. This development seems to indicate that once types of flexible employment have been introduced, for example in order to tide over companies at times of economic downturn, these precarious jobs tend to stay and gain wide acceptance even when the economy has recovered. It has been well documented that it is young people, as labour market outsiders, who are most at risk of holding a temporary contract. By contrast, older people, who are protected by seniority rules, are least likely to be employed in this way (Gebel and Giesecke, 2009, 242).

This trend seems to have been sharpened over the last decades. For example:

> [w]hile in 1996 [the youngest age cohort's] risk of holding a temporary contract was about four times higher than that faced by persons aged 46 to 55, this ratio had risen to about nine in 2005. At the same time, no other age group shows an increased risk of holding a temporary contract.
>
> (Gebel and Giesecke, 2009, 242)

Hence, concerning young people, while there has not been a watershed moment in which opportunities rapidly declined, there still has been a gradual process in which especially those with lower educational qualifications have experienced increasing difficulties in getting a foothold into VET and the labour market. These challenges can be attributed to a decrease in the demand for work requiring lower skills at the same time as there has been an increase in the proportion of youngsters with higher qualifications in the wake of educational expansion, resulting in the devaluation of lower-school leaving certificates (Protsch and Dieckhoff, 2011; Ahrens, 2014).[10] Such adverse developments for this group have further been exacerbated by public and political discourses about educational structures and the 'crisis of the *Hauptschule*' – a school type which evokes predominantly negative connotations, and whose students have become increasingly stigmatised. There is widespread belief amongst employers that *Hauptschule* graduates are neither trainable nor employable, mirrored in the fact that many training places remain 'vacant' for the alleged shortage of suitable candidates, when at the same time many school leavers are still waiting to be offered a place (Protsch and Dieckhodd, 2011). Hence, lower-secondary qualifications nowadays rarely lead to employment or training, so that the life paths of a large minority have become increasingly de-standardised (Völcker, 2012). The transition scheme, which has been designed to tie over those who have been unsuccessful in accessing vocational training, has proven to be counter-productive as it represents a discontinuity in a 'normal biography', thereby possibly placing its participant at a further disadvantage (Völcker, 2012). More than this, a discourse has been created which individualises the failure of securing an apprenticeship place, in many cases blaming the victim, rather than examining the contributing structural causes (Eckelt and Schmidt, 2015). This has affected some young people's views of the pathways available to them. In particular, youngsters who have witnessed their parents' precarious labour market positions quickly and readily accept that this may also represent their own future. They enter the labour market without any vocational qualifications, thereby occupying the most low-skilled, low-paid, and insecure dead-end jobs (Eckelt and Schmidt, 2015).

At the other end of the spectrum, *Gymnasium* graduates are reaping the fruits of the favourable economic climate, being highly sought after by employers. In order to fill VET places with the perceived most promising candidates, parents' influence over their children's decision-making processes has been recognised by industry. A case in point is the recent 'VET makes parents proud' (*Ausbildung macht Eltern stolz*) campaign of the Bavarian Chamber of Industry and Commerce, which is trying to convince parents of youngsters at the relevant transition stage, first, of the advantages associated with VET, and second, of their ability to persuade their children to take this avenue. [11]

Conclusions

This study of the significance of family background in social inequality and the transition to education and training in Germany has demonstrated that inequalities are clearly reproduced at each branching point of the education and training system. With regards to compulsory schooling, we have seen that family background plays a significant role in setting children on different tracks of unequal status and prospects very early on. Quantitative studies have demonstrated clear relationships between social class on the one hand and educational attainment and choices on the other, confirming Boudon's theory of the relevance of primary and secondary effects resulting from social origin. However, these studies have also raised many questions, in particular with regard to the mechanisms and processes which underpin unequal outcomes. While Bourdieu's concept of *habitus* in the context of educational establishments shaped by middle-class norms is likely to have relevance, we still lack the empirical evidence to understand underlying processes. Here, an aspect which deserves further study concerns the possible (positively reinforcing) coupling of the *habitus* of parents with academic backgrounds and that of teachers, the 'gatekeepers' at the transition from primary to secondary school. It would be interesting to find out whether parents with academic backgrounds are better able to instrumentalise the education-oriented *habitus* perspective of teachers for their own purposes and 'appropriate' it in order to support their children's educational career. The teachers' *habitus* would then possibly serve as an extension of the family *habitus* into the school context and enhance the children's academic progress.

In fact, it would be hard to overemphasise the role of the teachers in the decision-making processes of those families who do not share the teacher's *habitus*, and who have decided against *Gymnasium* education. While some evidence suggests that most parents hold *Gymnasium* education as an ideal for their children, those who have not attended *Gymnasium* themselves are reluctant to choose this school type for their offspring, not least because they feel unable to offer academic support. In cases where a child's grades do not allow for direct access to a *Gymnasium* but do raise the possibility of sitting an optional admission exam to demonstrate suitability, this reluctance may prove decisive. Parents without advanced education may also be hesitant to consider moving their children to *Gymnasium* if their grades proved sufficient in the first year of *Realschule*. In these cases, teachers' role in constructively encouraging these families to attempt an unfamiliar experience seems an indispensable precondition for addressing an important barrier to educational equality.

Young Germans are very aware of the importance of formal qualifications for employment opportunities, and almost all young people strive at least for fully qualifying VET. While the *Hauptschule* curriculum does result in its graduates having lower measures on (academic) competence than their counterparts from other school types, the school's very goal is to prepare its students for vocational training. The fact that employers sometimes prefer to keep training places vacant rather than offering them to a *Hauptschule* graduate has its roots at least in part in assumed deficiencies, such as an inadequate work ethos, which is ascribed to students from this stigmatised school type. Students' educational options are thus clearly circumscribed, and indeed damaged, by institutional factors. Educational origins influence employers' judgments as to whether an applicant may 'fit in'.

While the focus of research has been understandably on the plight of people with low educational credentials, it would also be interesting to examine what factors and processes support those graduates from lower-secondary institutions who immediately succeed in the VET system. Indeed, further research should also seek to explore outcomes relating to family-un/supported youth transitions from compulsory education to VET, higher education or work. It is important to better understand how family solidarity and support unfolds within the structural and institutional frame of opportunities. This would also better explain the familial influences on decisions and choices. However 'rational' such decisions may be conceived of in popular or policy terms, they are always influenced by the family of origin (even if they imply a dissociation from the family of origin, just as *habitus* remains predetermined even if it implies a break with tradition).

Family background and intergenerational inheritances of values and resources are thus crucial for understanding young people's pathways and transitions to adulthood. Because of the early branching points, such stratification is especially important in the German context. In addition, due to the stratification of the apprenticeship system, a German case study seems to be particularly fruitful for developing research questions into the reproduction of social inequality. On the one hand, the dual VET system seems to have particular relevance for families who do not prioritise academic education for their children and have first-hand experience with VET. On the other hand, dual VET proves to be attractive for some parents who may have tertiary education themselves, but they also act to support their children in creaming off the best career opportunities which the VET system offers.

Finally, it is worthwhile remembering that despite the apparent advantages which structural, institutional and familial factors may confer on the more privileged children and youth, this can be accompanied with considerable drawbacks for this group. Paradoxically, the well-intended support lent to young people can also interfere with their own life plans. A young person's identity and the perceived status attached to it may be privileged over life satisfaction and even potentially material interests due to the particular (middle-class) value which prioritises the academic pathway. This can prevent some young adults from pursuing a vocational route which may be better aligned with their abilities and inclinations. This seems particularly relevant in the German context, where skilled workers who have undergone the dual VET programme are in high demand and are offered attractive career progression opportunities by employers, which are similar to those of tertiary education graduates. The perhaps surprising lack of interest in this avenue has resulted in calls for changes in education policies. While the focus has hereby been mainly on the needs of the German economy, it should also be a key concern to consider how policies can ensure a better equilibrium between young people's abilities and interests. Addressing the barriers young people face when some options are equated with actual 'downward mobility' is an important part of this discussion.

Notes

1 The reason why the publication of the first round of PISA results had such a profound effect in Germany has in part been explained by the fact that, from the early 1970s to the 1990s, there had been a gap of German participation in international large-scale assessments, as standardised methods of measurement in education had not been popular. Hence, the country was unprepared for the comparatively poor results that emerged, including the enormous differences in educational achievement and opportunities by social background (Waldow, 2009).

2 The representation of the German education system is necessarily simplified here. For detailed information about this education system consult the *National Dossier for Germany*, which covers responsibilities and structures in the education system, as well as key developments in German educational policy up to the middle of 2014 (Lohmar and Eckhardt, 2015). For a recent mapping of education systems according to the UNESCO's International Standard Classification of Education (ISCED) see: http://uis.unesco.org/en/isced-mappings (26 April 2017)

3 There are also school types comprising two educational pathways, which offer *Hauptschule* and *Realschule* courses of education, or three pathways, which in addition provide *Gymnasium* courses of education (*Gesamtschule*). Moreover, at integrated comprehensive schools (*integrierte Gesamtschule*), subjects are made available at different ability levels, but no different courses of education exist (Edelstein, 2013).

4 Vocational qualifications and certain years of experience in the job can also allow for studying in tertiary education. However, criteria for access differ amongst institutions; extra tests, an interview and a probation period may be required. Moreover, the chosen course needs to be related to that previous experience.

5 Over the last decade, the percentage of pupils attending *Hauptschule* dropped by nine points (Statistisches Bundesamt, 2016a, 13).

6 Reference has been the highest educational qualification that (one of) the parents has achieved. High educational level equates with *Abitur* or higher; middle educational qualification with *Realschule* qualification, and low qualification refers to a *Hauptschule* certificate or less (for example, no secondary school qualification).

7 See, for example, Müller-Benedict (2007), who in this context analyses parental decisions on the transition to different secondary school types on the basis of PISA 2000 data.

8 For example, in 2015, more than half of the trainees in occupations such as baker, hairdresser, and mason had *Hauptschul*qualifications (Ebner and Uhly, 2016).

9 This compensation consists of 60% or 67% of the net wage lost through the reduced working hours Giesecke and Wotschack, 2009, 5).

10 The German labour market is generally regarded as having been geared to the skilled and highly skilled worker, holding very few opportunities for the low skilled. For example, from 2006 to 2010 the number of employees in the low-skilled employment segment dropped continually from 5.7 million to 5.1 million. Projections until the year 2030 suggest a further modest reduction in the demand for low-skilled workers in Germany (Weber and Weber, 2013, 2).

11 The internet campaign 'VET makes parents proud' provides arguments in favour of VET, followed by advice for parents on how to enter into an appropriate dialogue with their children (see www.elternstolz.de/start/).

References

Ahrens, D. (2014) Zwischen Reformeifer und Ernüchterung: Übergänge in beruflichen Lebensläufen, in: Ahrens, D. (ed) *Zwischen Reformeifer und Ernüchterung*, Wiesbaden: Springer VS, 7–34.

Allmendinger, J. and von den Driesch, E. (2014) *Social Inequalities in Europe: Facing the Challenge*. Discussion Paper P 2014–005, Berlin: WZB.

Beicht, U., Granato, M., Ulrich, J.G. (2011) Mindert Berufsausbildung die soziale Ungleichheit von Jugendlichen mit und ohne Migrationshintergrund? in: Granato, M., Münk, D., Weiß, R. (eds.) *Migration als Chance*, Bundesinstitut für Berufsbildung: Bonn, 177–207.

Boudon, R. (1974) *Education, Opportunity, and Social Inequality: Changing Prospects in Western Society*, New York: Wiley.

Bourdieu, P. (1983) Ökonomisches Kapital, kulturelles Kapital, soziales Kapital, in: Kreckel, R. (ed.) *Soziale Ungleichheiten*, Göttingen: Schwartzt, 183–198.

Bourdieu, P. (1984) *Distinction: A Social Critique of the Judgement of Taste*, Cambridge, MA: Harvard University Press.

Braun, F. and Lex, T. (2007) Hauptschulen in Deutschland: Ein Auslaufmodell oder besser als ihr Ruf? *DJI Online*, July 2007, www.dji.de/themen/dji-top-themen/dji-on line-juli-2007-hauptschulen-in-deutschland-ein-auslaufmodell-oder-besser-als-ihr-ruf/ auf-einen-blick.html

Brenke, K., Rinne, U. and Zimmermann, K.F. (2011) *Short-term Work: The German Answer to the Great Recession*. Discussion Paper No. 5780, Bonn: Institute for the Study of Labour.

Bundesministerium für Bildung und Forschung (BMBF) (2016) *Bildung und Forschung in Zahlen 2016*, Bonn/Berlin: BMBF.

Bundesministerium für Bildung und Forschung (BMBF) (2017) *Berufsbildungsbericht 2017*, Bonn: BMBF.

Debuschewitz, P. and Bujard, M. (2014) Determinanten von Bildungsdifferenzen in Deutschland: Lehren und Grenzen der PISA-Studie, *Bildungsforschung*, 1, 1–16.

Dumais, S.A. (2002) Cultural capital, gender, and school success: The role of habitus. *Sociology of Education*, 75, 1, 44–68.

Dumont, H., Maaz, K., Neumann, M. and Becker, M. (2014) Soziale Ungleichheit beim Übergang von der Grundschule in die Sekundarstufe I: Theorie, Forschungsstand, Interventions- und Fördermöglichkeiten, *Zeitschrift für Erziehungswissenschaft*, 17, 141–165.

Dustman, C. (2004) Parental background, secondary school track choice, and wages, *Oxford Economic Papers*, 56, 209–230.

Ebner, C. and Uhly, A. (2016) Beruf, Berufswahl und Übergang in Ausbildung, Bundeszentrale für politische Bildung (bpb), www.bpb.de/gesellschaft/kultur/zukunft-bil dung/228400/beruf-berufswahl-ausbildung

Eckelt, M. and Schmidt, G. (2015) Learning to be precarious – The transition of young people from school into precarious work in Germany. *Journal for Critical Education Policy Studies*, 12, 3, 130–155.

Edelstein, B. (2013) Das Bildungssystem in Deutschland. Bildungseinrichtungen, Übergänge und Abschlüsse, Bundeszentrale für politische Bildung (bpb), www.bpb. de/gesellschaft/kultur/zukunft-bildung/163283/das-bildungssystem-in-deutschland

Fend, H. (2014) Bildungslaufbahnen von Generationen: Befunde der LifE-Studie zur Interaktion von Elternhaus und Schule, *Zeitschrift für Erziehungswissenschaft*, 17, 37–72.

Gebel, M. and Giesecke, J. (2009) Labour market flexibility and inequality: The changing risk patterns of temporary employment in West Germany, *ZAF*, 42, 234–251.

Giesecke, J. and Wotschack, P. (2009) Flexibilisierung in Zeiten der Krise: Verlierer sind junge und gering qualifizierte Beschäftigte, *WZBrief Arbeit*, 1.

Granato, M. and Ulrich, G. J. (2014) Soziale Ungleichheit beim Zugang in eine Berufsausbildung: Welch Bedeutung haben die Institutionen? *Z Erziehungswissenschaften*, 17, 205–232.

Helbig, M. and Nikolai, R. (2015*) Die Unvergleichbaren: Der Wandel der Schulsysteme in den deutschen Bundesländern seit 1949*, Bad Heilbrunn: Klinkhardt.

Hillmert, S. (2014) Bildung, Ausbildung und soziale Ungleichheiten im Lebenslauf, *Zeitschrift für Erziehungswissenschaft*, 17, 73–94.

Hillmert, S. and Jacob, M. (2008) Selections and social selectivity on the academic track: A life-course analysis of educational attainment in Germany. Paper presented at the *Equalsoc Midterm Conference*, Berlin, May 11–12, 2008.

Jackson, M., Erikson, R., Goldthorpe, J.H. and Yaish, M. (2007) Primary and secondary effects in class differentials in educational attainment, *Acta Sociologica*, 50, 3, 211–229.

Keller, T. and Neidhöfer, G. (2014) Who dares wins?: A sibling analysis of tertiary education transition in Germany, *SOEPpapers*, 713, Berlin: DIW.

Kohli, M. and Albertini, M. (2008) *Families, Ageing and Social Policy*, Cheltenham: Edward Elgar.

Kohli, M., Albertini, M. and Künemund, H. (2010) Linkages among adult family generations: Evidence from comparative survey research, in: Heady, P. and Kohli M. (eds.) *Family, Kinship and State in Contemporary Europe*, Frankfurt/New York: Campus Verlag, 195–220.

Lohmar, B. and Eckhardt, T. (2015) *The Education System in the Federal Republic of Germany* 2013/14, Bonn: Sekretariat der Ständige Konferenz der Kultusminister der Länder in der Bundesrepublik Deutschland (KMK).

Maaz, K. and Nagy, G. (2009). Der Übergang von der Grundschule in die weiterführenden Schulen des Sekundarschulsystems: Definition, Spezifikation und Quantifizierung primärer und sekundärer Herkunftseffekte. *Zeitschrift für Erziehungswissenschaft*, Special Issue 12, 153–182.

Marginson, S. (2016) The worldwide trend to high participation higher education: Dynamics of social stratification in inclusive systems, *Higher Education* 72, 413–434.

Mayer, K.U., Müller, W. and Pollak, R. (2007) Institutional change and inequalities of access in German higher education, in: Shavit, Y., Arum, R. and Gamoran, A. (eds) *Stratification in Higher Education: A Comparative Study*, Stanford: Stanford University Press, 240–265.

Minello, A. and Blossfeld, H.P. (2016) From parents to children: The impact of mothers' and fathers' educational attainments on those of their sons and daughters in West Germany, *British Journal of Sociology of Education*, doi:10.1080/01425692.2016.1150156

Müller-Benedict, V. (2007) Wodurch kann die soziale Ungleichheit des Schulerfolgs am stärksten verringert werden *? Kölner Zeitschrift für Soziologie und Sozialpsychologie*, 59, 615–639.

Neugebauer, M. (2010) Bildungsungleichheit und Grundschulempfehlung beim Übergang auf das Gymnasium, *Zeitschrift für Soziologie*, 39, 3, 202–214.

OECD (2016a) *PISA 2015 Ergebnisse Deutschland*, www.oecd.org/pisa/PISA-2015-Germany-DEU.pdf

OECD (2016b) *Education at a Glance 2016: OECD Indicators*, Paris: OECD Publishing.

OECD (2016c) *Education at a Glance 2016. OECD Indicators. Germany – Country Note*, Paris: OECD Publishing.

Paulus, W. and Blossfeld, H.-P. (2007) Schichtspezifische Präferenzen oder sozioökonomisches Entscheidungskalkül? Zur Rolle elterlicher Bildungsaspirationen im Entscheidungsprozess beim Übergang von der Grundschule in die Sekundarstufe. *Zeitschrift für Pädagogik*, 53, 491–508.

Piketty, T. (2000) Theories of persistent inequality and the family transmission of wealth, in: A.B. Atkinson and F. Bourguignon (eds.) *Handbook of Income Distribution*, Vol. 1, Amsterdam: Elsevier, 429–476.

Powell, J.J.W. and Solga, H. (2012) Why are higher education participation rates in Germany so low? Institutional barriers to higher education expansion, in: Kupfer, A. (ed.) *Globalisation, Higher Education, the Labour Market and Inequality*, Oxon/ New York: Routledge.

Protsch, P. and Dieckhoff, M. (2011) What matters in the transition from school to vocational training in Germany, *European Societies*, 13, 1, 69–91.

Rinne, U. and Zimmermann, K.F. (2012). Another economic miracle? The German labor market and the great recession, *IZA Journal of Labor Policy*, 1, 3, www.iza jolp.com/content/1/1/3

Schneider, T. (2004) Hauptschule, Realschule oder Gymnasium? Soziale Herkunft als Determinante der Schulwahl, in: Szydlik, M. (ed), *Generation und Ungleichheit*, Wiesbaden: Verlag für Sozialwissenschaften, 77–103.

Schneider, T. (2008) Social inequality in educational participation in the German school system in a longitudinal perspective: Pathways into and out of the most prestigious school track, *European Sociological Review*, 24, 4, 511–526.

Schnitzlein, D. (2013) Wenig Chancengleichheit in Deutschland: Familienhintergrund prägt eigenen ökonomischen Erfolg, *DIW Wochenbericht*, 4, 3–9.

Solga, H. and Dombrowski, R. (2009). *Soziale Ungleichheiten in schulischer und ausserschulischer Bildung – Stand der Forschung und Forschungsbedarf*. Düsseldorf: Hans-Böckler-Stiftung.

Statistika (2017) Veränderung des Bestands an Kurzarbeitern in Deutschland im Vergleich zum Vorjahr von 1991 bis 2015, https://de.statista.com/statistik/daten/studie/ 2897/umfrage/prozentuale-veraenderung-des-bestands-an-kurzarbeitern/

Statistisches Bundesamt (2016a) *Schulen auf einen Blick, 2016*, Wiesbaden: Statistisches Bundesamt.

Statistisches Bundesamt (2016b) *Bildung der Eltern beeinflusst die Schulwahl für Kinder*, Wiesbaden: Statistisches Bundesamt.

Stompe, A. (2005) Armut und Bildung: Pisa im Spiegel sozialer Ungleichheit. *Armut und Geschlecht*, 29/30, 16, 132–144, www.gender.hu-berlin.de/de/publikationen/ gender...29.../texte2930pkt13.pdf

Sullivan, A. (2002) Bourdieu and education: How useful is Bourdieu's theory for researchers? *The Netherlands Journal of Social Sciences*, 38, 2, 144–166.

Triventi, M. (2013) Stratification in higher education and its relationship with social inequality: A comparative study of 11 European countries, *European Sociological Review*, 29, 3, 489–502.

Völcker, M. (2012) Identität und Schule: Zur Identitätsbildung bei Hauptschülern – zwischen Inklusionswünschen und Exklusionserfahrungen, in: *Tagungsreader des Pädagogik Symposiums*, 2012, Hamburg.

Wacquant, L. (2016) A concise genealogy and anatomy of habitus, *The Sociological Review*, 64, 64–72.

Waldow, F. (2009) What PISA did and did not do: Germany after the 'Pisa shock', *European Educational Research Journal*, 8, 3, 476–483.

Weber, B. and Weber, E. (2013) Qualifikation und Arbeitsmarkt: Bildung ist der beste Schutz vor Arbeitslosigkeit, *Institut für Arbeitsmarkt- und Berufsforschung (IAB) Kurzbericht*, 4, 1–8.

Will, H. (2010) Kurzarbeit als Flexibilisierungsinstrument: Hemmnis strukturellen Wandels oder konjunkturelle Brücke für Beschäftigung?*IMK Studies*, 5. Düsseldorf: IMK, www.boeckler.de/pdf/p_imk_study_5_2010.pdf

7 Youth transitions and generations in Portugal

Examining change between baby-boomers and millennials

Nuno Almeida Alves

Introduction

This text aims to analyse the pattern of change in youth transitions in Portugal, a country whose contemporary history is clearly detached from the path followed by the majority of its partner states in Western Europe, due to an extraordinary long autocratic rule, a fragile economy and a limited welfare state, especially in respect of public policies and benefits relevant for young people. The traits that set Portugal apart from other European countries have been important for prolonging the already difficult transitions of young people, especially when facing a deep economic and social crisis such as the one started in 2008.

Youth transitions changed in Portugal throughout the national construction of a European-like democracy and market economy. This process will be described in this chapter through the analysis of a set of historical statistical series on youth transitions in the age group 15 to 29. These comprise indicators of employment/unemployment, educational attainment and activity status, financial dependency and autonomy and civil status. This quantitative account will be complemented by the presentation of a number of qualitative interviews where the transitional process is in focus. This set of cases consists of diverse trajectories which reveal novel generational challenges in respect to income, education, labour relations and other personal circumstances. This selection was drawn from a set of 56 interviews undertaken during the peak of the financial and economic crisis in Portugal, between 2012 and 2013.

Changing transitions through time and place

The youth transitions paradigm has been helpful for describing, analysing and understanding social change among the succession of generations in late modern western societies (Furlong & Cartmel 1997, 2007; Wyn & White 1997; Furlong & Kelly 2005; Wyn & Woodman 2007; and Chapter 2 in this volume). The *transition processes* involve a series of biographical status changes that young people go through immediately after leaving education: from students to workers and ultimately for many to partners, spouses and parents. The narrative popularised in western societies states that this transitional process occurred quickly and smoothly (although modulated by class and gender) in the years after the Second World War, a golden period that started to change in the 1970s, along with the economic changes of the globalised late capitalism in the transition from the twentieth to the twenty-first century (see Chapter 3 in this volume). This *smooth transitions model* has been challenged by a number of authors, who have stated that even in this period transitions were far more complex and intricate than we currently suppose (Vickerstaff 2003; Goodwin & O'Connor 2005). However, in general we may assume that youth transitions have become longer and less standardised, meaning that they take more time to accomplish and are less orderly in the progression through the stages: education lasts longer due to the massification of higher education and the decreased demand for low-skilled work. Obtaining a stable position in the labour market takes more time to achieve because of the deregulation of the labour market and growth of atypical contracts, characteristic of a flourishing service sector. Achieving residential autonomy takes longer and involves more steps (co-residence with friends or partner before the constitution of a new family), linked experimentation but also extensive constraint. The order in which these steps are taken has also become more diversified, with a growing proportion of people returning to education due to the instability of employment or change of family statuses. The coincidence of these changes has generated a less standardised transition process for young people

Class and context

This narrative of changing youth transitions in late modern capitalist societies must not be seen as independent of social class and context, however. If transitions have become longer and less standardised for the 'the missing middle' (Roberts 2011), they have remained largely unchanged among the wealthier or poorer. As well-off families may provide a smooth transition for their offspring through a privileged education and mobilisation of social capital to obtain a satisfactory position, the children of the worse-off may still follow their parents' path into early drop-out of education and immediate integration in the minimum-wage services and blue-collar positions still available. However, if social inequalities still have a determinant role in the modulation of young people's transitions, what can be said about context, and more specifically about the country and time in which transitions occur? Each country's structural features (economic, regulatory, social and cultural) also play a significant role in the modulation of youth transitions and this process must be accounted for when we reflect generally and specifically on the overall pattern of change on youth transitions throughout western societies (Nilsen & Brannen 2014). Such trends will be explored in the next sections with reference to Portugal, including an account of the influence of diverse class contexts on the transition processes of young people in the last part of the chapter, based on the exploration of new qualitative data.

The singularity of Portuguese contemporary history

Portugal is a very interesting case for studying impacts of context on youth transitions. The country did not enjoy the golden post-war period of economic development and social progress obtained through the institutionalisation of welfare states that most of Western Europe went through in this period. Current Portuguese youth transitions are usefully understood against this historical backdrop.

The dictatorship period

The third quarter of the Portuguese twentieth century was characterised by a long-lasting dictatorship with a conservative and backward mind-set which idealised the country as a traditional catholic society with an agriculture-based economy. This stance was fostered and protected through an isolationist posture in the international arena and a strict dependence on very close political, economic and demographic relations with the African colonies fiercely maintained until 1974. The country was concentrated on guaranteeing its self-sufficiency, first in the agricultural field and later on the industrial side, with the aim of protecting the national production and substitution of imported goods. These objectives were also guaranteed by government control of the opening of new businesses, limiting internal free competition and protecting national business conglomerates close to the regime. The country was politically organised in a corporatist fashion, and the labour market was organised between guilds of employers and the workers in (national) trade unions controlled by the government. Strikes were forbidden and wages strictly controlled at a low level to prevent inflation. Education was highly selective and literacy rates substantially low, reaching 62 % in 1960 (Lains et al 2013: 290). Women were discriminated against throughout the whole dictatorship period: in 1960, 39% of women were illiterate against 27% of men; they represented 19% of the employed population and earned an average of 22% less than men in 1985 (GEP-MTSS 1985). Income inequalities were endemic during the dictatorship period: based on the calculations made by Pereirinha on a series of different family expenses and budget surveys, the Gini coefficient changed from 0.45 in 1967/1968 to 0.44 in 1973/1974 and finally to 0.38 in 1981 (Pereirinha 1988: 254), a figure reduced to 0.34 in 2015 (Eurostat 2016) but still significantly higher than other European countries.

The last 13 years of the dictatorship were marked by a Colonial War fought in three different territories – Angola, Mozambique and Guinea-Bissau – thousands of miles away. This historical event changed the country deeply and ultimately brought about the end of the regime in April 1974. The Colonial Wars fostered a massive move of Portuguese young nationals either to fight (if they were male), to go into exile in order to avoid combat in Africa or for political reasons or, finally, to emigrate across Europe (mainly to France, Germany or Switzerland) to make a living, especially if they came from the deprived countryside. Estimations of the emigration numbers during the dictatorship vary but it seems likely that over 1 million people emigrated between 1960 and 1974 (Carrilho 1991, Baganha 2003).

The post-revolutionary period

The change of the political, social and economic profile of the country has been dramatic since the end of the dictatorship. The non-competitive environment that a few national conglomerates enjoyed during the dictatorship ended, leaving an outdated production system specialising in substandard products, operated by a low-skilled labour force with a low-profile consumer society based on low wages and economic scarcity. The (one-year) revolutionary process subsequent to the downfall of the dictatorship was tumultuous and did not improve the country's economic prospects. The nationalisation of strategic sectors of the economy, designed to prevent the massive transfer of capital to other countries, not only disorganised the economy and markets but also contributed to a significant period of social unrest. The economic changes and social and political pressure to raise wages and build a European-like welfare state led to the first intervention of the International Monetary Fund in 1977 and the second in 1983, aimed to correct the imbalance of the economy and the dramatic budget deficit. However, the post-revolutionary decades were dedicated to the construction of a European-like liberal democracy, a welfare state, a universal education system and to the modernisation of the economy at a time when some of these features were challenged by neoliberal visions of the economy, the society and the state. Helped by European structural funds and regulation after integration into the European Economic Community in 1986, the country was able to create and maintain some European-like economic and social features.

Portugal has made significant progress from the 1970s to the present, both in economic and in social terms, although still showing signs of fragility in both domains when compared with the European averages (Machado & Costa 1998). This path of progress was severely hindered by the financial, economic and social crisis that started in 2008. The massive reduction of the gross domestic product and rampant rise of public and private debt (precipitating a painful third intervention of the International Monetary Fund in 2011) had severe implications for public spending, and the austerity programme that followed (with social services budget cuts, raised taxes and reduced wages and pensions) hit the most fragile groupings in Portuguese society: the poorer, the elderly and younger people.

This historical account describes the recent development of Portuguese society, which is very different from the path followed by other countries in the post-war years of western European economic and social development. However, youth transitions from education to the labour market were relatively smooth. Compulsory education was finished at 10, or 15 if families could afford vocational training. The integration in the labour market was swift as an apprentice or a junior clerk. Work was low paid but secure, fostered by a labour-intensive and archaic production system, complemented by a massive emigration of young workers that acted as a safety valve for the system. The post-revolutionary period modernised the economy and subjected businesses to globalisation, pushed education close to European standards and changed the labour market regulation, fostering flexibility and adaptation to current economic conditions. How have these changes turned out for young people?

Young people and the changing labour market

The Portuguese economy and labour market have changed substantially over the past decades, in line with political, regulatory and cultural changes. The structure of the Portuguese economy changed significantly, with the emergence of the services sector as the dominant employer of young people as for the total population. Employment became significantly more segmented between secure tenured jobs and diverse categories of precarious work. Both changes had a significant impact on the occupational prospects of young people.

Restructuring of the economy and emergence of precarity

One of the most significant changes with impact on the quality of employment available to young people was the restructuring of economic sectors shown in Figure 7.1. The tertiary sector has grown to absorb almost three-quarters of young people's employment.

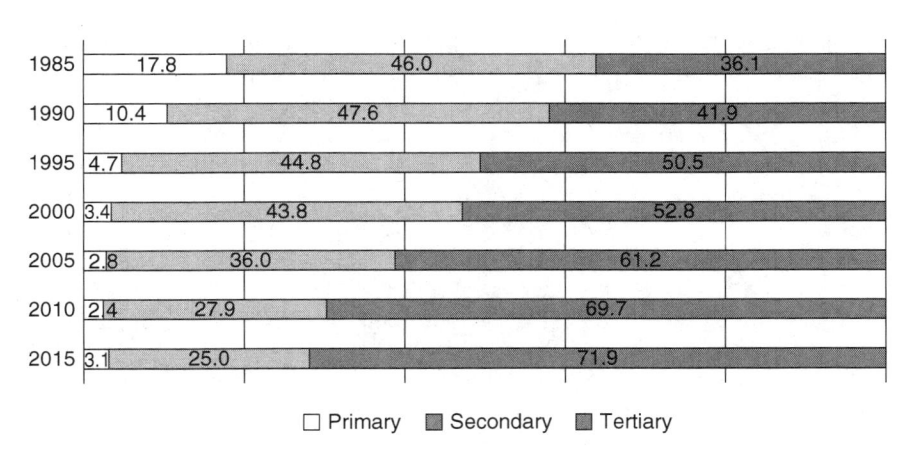

□ Primary ■ Secondary ■ Tertiary

Figure 7.1 Employment of the age group 15–29 by economic sector, Portugal, 1985–2015 (%)
Source: INE, Labour Force Survey 1985–2015

Agriculture was still a significant sector in terms of employment at the beginning of the 1980s (employing 18% of young people), and this may be explained by the traditional and manual-intensive character of this sector in Portugal due to the smallness of the agricultural estates and consequent low level of mechanisation. During the period, Portuguese agriculture slowly changed into a more modernised and knowledge-intensive sector at the expense of a reduction of labour (employing 3% of young people in 2016). The secondary sector was the largest employer in the early 1980s, partly due to limited automation of production and specialisation in low value-added products (e.g. textiles and shoes) (Pontes 1982: 222). The manufacturing sector maintained its prominence until the end of the century, accounting for almost half of the total employment of young people. However, by the end of the period, the secondary sector recruited only a quarter of young people, due to the demise of the traditional Portuguese manufacturing sector. The tertiary sector accounted for almost three-quarters of the total employment of young people, showing convergence with the European average distribution of economic sectors (Eurostat 2016).

The main types of employment available to young people in the service sector are located in retail (supermarkets, international retail chains present in the high streets and shopping malls) and personal services (restaurants, cafés, call centres, etc.). These kinds of unskilled positions are usually paid at the minimum-wage level (557 euros before taxes in 2017, approximately 3.2 euros per hour) and include a high proportion of part-time work. The majority of these service positions are extremely individualised in job content and labour relations, leading to a very low level of unionisation, features that leave young employees at the mercy of employers or supervisors. Several studies show how the growth of the service sector and the deregulation of labour were significant for the widening of employment precarity among young people in Portugal (Alves et al 2011; Carmo et al 2014; Cairns et al 2014, 2016; Nico & Alves 2017) as in most of the western world (Furlong and Kelly 2005).

Unemployment varies with economic cycles but increases more quickly in a downturn phase than it declines in the upturn stage. Young people are especially vulnerable to unemployment: usually the last to be hired but the first to get fired in the coming of a crisis. Figure 7.2 shows unemployment rates from 1983 to 2015, with the last peak linked to the world financial crisis in 2008. It is quite common for youth unemployment to be double that of the general population rates. However, this exceptionally high rate of unemployment reinforced the increasing precarity of youth employment, with youth acting as a sort of reserve industrial army (to use the Marxian expression) in order to press down wages, working hours, contractual conditions and statutory benefits (Antunes 2013)

One other factor contributing to the precarity of young people's employment in Portugal is the changing incidence of permanent and temporary work. The proportion of permanent contracts was about 75% in the 1980s (Figure 7.3) and decreased to 48% by 2015.[1] This means that Portuguese employers prefer

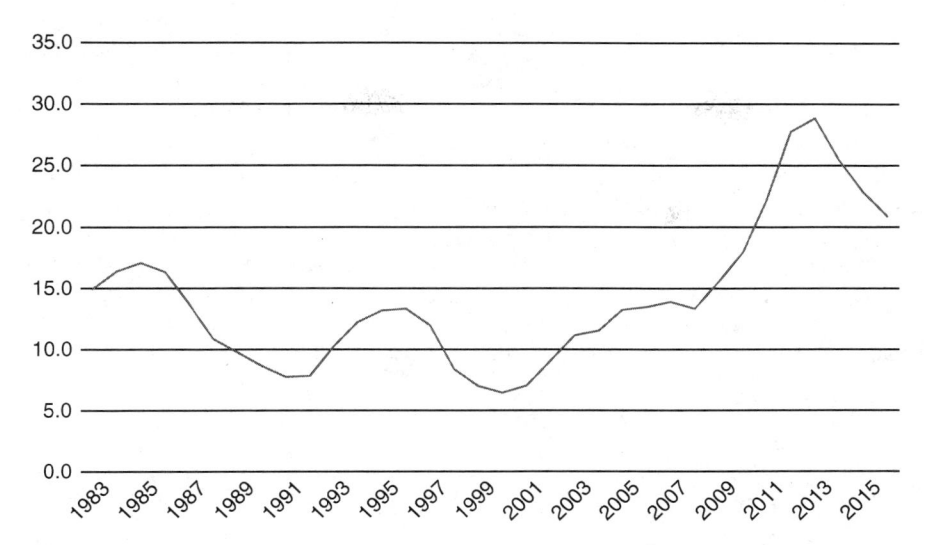

Figure 7.2 Unemployment rate of the age group 15–29, Portugal, 1983–2016 (%)
Source: INE, Labour Force Survey 1983–2016

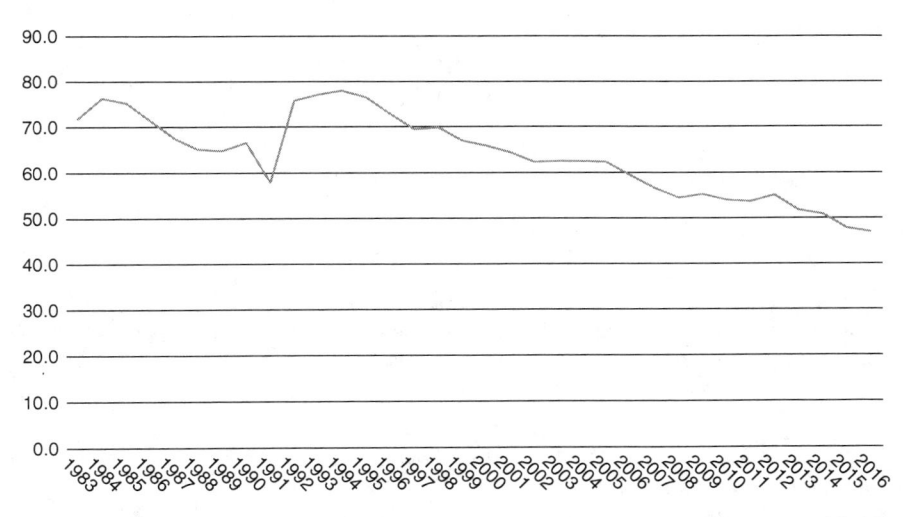

Figure 7.3 Proportion of employees with permanent contracts (age group 15–29), Portugal, 1983–2016 (%)
Source: INE, Labour Force Survey 1983–2016

to hire young people temporarily but under successive contracts, sometimes with very short cycles of 15 days, a week or even one day, even when the positions for which they are hired are of a permanent nature (Alves et al 2011).

Longer educational trajectories and current employment conditions offered to young people seem to extend already long transitions. After leaving secondary or tertiary education, the usual work trajectory is alternating between short-term jobs, internships, scholarships,[2] periods of unemployment and short-term jobs again. In addition, the most probable situation is that this trajectory is accompanied by an absence of labour rights such as social security (fundamental to gain access to statutory entitlements such as unemployment benefits, illness or maternity leaves or to a pension in case of early involuntary retirement) and holidays and Christmas bonus wages. These employment conditions add precarity to other dimensions of young peoples' lives (Alves et al 2011; Carmo et al 2014), namely the opportunity to find and maintain affordable housing (either alone, with friends or with a partner) or even to form a family.

The statistical indicators analysed show evidence of a structural change in some of the fundamental dimensions relevant for young people's transitions into adulthood in Portugal. The changes in education and employment have extended and disrupted transitions compared to those of previous generations.

Young people and sociodemographic change

The emergence of labour precarity has contributed to progressively protracted youth transitions in Portugal. However, before precarity there were a series of social and demographic processes led by educational change that have significantly contributed to delay in youth transitions in the last decades.

Significant progress in education

The educational status of successive cohorts of young people is one of the most significant changes in Portugal in the last 30 years (Figure 7.4). The educational heritage of the dictatorship was poor: total enrolment by children aged 6 to 9 in the four years of elementary education was obtained only in 1980 (INE/GEPE 2005: 65); early leaving of secondary education was typical, and higher education served the reproduction of the educational/professional capital of the elites (Vieira 1995: 316–319).

In 1981, the large majority of the population aged 15–19 had only elementary education (ISCED 0–2); secondary and tertiary education were scarcely distributed, the former essentially a means of access to higher education and the latter a passage to a secure and high-skilled occupation and consequently a better life. By 2011, the numbers changed substantially: the proportion of young people with only elementary schooling was significantly reduced to less then one-third of the population of the three age groups (and this number is still being reduced with the policies to tackle early school leaving); secondary

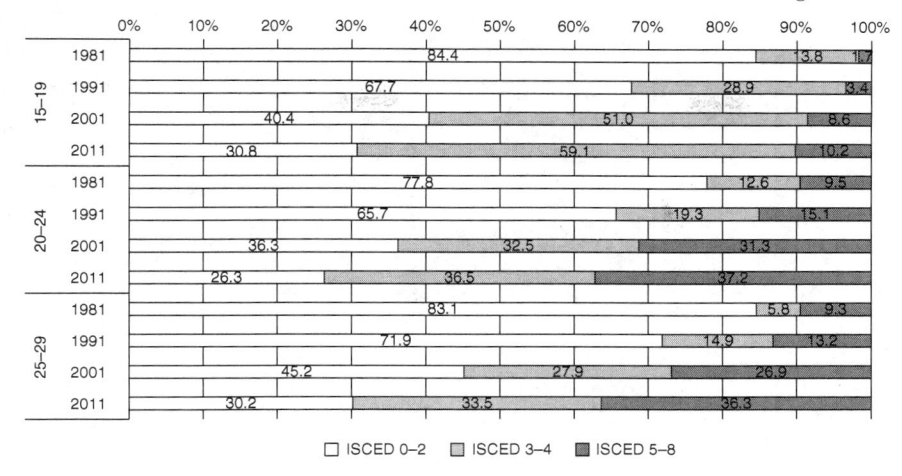

Figure 7.4 Education by age group, Portugal, 1981–2011 (%)
Source: INE, Population Censuses 1981–2011

education grew to about one-third in older age groups and 60% in the younger group. Tertiary education reached numbers closer to the European average.

A delayed transition from education to work

The young people that used to leave school immediately after completing elementary education or even before finishing compulsory education did so because of the number of low-skilled blue-collar or service jobs available in Portugal at that time, and it became a first step to financial autonomy. The massive mobilisation of young people into further education in this period has had the expected effect of delaying youth transitions to adulthood and becoming more like other European countries (Furlong and Cartmel 1997, 2007). The changes of young people's educational status in the past decades resulted from both the efforts made by the fragile post-revolutionary Portuguese welfare state in order to improve the educational records of its citizenry, as well as by families that continuously considered tertiary educational credentials as a decisive factor for social mobility (Machado et al 2003).

The change from early integration into the labour market to longer education by young people, particularly among the youngest group, is clearly demonstrated by Figure 7.5.

Protracted financial autonomy

The progressively delayed entrance of Portuguese young people into work is evident in the indicator 'origin of income' (Figure 7.6). In 1981, about 42% in

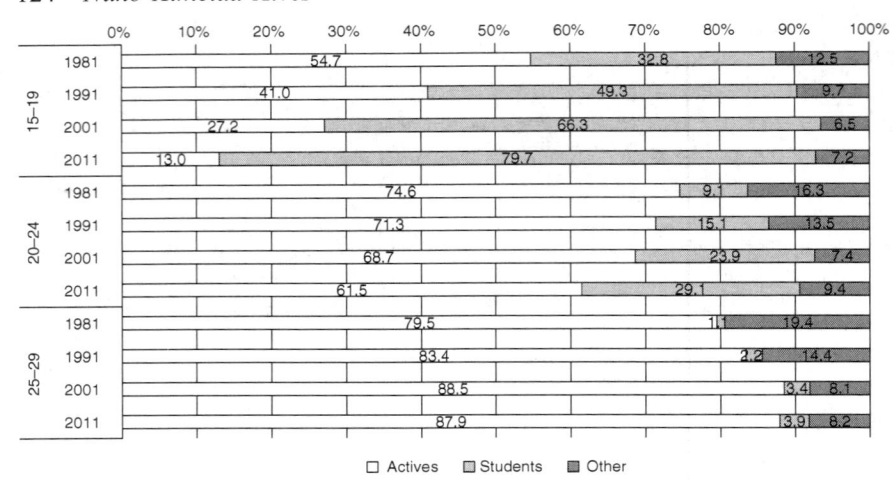

Figure 7.5 Economic activity status by age group, Portugal (%)
Source: INE, Population Censuses 1981–2011

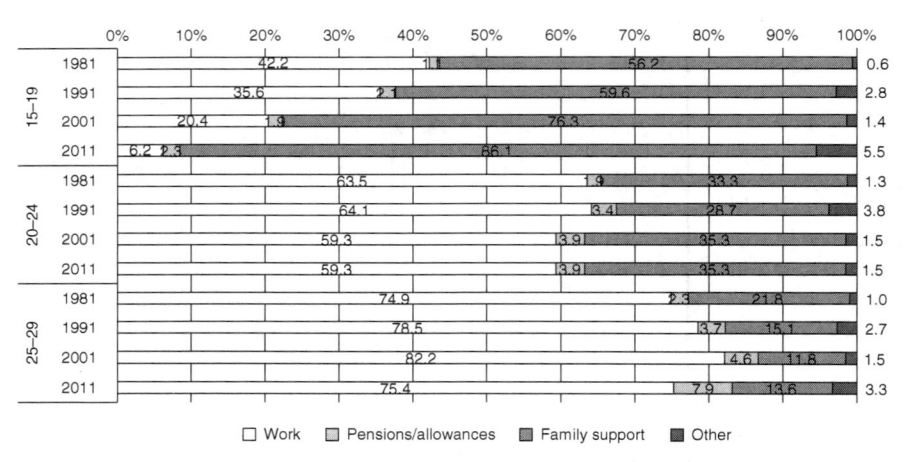

Figure 7.6 Origin of income by age group, Portugal 1981–2011 (%)
Source: INE, Population Censuses 1981–2011

the age group 15–19 already earned a living based on paid work and 56% of this age group still depended on their families. This balance shifted in the following censuses, with the proportion of workers decreasing to 6% in 2011 and the segment of young people depending on their families reaching 86%. Among 20–24 year olds the proportion of young people living on their wages reached almost two-thirds in 1981 and 1991 and then slightly decreased to 59% in 2011. The proportion of young people depending on their families is rather stable, around one-third of the age group in the four censuses observed. The 25–29 age group shows a higher dependence on work for living arrangements, between 75% and 82% in 2001, with a correspondingly smaller proportion of young people dependent on their families (between 12% and 21%). In this age group the 'pensions and allowances' category turned more visible (especially in 2011) due to the peak of the financial and economic crisis, as unemployment benefits rose substantially and helped young people to live through the crisis.

Postponing family formation

Longer educational paths and delayed entrances to the labour market are two factors affecting the timing of transitions into adulthood. Others are related to young people's residential arrangements and family formation. There is not much data available to cover the first of these topics, but the censuses that have been analysed here contain the necessary information to characterise the change in Portuguese young people's family statuses in the last decades (Figure 7.7).

There are no significant changes in the youngest age group in the last 30 years. In the intermediate age group, the proportion of single young people rose from 59% in 1981 to 84% in 2011, meaning that early marriages/cohabitations are reduced to a very small proportion (16%). It is also interesting that the proportion of cohabitations is increasing in this age group: in 2011 the proportion of cohabitees was higher than the one of married young people. This means that the traditional (conservative/catholic) path from the family home directly to marriage is losing ground in favour of a more experimental

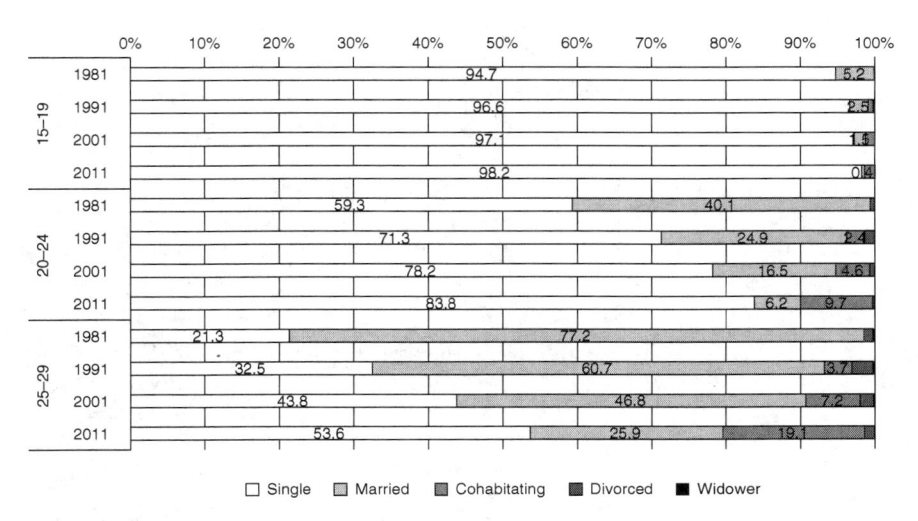

Figure 7.7 Family status by age group, Portugal 1981–2011 (%)
Source: INE, Population Censuses 1981–2011

approach of young people in respect to the development of new families and households (Guerreiro and Abrantes 2004). The older age group also shows important changes in respect to this indicator. The minority of single people between 25 and 29 in 1981 (21%) is transformed to a majority of 54% in 2011. The proportion of married young people (77%), which constituted the only alternative to being single, is reduced to a quarter of the age group and is being clearly challenged by a growing cohabitating alternative (19%).

The immediate consequence of the way these indicators have developed over the last 30 years is the postponement of motherhood/fatherhood. In the 1970s, the average age of the mother at the birth of the first child was 24 and this persisted until the mid-1980s. After this period the average age at the birth of the first child has increased to 30 in 2016 (INE 2016). These trends affect other demographics such as fertility rates, ageing of the population, and substitution of generations, labour force and welfare rights. The increased freedom of option for delaying marriage/partnership and having children in exchange for more experimental living arrangements and partnerships is also shaped by structural change in education, the labour market and housing access for young people. All of these structural constraints impel young people onto longer educational paths aimed to facilitate employment chances and more successful occupational careers that also take time to consolidate and provide the resources needed for other transitional steps (residential autonomy, partnerships, and children).

An ageing society

One of the most immediate consequences of these social processes is the demographic change of the Portuguese population, with a shrinking proportion of young people. The two age pyramids below (Figure 7.8) show clearly the profound demographic change in Portugal in the last decades. A rise in the life expectancy at birth and the massive reduction of the cohorts of young people made Portugal the country with the fifth oldest population in 2015, with an average age of 44 years (UN 2015: 32). Younger cohorts (0–24) have been significantly reduced due to decades of sinking birth rates; young adults (25–34) are notably stable because these are the cohorts born during the last baby-boom in the years after the revolution; from 35 years on the cohorts are systematically more numerous with a little more prominence on the female side.

This means that the youth population is decreasing and the total population is ageing at a swift pace (the population between 15 and 29 years decreased by 28% in the last 30 years). The causes for this demographic shift are deeply rooted in Portuguese history and society, as addressed in earlier sections.

Generations and transitions

The protracted transitions into adulthood in Portugal are demonstrated in the quantitative data. However, the diversity of causes and consequences behind

Figure 7.8 Age pyramids, Portugal 1970 and 2015 (%)
Source: INE, Population Estimates, 1970–

the numbers come to the fore in qualitative accounts of young people's thoughts and experiences. The crisis that hit the country in the last few years amplified social and economic problems, turning them into a daily topic of discussion that clearly emerged in the interviews. These interviews[3] were undertaken in 2012 and 2013, as a follow-up of a previous survey, and the main objective was to observe and describe the potential for political radicalization of Portuguese young people. The material analysed here was collected from the answers given to the question "What is going on now that is really affecting people (and your family) in Portugal?"

The data is presented in a series of eight cases that illustrate the diversity of the interviewees' backgrounds, educational patterns, employment situation, the general situation in the present and expectations for the future. The cases were selected with reference to location, social background, gender, age (the most unbalanced due to the initial stage in the transition process and lesser reflexivity of teenagers) and transition process. The order of presentation follows a scale of increasing difficulties for young people accomplishing a smooth transition from education to work, with difficulties emerging from different sources: reduction of income, educational hurdles, precarity and an articulation of these with each other in the worst cases. These hurdles are linked to interviewees' experiences and to structural factors such as social background and neighbourhood.

The first two cases illustrate young people barely affected by the crisis. Coming from privileged backgrounds, they managed to maintain their standards of living, hold on to their academic trajectories and aim for a bright future, helped by their respective encouraging networks.

Distance from crisis and optimism for the future

Paulo was born in Lisbon and is 23. He studied in a well-known private school and obtained a degree in Business Administration from the Catholic University in Lisbon. He is currently enrolled in a Masters in Marketing but already has some employment experience in the digitalization of architecture projects, where he has had a chance to coordinate a small team. He considers that the trouble the country is going through has emerged mainly from a crisis of values, because people are going only after material values and forget the well-being that surrounds them, a consideration that clearly comes from his conservative catholic upbringing. Paulo is firmly convinced that Portuguese people over the last decades were used to easy living, consuming whatever they wanted supported on credit, living well and retiring early. Today, with the globalisation of the economy, with the cheap products coming from China and India, this is no longer affordable. And when people had to change their expectations they blamed the government instead of blaming themselves. This vision of the Portuguese economic and social crisis was popularised by the neoliberal-inspired government that ruled the country during the peak of the crisis (2011–2015).

(Paulo, 23, male, Lumiar, higher education)

Maria João is 21, lives in Lumiar with her family and is a Nutrition Science undergraduate in a small private university across the river Tagus. Coming from an upper-middle-class background, she has until now not been affected by the crisis. However, she is aware of its effects through her peers with unemployed parents who can hardly cope with higher education expenses. Although coming from a privileged background, Maria João is concerned with social and environmental matters and engages in some voluntary work and political demonstrations such as 'Ocupar o Rossio' in a sort of Portuguese light version of Occupy Wall Street or Ocupar Puerta del Sol in Madrid. Although she acknowledges that young people are going though severe difficulties in Portugal, Maria João is optimistic about the future and really believes that things are going to get better, with more employment opportunities and better living prospects for all.

(Maria João, 21, female, Lumiar, enrolled in higher education)

These are examples of young people untouched by the crisis. Their parents were highly educated and in permanent employment, able to maintain their family's standard of living. However, there is an important difference between them: Paulo is a neoliberal catholic who considers that the worst-off are being punished by their wrongdoings while Maria João tries to appease her more progressive conscience with voluntary work.

The two following cases are also from Lumiar and introduce two young people going through higher education and living autonomously but whose families are going through economic difficulties, with direct implications for their standard of living. They are examples of the middle classes who were used to living comfortably until things went wrong (either because of unexpected unemployment, illness or wage cuts).

Middle-class immersion in the crisis and perceptions of a changed future

Fernando is 25 and has always lived in Lumiar, first with his parents and now with his girlfriend. He has studied Geography, holding an undergraduate and master's degree in this field and is now a PhD student with a scholarship from the Portuguese Science Foundation. He is very committed to his neighbourhood and has been on the board of the Resident's Association. Fernando's closest family are all suffering from precarity: his girlfriend has had a series of precarious jobs in the last few years and his sister and sister-in-law are in the same situation. He is really worried by this situation because his scholarship does not entitle him to illness or unemployment benefits, not being very different from any other typical temporary job. The employment precarity and severe unemployment that drive Portuguese youth to emigration is demoralising Fernando because he is investing in a career that he will certainly not be able to pursue in his country. The situation that young Portuguese are going through drives Fernando to think that there is a generational fracture in Portugal at this time. He thinks that young people in Portugal are going through a double feeling of loss: "They are not going to have the future that was promised to them; but they are not going to have the quiet past their parents had, either. It is a loss of future and a loss of memory and this is very hard for us!"

(Fernando, male, 25, Lumiar, higher education)

Daniela is 22, and lived in Oporto until she came to Lisbon three years ago to study Criminal Psychology at a local private university. She lives alone in Lisbon and all her family lives abroad due to recent emigration trajectories. Her father is in Brazil, her older brother in Norway, her mother and younger brother in the UK. Both she and her family were deeply affected by the crisis. Her mother was a retired teacher but the rise of taxes and pension cuts reduced her income to a level that made it impossible for her to pay her expenses. She moved to London with her youngest son to work as a cleaner in a hotel. Daniela used to live well in Lisbon just on her family's allowance but the crisis reduced her income significantly; in spite of this she never looked for a part-time job to earn some money and reduce the burden on her family. With the crisis and all the problems with youth employment, Daniela does not expect to find a job in Portugal after finishing university. But she already has a plan: first she is going to London in order to find an internship in her area of expertise and improve her English and afterwards she will move to Brazil to live with her father and make a living.

(Daniela, 22, female, Lumiar, enrolled in higher education)

Precariousness and the other cuts in pensions pushed people to change their way of living to be able to cope with the reduction of income, demonstrating that the crisis has affected not only young people but their parents as well. Fernando offers a comparison across generations and their different employment and transitional trajectories. Despite the difficulties of the past, the transition of the previous generation is considered smooth and unproblematic compared to the difficulties in the present. Both cases introduce the theme of emigration as the only way out for qualified young people due to the current situation of the labour market in the country, an option chosen by 40,000 young Portuguese graduates between 2011 and 2013 (Gomes et al 2015).

The next four cases come from Barreiro, a post-industrial suburb of Lisbon. All interviewees have working-class or lower-middle-class backgrounds. Three of them entered higher education, with only one completing a degree and the fourth still being a teenager. Despite these very different educational experiences, their employment and life prospects have not differed significantly until now. This has made them consider the current value of higher education, particularly in the absence of a protective network that could help their prospects.

Working classes coping with the present with no expectations for the future

Nélson is 23 and lives in Barreiro with his mother and younger brother. He was enrolled in higher education immediately after finishing high school but he dropped out for financial reasons. His mother's was the only income and that was not enough. After leaving university he started to work as a mechanic in his mother's shop, helping her in the driving school she owns. Working for his mother was not at all his first choice because work and family should not mix, in his opinion, but there was no other option available due to the crisis. The economic situation is also affecting the family business. In the last year they had to sell the house where they lived to keep the business alive. His grandfather, recently deceased, was an important reference point for him, because he was a soldier who made several commissions in the Colonial Wars and then returned to Portugal and was involved in the revolution that brought about democracy. In his talks with his grandfather Nélson started to grow an interest in politics that motivated him to have a role in student unions, in the youth branch of the Communist Party and later to be an active militant of the Portuguese Communist Party. The way that things have worked out in his life and his political experience gave Nélson an acute perspective on the social inequalities in Portugal, in particular the difficulties that young people go through, almost leaving emigration as the only way out. In his perspective, young people's prospects in Portugal these days are worse than those for the previous generation, and this is not a bright perspective for the future.

(Nélson, 23, male, Barreiro, higher education drop-out)

Júlio is 25 and has always lived in Barreiro. He is a Sociology graduate, after having started his higher education in Communication and Culture. Júlio finished his degree in 2010 and since then has been working in a call centre, first as a back-office operator and afterwards as the manager of the commercial department. He is not happy at all with his employment situation since it is a temporary job with no career prospects, but a more attractive opportunity has still not shown up and Júlio needs his wages to keep up with his monthly responsibilities. In the crisis context the country is going through, his only objective is to make ends meet. All the money he earns is aimed at surviving for another month. Júlio firmly believes that he is now paying for a crisis that was caused by years of bad government, corruption and wrong options, a crisis he had no responsibilities for but that will last for ten or more years, turning his generation into a lost generation. The crisis, the raised taxes and loss of income and the absence of good prospects is driving Júlio to hopelessness and depression.

(Júlio, male, 25, Barreiro, higher education)

Nélson and Júlio both come from working-class families and have always lived in Barreiro. Both circumstances gave these young men an acute awareness of the social inequalities they live through and the difficulties involved in overcoming them, particularly in the depressive economic environment the country has gone through recently. They both have gone through higher education, although with different outcomes. However, until now this has not made a significant difference for their employment or life prospects. They are very pessimistic about their futures: Júlio is deeply affected and demoralised by precariousness and Nélson by the lack of opportunities offered to his generation. Once more, the comparison between generations is present here as well as the reference to emigration as the only way out for young people.

The next two cases are young people deeply scarred by the crisis and unemployment, either personal or from their parents. They both have difficulties due to lack of funds to stay in education.

Unemployed and procrastinating through the crisis

Rui is 24 and lives in Barreiro. He started his education in Barreiro but changed to a vocational school in Lisbon for his secondary education. After finishing secondary education, he started a postsecondary course as a showbusiness technician while working for the postal services. He later dropped out from the postsecondary course and enrolled in Science and Technology of Sound at a Lisbon private university. When the employment contract ended he was forced to drop out of university because the fees were expensive and his family had no resources (his mother is a precariously employed high school teacher although she has a PhD degree). His view of the future is rather pessimistic because people of his age are finishing their university degrees and cannot find a job (something which also gave him an argument for justifying his drop-out from university). He felt that when they find one, they are underpaid and cannot afford a house or children. When he compares his parents' generation with his own, he notices that at his age his parents had already moved from home and had children while he is still stuck in his parents' home.

(Rui, 24, male, Barreiro, higher education drop-out)

Living with constraint

Diana was born in Cape Verde, she is 16 and lives in Barreiro. Initially she lived with her mother in Lisbon but she moved to Barreiro three years ago. She is enrolled in the 10th grade and would like to go to university to study Business Administration. The crisis forced the families that employed Diana's mother as a cleaner to reduce their expenses, and since then they have both been depending on the minimum guaranteed income to survive, a circumstance that affects almost the entire neighbourhood. Money is tight but Diana is used to living on a limited budget and she has modest expectations.

(Diana, 16, female, Barreiro, enrolled in secondary education)

Rui and Diana have suffered the loss of income, which was common in Portugal during the crisis, a process that had more severe consequences in the lower middle classes and in the working class. Diana has accumulated a series of disadvantages that are difficult to overcome. Rui is quite a different case. Coming from a highly educated background, he seemed to have made a series of wrong choices in his educational path. With the present situation in the labour market, he also has some difficulties in finding and holding down a secure job, leaving him with few opportunities for the future. However, the labour market does not present better prospects for those who have a degree.

Although socially diverse, this set of cases clearly illustrates the difficulties that the majority of Portuguese young people are going through in the face of the deepest financial and economic crisis since the Great Depression of the twentieth century. They are simultaneously the best educationally qualified cohort Portugal has ever had and the one with the fewest employment opportunities and future prospects. A significant proportion of them are deeply scarred by the crisis and reduction of income, by being constantly rejected or ignored by employers, or alternatively being submitted to diverse forms of employment precariousness. Having lived with these conditions for such a long time and seeing no light at the end of the tunnel, they are losing hope and the means to think positively about the future. The only solution available seems to be emigration, precisely the same one adopted by diverse generations of Portuguese citizens in the twentieth century and even beforehand.

Apart from the difficult transitions, the most curious fact emerging from these interviews, although not present in all the cases, is the comparisons they make with their parents' generation. These comparisons occurred unprompted and it would therefore be interesting to explore the reasons for this way of thinking. Was it an issue of debate in families? Was it something popularised in the media around the theme "This generation will be the first to have worst prospects of living than the previous one"? This is a valuable focus for further research.

Conclusion

Portugal has followed a very different path through the twentieth century compared to its European counterparts, one that was characterised by a long period of dictatorship and a closed and underdeveloped economy. In spite of this, youth transitions into adulthood were rather linear and short, although a significant number emigrated to Europe and life expectancy was lower for the ones that remained. Along with other Southern European economies and societies, the definitive developmental step was the integration of the country in the European Economic Community, a strategic decision that provided the economic, political and regulatory frameworks that fostered the development of the country into a democracy and market-driven economy.

During the last four decades the country has made remarkable progress, with the development of strongly rooted democratic institutions and processes, a widely based although frail welfare state and public provision of education and health services, and a modern although severely European-dependent economy. This significant social change is also evident in the Portuguese youth statistical indicators. Although shrinking in volume and proportion to the total population, young Portuguese show similar trends to their European counterparts. Their educational paths are longer and their first approach to the labour market is made later in the life course, and they are more qualified than previous generations. The prolonged period in education has led to less autonomous lives: young Portuguese tend to stay at their parents' home and to be financially dependent on them until very late in life. When leaving the parental home, they tend to be more experimental in residential and emotional arrangements, changing the tradition of leaving the parental home directly into marriage. On the negative side, part of these changes may also be attributed to the dramatic changes in the labour market. The neoliberal globalised economy, with its fierce fight for profits and deregulated *modus operandi*, has been very important in shaping the prospects of recent cohorts of young adults.

Qualified and well-paid jobs are scarce and only available to those with the talent or networks needed to capture it; underpaid and insecure tertiary jobs are the most widely available job opportunities for young people, opening the door to indefinite periods of precarious work, eventually leading to a precarious life. The global financial crisis that started in 2008 had dramatic effects in the country. The rampant public debt contaminated the state's budget and all economic activity. Income has decreased and taxes increased, exhausting the capacity of the economy to grow and create employment. High unemployment rates turned youth employment prospects even worse, boosting emigration as a viable solution. After 40 years of democracy and social change, young people were facing virtually the same problems with the same and only solution. The notion of continuous progress from one generation to the other was lost, replaced by a contrast between constructed memories of the past and the perceived bleakness of the future. This comparison process of past and current transitions made among young people was an interesting and unexpected outcome that emerged from the qualitative research explored in this chapter.

Notes

1 Although there is a bizarre behaviour of the series between 1989 and 1991, attributable to the coincidence of a significant cyclical crisis with a break in the series, the downward slope of the curve is very consistent.
2 Very common in academia in order to obtain cheap labour that may be included in technical or menial positions in scientific research or even in administrative tasks.
3 The interviews were part of the fieldwork undertaken by the MYPLACE research project, financed by the 7th Framework Programme of the European Commission, coordinated by Professor Hilary Pilkington of the University of Manchester. A total of 56 interviews were conducted in two different locations in the Lisbon Metropolitan Area: Lumiar, a predominantly middle-class newly constructed neighbourhood in the north-eastern part of Lisbon; and Barreiro, a post-industrial town largely inhabited by working-class people on the south bank of the river Tagus, currently evolving into another suburban neighbourhood of Lisbon. The sample was quite even in terms of gender but less so in respect of age and education. Lumiar: 15 male/12 female; age: 4 (16–19), 9 (20–22), 13 (23–25); 3 (ISCED 2), 24 (ISCED 3). Barreiro: 15 male/14 female; age: 12 (16–19); 7 (20–22); 7 (23–25). ISCED 3 refers mainly to interviewees that were enrolled in tertiary education at the time.

References

Alves, Nuno de Almeida, Frederico Cantante, Inês Baptista and Renato Miguel do Carmo (2011), *Jovens em Transições Precárias: Trabalho, quotidiano e futuro*, Lisbon: Mundos Sociais.

Antunes, Ricardo (2013), *The Meanings of Work. Essay on the Affirmation and Negation of Work*, Leiden and Boston: Brill.

Baganha, Maria Ioannis B. (2003), "Portuguese emigration under the corporatist regime", *e-JPH* 1(1): 1–16.

Beck, Ulrich (1992), *Risk Society: Towards a New Modernity*, London: Sage.

Cairns, David, Nuno de Almeida Alves, Ana Alexandre and Augusta Correia (2016), *Youth Unemployment and Job Precariousness: Political Participation in the Austerity Era*, Basingstoke: Palgrave Macmillan.

Cairns, David, Katarzyna Growiec and Nuno de Almeida Alves (2014), "Another 'missing middle'? The marginalised majority of tertiary-educated youth in Portugal during the economic crisis", *Journal of Youth Studies* 17(8): 1046–1060.

Carmo, Renato Miguel do, FredericoCantante and Nuno de Almeida Alves (2014), "Time projections: Youth and precarious employment", *Time & Society* 23(3): 337–357.

Carrilho, Maria José (1991), "A Evolução da Produção Estatística e da População através dos Censos", in: Instituto Nacional de Estatística, *Atas do Seminário Censos 91*, Lisbon: INE.

Furlong, Andy and Fred Cartmel (1997), *Young People and Social Change: Individualisation and Risk in Late Modernity*, Buckingham: Open University Press.

Furlong, Andy and Fred Cartmel (2007), *Young People and Social Change: New Perspectives*, 2nd Edition, Maidenhead and New York: McGraw Hill and Open University Press.

Furlong, Andy and Peter Kelly (2005), "The Brazilianisation of youth transitions in Australia and the UK?", *Australian Journal of Social Issues* 40(2): 207–225.

Gomes, Rui Machado (Ed.), João Teixeira Lopes, Henrique Vaz, Luísa Cerdeira, Paulo Peixoto, Rafaela Ganga, Sílvia Silva, Maria de Lourdes Machado, José Pedro Silva, Rui Brites, Dulce Magalhães, Tomás Patrício and Belmiro Cabrito (2015), *Entre a periferia e o centro: Percursos de emigrantes portugueses qualificados*, Coimbra: Coimbra University Press.

Goodwin, John and Henrietta O'Connor (2005), "Exploring complex transitions: Looking back at the 'golden age' from school to work", *Sociology* 39(2): 201–220.

Guerreiro, Maria das Dores and Pedro Abrantes (2004), "Moving into adulthood in a Southern European country: Transitions in Portugal", *Portuguese Journal of Social Sciences* 3(3): 191–209.

Lains, Pedro, Ester Gomes da Silva and Jordi Guilera (2013), "Wage inequality in a developing economy: Portugal 1944–1984", *Scandinavian Economic History Review* 61(3): 287–311.

Machado, Fernando Luís and António Firmino da Costa (1998), "Processos de uma Modernidade Inacabada: Mudanças estruturais e mobilidade social", in: José Manuel Leite Viegas and António Firmino da Costa (Eds.) *Portugal, que modernidade?*, Oeiras: Celta, 17–44.

Machado, Fernando Luís, António Firmino da Costa, Rosário Mauritti, Susana da Cruz Martins, José Luís Casanova and João Ferreira de Almeida (2003), "Classes sociais e estudantes universitários: Origens, oportunidades e orientações", *Revista Crítica de Ciências Sociais* 66: 45–80.

Nico, Magda and Nuno de Almeida Alves (2017), "Young people of the 'austere period': Mechanisms and effects of inequalities over time in Portugal", in: Joe Pike and Peter Kelly, *Neoliberalism, Austerity and the Moral Economies of Young People's Health and Well-being*, Basingstoke: Palgrave MacMillan, 125–140.

Nilsen, Ann and Julia Brannen (2014), "An intergenerational approach to transitions to adulthood: The importance of history and biography", *Sociological Research Online* 19(2): 9.

Pereirinha, José A. (1988), *Inequalities, Household Income Distribution and Development in Portugal*, Thesis submitted in full requirement for the award of the degree of Doctor of Philosophy in Development Studies at the Institute of Social Studies, The Hague, available at www.repository.utl.pt/handle/10400.5/2294

Pontes, José Pedro (1982), "Tecnologia e especialização industrial na adesão à CEE", *Análise Social*, 18, 70: 215–229.

Roberts, Ken (1997), "Is there an emerging British 'underclass'? The evidence from youth research", in: Robert MacDonald (Ed.) *Youth, the 'Underclass' and Social Exclusion*, London and New York: Routledge, 39–54.

Roberts, Steven (2011), "Beyond 'NEET' and 'tidy' pathways: Considering the 'missing middle' of Youth Transition Studies", *Journal of Youth Studies* 14(1): 21–39.

United Nations (2015), *World Population Prospects – 2015 Revision*, New York: UN.

Vieira, Maria Manuel (1995), "Transformação Recente no Campo do Ensino Superior", *Análise Social* 30, 131–132, 315–373.

Vickerstaff, Sarah (2003), "Apprenticeship in the 'golden age': Were youth transitions really smooth and unproblematic back then?", *Work Employment & Society* 17(2): 269–287.

Wyn, Johanna and Dan Woodman (2007), "Generation, youth and social change in Australia", *Journal of Youth Studies* 9(5): 495–514

Wyn, Johanna and Rob White (1997), *Rethinking Youth*, London: Sage.

Sources

GEP-MTSS, Employment Registry 1985

Eurostat, Labour Force Survey 2016

INE, Demographic Indicators 2016

INE/GEPE, 50 Years of Statistics on Education, 2005

INE, Population Estimates, 1970–2015

INE, Labour Force Survey, 1983–2016

INE, Population Censuses, 1981–2011

8 Young people and housing transitions
Moral obligations of intergenerational support in an Italian working-class context

Elena Mattioli and Nicola De Luigi

Introduction

Even before the financial crisis of 2008, Italy was depicted as 'no country for young people', characterized by a distinctive, late and prolonged transition out of the parental home. Considering young people's age at home-leaving in Europe, two opposite patterns can be distinguished (Billari 2004). Italy and the other southern European countries follow a 'latest-late' pattern with prolonged residence in the parental home (even into their 30s) and high synchronization between leaving home, union formation and parenthood. In contrast, in Nordic countries young people tend to adopt an 'earliest-early' pattern: leaving home around the age of 20 is not connected with union formation and parenthood, but it is rather characterized by living as a single or in shared flats. Other European countries fall in between these extremes.

To explain these differences, two main factors are primarily taken into account (Mulder 2009). One explanation stresses the persistent cultural differences with regard to family formation. Italy has long been characterized by strong kinship networks and patrilocal residence (couples settling in the husband's home or community). Another explanation refers to the characteristics of welfare regimes, stressing the absence of Italian social policies to support young people's transition to adulthood and the protective role of the family for all its members.

However, some scholars have been concerned with the specific characteristics of the housing system. Similar to other southern European countries and Ireland, the Italian housing system presents high rates of homeownership and scarce offer of affordable rented housing in a poorly regulated housing market (Allen et al. 2004; Kurz & Blossfeld 2004). Therefore, within the Italian context, young people willing to leave their family can hardly find affordable rented housing and often do not have the economic resources to buy. Research has documented that transition to independent living occurs in the form of homeownership and is dependent largely on family resources (Bernardi & Poggio, 2004). Studies have also tried to measure the amount of resources transferred and the types of support given by family members, analysing their influence on housing market behaviours. The most common forms of family support in Italy are identified in help within self-building strategies, transmission to family members of properties or financial transfers to allow the purchase of a house. The first form has been particularly important for working classes until the 1980s, while the latter – once only possible for middle and upper classes – can be considered a current form of adaptation in the working class and families that try to negotiate the heavy constraints of the Italian mortgage market, offering their adult children houses inherited from grandparents (often bought after a life of hard work and saving), or helping them with economic resources deriving from inheritance and part of their income and savings, often being two-income families.

However, these studies say little about the normative obligations structuring intergenerational support; how this support is understood by 'givers' and 'receivers' and how it is negotiated in practice (Druta & Ronald, 2016). Every kind of family support is not only an exchange of material commodities; it also raises issues about duty and responsibilities, dependency and independency, legitimacy and worthiness. The processes whereby these moral norms and 'guidelines' for 'proper' behaviours are translated into practices often cause tensions between the parents' obligation of giving and children's responsibilities related to receiving. When supporting children leaving home, parents can exercise control over their lives, imposing for example their own moral standards about family formation. At the same time, young people's protracted dependence on family resources may lead them to negotiate supports in trying to manage the so-called 'shame of dependence' that is said to characterize contemporary Western societies (Sennett, 2003).

This chapter explores practices of intergenerational support for leaving home in working-class families, drawing on experiences of parents giving financial and in-kind support and of adult children receiving it. Examining how this is negotiated and understood allows us to explore how moral obligations are translated into actions and the tensions that may arise. A focus on leaving home in working-class families means paying attention to the specific contexts in which support is performed and negotiated, and which are currently undergoing profound changes. Indeed, the global financial crisis of 2008 and the following austerity policies have negatively affected the already weak Italian welfare state, increasing young people's structural dependency on their families. In the second section, we give an overview of the contemporary understanding of the relevance of moral dimensions of intergenerational support for leaving home and provide a framework of the Italian housing system and the challenges faced by the working class. The third section presents the methodological approach of the research that is the basis of this chapter, while the next three sections present our findings. Here we will focus on the practices of independence and on the role of parental housing support, then we will introduce ideas about 'independence' and 'housing autonomy' across young people and parents. Finally, we will discuss the processes of negotiation of parental support, reflecting on how adult children react to informal parental support, which is generally used as a way to socialize adult children to specific values.

Intergenerational support in the Italian housing system: Leaving home in working-class contexts

Over the last decades, scholars and policy makers have become increasingly concerned with the leaving-home experiences of young people in many Western societies (Forrest & Hirayama 2009). The transition from family home into independent living represents one of the most difficult aspects of the transition to adulthood. It is becoming more delayed, protracted and complex (Billari & Liefbroer, 2010), although with considerable variations across countries.

Research has highlighted the primary role of the family in providing continued practical and economic support to their adult children to cope with the accomplishment of emotional and economic independence (Jones, 1995), arguing that in the last few years pathways to independent living have become more dependent on intergenerational supports. As Holdsworth and Morgan (2005, p. 125) suggest, 'young people do not leave home on their own but a whole host of different actors are brought into play'. Studies have emphasized the *social embeddedness* of acquiring independence, especially highlighting the importance of family support on young people's experiences of both living at home and leaving home. Research has documented how parental support and intergenerational transfers favour or hinder access to housing and home-ownership. Such studies have often been concerned with measuring the length of time young people spend in the parental home or the transfer varieties (financial, inheritance and in-kind) and amounts, analysing also their influence on housing market behaviours such as how parents' financial support impacts down-payments on a house, ensuring better mortgage conditions. Many authors have investigated access to housing as a function of young people's socio-economic background, focusing on different forms that material family support may take (market or non-market), depending on the context and resources available (Albertini & Kohli, 2012).

However, analysing the embeddedness of leaving-home practices does not merely serve to assess the extent to which parents help children in the transition to independent leaving, or support them while at home, nor to detail the different kinds of support that young people might receive. Within intergenerational family network support, the material dimension (the actual amount of resources given and received) always intersects with the moral dimension that inevitably springs from the ongoing tension between autonomy and dependency in intergenerational relationships, yet less attention has been paid to the role played by the normative obligations in modelling the intergenerational exchanges within family networks (Finch & Mason, 1993).

According to Finch and Mason (1993), who analysed the role of the moral dimension in the context of family and kin relationships, family support can be considered a moral practice in which the person's identity and reputation are at stake. This means that although parents' support may be helpful on a material level, it may not succeed on a moral level, affecting in particular young people's sense of independence and adulthood. This happens, for example, not only when a young person returns to the parental home after the end of a marriage, in need of financial support or assistance with childcare, but also when adult children are unable to leave the family home and receive in-kind support yet still value autonomy and individual responsibility. Moreover, even if family support tends to be taken for granted, especially in southern European countries, where familial welfare regimes push parents to take greater responsibility in preserving young people's well-being (Holdsworth, 2004), research show that kinds and types of support often depend on the circumstances and expectations of all family members. As suggested by Finch and Mason (1993), fundamental aspects that should be taken into account in analysing family support are both the 'legitimacy' of the request and the 'deservedness'· of the person asking for it. A study carried out in 2010 by Heath and Calvert (2013) in a southeastern city in the UK suggested interesting insights into young adults' negotiations of parental support in terms of gift or loans. Recalling the study by Finch and Mason (1993), the authors refer to the key role played not only by the difference between loan (i.e. supposed to be given back) and gift (which is presumed not to be returned), but also by issues concerning the legitimacy of the support requested and whether 'applicants' are worthy of it. The research also showed that young people express an ambivalent sense of gratitude and discomfort towards material and financial support received from parents, and manage this feeling by 'blurring' the boundaries between what is to be considered a gift or a loan.

A recent UK study by Druta and Ronald (2016) focused on relationships occurring within processes of family negotiations, identifying four types of negotiations of parental housing support.[1] They found out that support given as a loan often implies clear contractual terms and repayments. Alternatively, support given as a gift can create some feeling of discomfort, especially when it is the case of imbalanced support as, for example, in prolonged co-residence with parents, which can result in distress and frustration. In cases of small gifts with young people receiving 'easy money' (Druta & Ronald 2016), there is not too much feeling of indebtedness and reciprocations can be found. These few studies analyse the moral dimension of family support and how those giving and receiving support understand it, but they focused on northern European contexts characterized by more de-familialized welfare regimes. Italy, indeed, belongs to a southern European housing system (together with Greece, Spain and Portugal), where higher rates of homeownership make it difficult for young people to access affordable housing (Mencarini & Tanturri, 2006) and intra-family solidarity continues to play an important source of support in mediating housing transitions and well-being (Allen et al. 2004; Forrest & Yip, 2012).

Young people's experiences in accessing housing are heavily dependent on the characteristics of the national housing system and the availability of certain kinds of housing (Holdsworth & Solda, 2002). Young people entering the housing market are in a relatively weak position, because they often do not possess sufficient resources to buy a home and encounter difficulties in finding affordable accommodation. In this regard, it is important to consider the peculiar and longstanding characteristics of the Italian housing system: the high rate of homeownership and an inadequate offer of affordable housing in the rental sector.

Most of the expansion of homeownership in Italy took place during the 1970s and the 1980s (and stabilized in the 1990s). According to Italian census data, the rate of homeownership increased from 40% in 1951 to about 72% in 2011, with nearly 20% of households currently living in rented house (mainly in the private rental sector), and almost 10% live in loan-for-use houses, given them for free by the family of origin or informal networks.

Among Italian households with low economic resources, homeownership prevailed over renting both for cultural reasons (e.g. norms about the formation of family systems) and for the overall improvement of their economic conditions after the economic boom of the 1950s (Allen et al. 2004; Bernardi & Poggio 2004). The possibility to take advantage of low-cost channels for accessing housing also played an important role (Poggio 2009). Important options were the privatization of public housing (about 850,000 houses were privatized between 1951 and 1971), the tolerance towards unauthorized building, especially in the South and in smaller cities and industrial districts of the North (it was estimated that about 30% of the houses built between 1971 and 1984 were illegal), the recourse to practices of partial or total self-building (which accounted for 40% of house-building activities in the early 1980s, and 30% in the 1990s) and the underdevelopment of the mortgage market for funding homeownership (until 1980 home mortgage was limited to 50% of the property's overall value, but banks continued to ration credit when the loan-to-value threshold increased).

Over the last decades, the ways in which Italian families accessed home-ownership have changed significantly: a systemic reduction of renters among young people occurred, regardless of their social background (Filandri, 2015).[2] Barbagli et al. (2003) showed that 55% of the new households at the end of the 1940s opted for renting. This way of leaving home prevailed until mid 1970s, when it reached and exceeded 60%. Later, the rate of young couple renting drastically decreased, to about 35% during the 1990s.

In this way, the Italian system of accessing homeownership, once characterized by a *'career ownership'*, progressively moved toward a model marked by the so-called *'entry ownership'* (Poggio 2009). In the first pattern, access to ownership occurred in advanced stages of family life, after a period of renting, once people had accumulated enough money for the purchase or after the conclusion of a self-building process. In the pathway toward homeownership, however, it was not infrequent, especially for low-income households and those living in rural areas, to live 'under the same roof', sharing it with other family members and their relatives, traditionally with women moving to their husband's family according to a principle of *patrilocity*. In the *'entry ownership'* pattern, ownership characterizes the very first phase of entry into the housing market, following the leaving of the parental home. This model, increasing the amount of resources required for the transition to adulthood, resulted in making parental support even more essential, affecting matrimonial and reproductive behaviours, and the average age of young people leaving home.[3] Thus, the mobilization of family resources became a key aspect of the Italian leaving-home process, contributing to enhancing a system of reciprocity and mutual support within familial networks, increasing the difficulties already present in processes of transitions to adulthood. Indeed, leaving the parental home has become directly proportional to the probability of entering home-ownership, with consequences – as we will show in the following pages – for social norms and expectations concerning the timing and the ways in which young people leave home.

Thus, in this rigid housing system, homeownership is increasingly becoming the normal – and normative – answer to the problem of leaving home, even if for lower classes it can be considered a forced solution. According to Poggio (2009, 281), it is important to trace a distinction between 'rich ownership', characterizing those who opted to buy a house that is able to meet their family needs at a good standard, and a 'poor ownership', which derives from forced, difficult and complex choices oriented to the purchase, to be under-stood as a reaction to the lack of good and affordable alternatives in the renting sector.

The rigidity of the Italian housing market means that to achieve home-ownership, young people have to rely on family support. Leaving home has hence become an outcome of an extended family strategy by which family members exchange and manage different combinations of resources such as income, borrowing potential, marketable property, social aid for housing, self-help and mutual aid networks. However, homeownership still represents a strenuous option to pursue, notwithstanding the introduction of fiscal subsidies for the purchase of the first house and new forms of mortgages. When families lack economic resources, the purchase of a home is usually postponed until both partners reach a certain level of financial means. For these reasons, the average age of working-class young home leavers tends to be high compared to middle-class young home leavers, in particular among men, while women tend to leave the family nest earlier.

Methodology

This chapter draws on research focusing on housing pathways of working-class young people, and the role played by their family in the transition towards independent living, within a broader reflection on processes of reproduction and intergenerational transmission of social inequalities. This study opted for a *retrospective longitudinal qualitative* research design (Neale & Flowerdew 2003), interviewing both parents and their adult children. We asked young adults (both women and men) to think about their present con-dition, and asked their parents to reflect on their adult children's housing transitions and on their own experiences. This gave us insights into three generations (young adults of the sample, their parents and their grand-parents).The 'family histories' allowed us to enter the 'black box' of working-class families' attitudes and practices, in order to understand how individual and structural factors shape young people's housing practices.

We carried out fieldwork in 2013–2014 in Bologna (Emilia-Romagna, Northern Italy), a city where working-class culture is deeply rooted in the countryside and in rural families (Capecchi 1982). Until the 1950s half of the local population was employed in the primary sector, especially as *share-croppers* (*'mezzadro'*) and *'farm hand'* (*'bracciante'*) on a daily wage. Emilian peasant families were characterized by a high level of solidarity between members of different households and generations. Expression of this was the common recourse to practices of self-building (partial or total) to provide a house to young couples, generally living in the same community.

The sharecropping crisis and the advent of the big manufacturing industries resulted in many selling their land or unifying them in bigger farms, whose profits were invested in local artisan productions, while many *farm hands* moved to the city to search for new jobs. Rural working-class families thus became wealthier than their urban counterparts, which currently, due to changes in the occupational structure, notably the expanding tertiary sector, is constituted not only by workers of the metalworking and mechanical industry, but also by junior clerks, small retailers and artisans.

Considering this, we decided to adopt a broad definition of *'working-class families'*: following Lareau (2003), we considered those with (i) parents with an educational level equal to ISCED 0–2 (no title, primary and lower secondary education, short vocational training); (ii) employed as office workers, unskilled industrial workers, craftsmen, manual employees in the primary sector. As our *anchors* were parents, a variety of occupations and educational degrees can be observed among young adults. In consideration of the high rates of commuting from neighbouring municipalities to the capital town, and taking into account the specificity of the housing market in Bologna – which, since the early 1980s, saw an "escape" of residents from the centre to the periphery due to the high cost of housing (both for rent and for sale) – we decided to extend the sampling to municipalities in the urban belt.

Finally, we decided to include in our sampling young adults aged 25–40, in consideration of the characteristic patterns of leaving home and housing situations of Italian young people. Among European countries, Italian young people are the last to leave the parental home, at an average age of 29.9 years old (in 2013), with young women leaving before men (28.7 years old for women, against 31 years old for men).[4] Moreover, there is a high rate of co-residence between parents and young people in Italy. According to Istat, the percentage of young people aged 18–34 living with their parents in 2003 was 48%, in 2011 62.3%, and 61.2% in 2012, with 29.6% of 30–34 year olds and 13.8% of 35–39 year olds still living with their parents (Istat 2014). More recently, the rate of young people aged 18–34 living with parents has increased to 68% in 2016 (Istat 2017).

Considering all this through a *purposive sampling* strategy (Patton 2002), we decided to include families whose anchors were working-class parents living in Bologna or in the urban belt, with at least one adult child aged 25–40 in one of the following conditions at the time of the interview:

i   living independent from the family, or being about to leave;
ii   still living with the family;
iii having returned to the family after a period of independent living.

This would allow us to include a variety of housing transition stories and to understand which factors could positively or negatively affect the transition process. We collected 15 family histories and 32 life stories: 17 individual interviews with adult children (6 men and 11 women) and 15 interviews with parents (4 couples and 11 individuals – 3 fathers and 8 mothers).

Practices of independence among young people and the role of parental housing support

Observing our young adults' housing pathways at the level of *practices*, great complexity is revealed. Their living arrangements at the time of interviews varied: four lived independently, six shared a house with their partners, two lived in shared accommodation while five still lived with their parents (with three having returned after a period of independent living). Overall, out of the 17 interviewed young adults, the most common status was living in owned houses (8), while five rented in the private renting sector and four lived in houses given to them on a loan from parents or other close relatives.

Looking at their first destination out of the parental home and more generally at their housing biographies, their housing transitions seem not only prolonged, but also characterized by fragmentation and reversibility (Billari & Liefbroer 2010). One young man (27) had never left the family. Two young women left home at 18 to attend universities far from their city of origin. Six left to start a new family (four women and two men), while eight (aged 27–30) left to start independent living. Finally, during their housing careers, two women and one man (all almost 35 years old) had been forced to return to the parental home after separating from their partners.

The decision to leave home occurred as soon as the young people could afford it, without relying on their parents' finances. At the same time, they acknowledged the important role played by parental support in their transitions to independent living. The majority of them received help mainly from parents or other close relatives such as grandparents, while only a few benefitted from the government's support (student accommodation when enrolled in higher education, or council houses entitled to their parents, with whom they were living), confirming once again the residual role of the state in supporting young people's transitions and the determining role of the family. Only a few said that they reached independent living as a result of their own efforts, but interestingly none of them is a homeowner; rather, they are 'renters'.

Overall, housing support can take many forms, and can be divided into *formal* (i.e. financial help) and *informal* support (Holdsworth 2004). Within formal support, we find governmental benefits[5] such as tax deductions for renovations, for energy-efficient appliances, or incentives for first-time house buyers. Interestingly, some of the young people managed to obtain such aid, allowing parents to purchase the house as first-time buyers.

Formal support includes economic help (cash) from parents, which is used to purchase (both in part and in full) a house.[6] In other cases, young adults were helped by their parents acting as 'guarantors' to obtain a mortgage, which would otherwise have been difficult – if not impossible for young people, due to their precarious contracts.

> Mother: *So, the apartment is half mine and half my daughter's. (…) [I took it in my name] to have the facilitations for those buying their first house… Because this house where we're living is under my husband's name, so I could take the other one under mine… because my daughter otherwise could not obtain a mortgage, with her income…*
>
> Father: *Because today a bank would never have accepted to give my daughter a mortgage! Absolutely! And I had to guarantee, too!!*
>
> (Family no. 3: Mother, aged 62, retired, vocational training; Father, aged 65, retired, lower secondary education, living together, owners)

Alternatively, others had a house on loan from parent without having to pay rent; young adults could thus save money for their future needs.

Family support does not end with home purchasing, but continues after it, with furniture and home appliance purchasing (TVs, wardrobe, washing machine, refrigerators, and so on). Sometimes, especially for households with low income, this latter form of help was the only one possible, often coming from other relatives, for example grandparents. Siblings and friends, instead, seemed to play a marginal role, with the latter providing emotional support or helping with moving.

Parents supported their adult children even after they had left home. This is not particular to our study, as previous research showed that at the European level there is a net downward flow from the older to the younger generations, both through *inter vivos* financial transfers and through social support (Albertini et al. 2007), even if country-specific transfer patterns were found.[7] In our study, support after leaving home was represented in particular by house cleaning, food preparation, baby or pet caring, and even if these kinds of help are not properly financial, they represented important savings for young adults' limited budget.

> *They helped us with redecorating the doors, so we didn't have to change them, redecorating the radiators (…) we have been able to save money*

during all these years, also thanks to the fact that basically, our parents are feeding us. When we visit our parents we always come back with tons of boxes of vegetables from their garden (…) So if we could save money through these years, and could reach the budget to buy a home even with a low-paid job – because you know, the academic job is… we are both precarious (…) otherwise, you alone can't do anything. (…) for example, we thought to renounce having a car. We were living near the centre, so we could avoid the car and all its expenses, taxes, insurance, and so on… but my partner's father paid these things for us all these years. It was a big help.

(Family no. 13, eldest daughter, aged 36, junior researcher, Ph.D., living with partner, owner)

These exchanges happened on a frequent (sometimes daily) basis, and in some cases, represented a 'two-way' support. In other words, adult children often returned their parents' favours and help in different ways, for example by carrying heavy food supplies or doing small maintenance tasks.

R: *For example, I go to buy milk at the supermarket because they buy a huge quantity of it and of a certain brand… I buy Stevia (a kind of sweetener) online for my father from Colombia or Bolivia… I don't ask them to refund me… because maybe then my mum pays a bill for me, or she gives me some food (…), it's a 'do ut des', at a very basic level… I mean, we're talking about little sums, ten Euros more or less… little things.*

(Family no. 1, youngest son, 31, self-employed engineer, BA, living with partner, loan for use)

Our data show a higher level of support from mothers, who turned out to be the main caregivers in most of the cases. Also, a gender impact can be found regarding young adults. While sons were often in charge of manual work (small renovations and maintenance), daughters were more frequently asked to care for family members. For example, the older child of Family no. 5, (*eldest daughter, 30, part-time employee, upper secondary education, living with partner, loan for use*) was asked by her parents to see to her grandmother's needs.

For these reasons, young adults often decided to live near their parents, to take care of them while they were ageing. In some cases, parents tried to influence their adult children's decision in this direction, by buying a house for them in their own neighbourhood. In some families, especially those with two-income parents, homeownership was considered a 'safe investment' for family savings (Poggio 2009).

At the beginning of 2008, I left my parents' home… I went living alone, as I had this salary of 800 euros from the pub, and some more money from odd jobs. The house was already there… because they, already 13 years ago, bought this little apartment here nearby… they bought this tiny flat so that I could leave home once I was self-sufficient… very little, you know, but…! They've been really smart! They said 'we buy it near us, so she has to stay nearby. She leaves, but she stays near' (…) I seriously thought sometimes about going away… but I think about them, and I won't be able to leave them because they're getting old.

(Family no. 3, only daughter, aged 32,
tattoo artist, BA, living alone, owner)

Ideas of 'independence' and 'housing autonomy'

We asked young people and parents what 'independence' meant to them, and what it means to be 'autonomous'. Their answers revealed a variety of meanings of independence, which we can *analytically* divide into two categories: there is a *material independence* and a *cognitive* one, even if in reality these two dimensions are often intertwined.

First of all, independence seems to be linked to the idea of being able to 'rely on one's own resources' (*Family no. 11, Eldest son, 32, bachelor's degree, employee, living with partner, renter*). This does not reflect a sort of inclination toward an *individual autocracy* of the subject, but rather the need for creating an independent identity from that of parents, based on the ability to govern life through relevant choices. Some said that being independent went along with *'responsibilization'*, i.e. becoming a reliable person, both from a moral and an economic perspective, who did not need help from others:

It means to become responsible and get satisfaction from this… that is, you know that nothing is going to be done if you don't do it… and you can experience it and say, 'I did this by myself, and I did it right for myself'.

(Family no. 1, youngest son, 31, bachelor's degree,
employee, living with partner, loan for use)

Others interpreted 'independence' more in terms of 'freedom', both *from* somebody (namely, from parents' ties) and *of* doing something. For example, no one interfering with the management of personal space and objects in the house, and no one asking you about your day once back home. Also, independence can be associated with the creation of one's own family. *'I will be independent when I find a person with whom I will start a family when I have children'* (Family no. 7, only daughter, 34, bachelor's degree, back to family home).

Interestingly, young adults were aware of the difficulties with total and permanent conditions of independence. In their reflections there were increasing worries about the future and the feeling of facing hard times, as a reflection of uncertainty due to precarization processes and its impact on young people's transitions to work, which are strengthened by the effect of the global financial crisis. This resulted in an increased feeling of dependence upon parents, not only because of income precariousness but also due to limited access to the credit and mortgage market for temporary workers, who need supplementary guarantors (Baldini & Poggio 2014).

A young woman experiencing a 'yo-yo transition' (Walther et al. 2002), who returned to her parents' home after her divorce, said it is impossible to talk about independence as in the past:

> *I believe that my generation can't talk about 'pure independence' because there aren't anymore the social conditions that allow you to do so... 'Cos willing or not... in my opinion I am going to be tied to my parents for many years...*
>
> (Family no. 7, only daughter, 34, bachelor's degree, back to family home)

Given the strong ties between young adults and the older generations and the key role played by the latter in young people's lives, we turned our attention to parents' ideas about 'independence' and 'autonomy'. First, they stressed the importance of working in order to be economically self-sufficient, as *'you can say someone is independent when he has a job; this is at the root of everything'* (Family no. 13, Mother, 55, lower secondary education, employee, living with husband, owner). Second, independence did not concern merely economic issues – even if this aspect was strongly present in parents' words. Independence must also be understood in terms of personal growth of subjects, in relation to the ability to think strategically about life-planning and to be able *'to think with your own head'* (Family no. 12, Mother, 60, lower secondary education, employee, living with her only daughter, renter). According to parents, this latter understanding of individuals' independence was also represented by the ability to acknowledge being in need of parents' help in the future, and to explicitly ask for it.

Data so far shows that, like the young adults, parents distinguished between an economic meaning of independence and a cognitive one. Again, like their children, they seemed to be aware of the impact of the present socio-economic conditions, in particular in terms of the 'postponement' of adulthood: *'my daughter is 33 years old... In the past when someone was 33 he or she was considered an old person already!'* (Father, Family no. 7, 62, retired, lower secondary education, living with wife and his mother, owned house of his mother). Also, they were informed about the increasing risks young people faced in their lives, especially in relation to the job market. Parents thought that the effects of this situation were out of the control of young people, and were therefore ready to help them during their entire life course, even once out of the family nest, resorting to family wealth, constituted by previous inheritance and lifetime saving, often deriving from being two-income families (Poggio 2009).

However, this came with some feelings of discomfort for the present situation, evidence of a cognitive uncertainty, a structural trait in contemporary society (Bauman 2013)

> *Everything's changed! That is, the relations of independence are changed. According to me, they turned upside down... 'Cos in the past, independence*

was being more or less 20–22 years old, done with the military service, getting a job and going away, to build your own life... Today everything's changing... the job is unstable... parents are getting divorced, children see wrong examples, and then there is also this bombing from mass media... without realizing it you go buying this and that.... 'well it's just 20 euros'... people are falling apart from the inside... If you don't have something stable, even if it is just a slum, you are then devastated, aren't you?'
(Family no. 4, Father, 57, lower secondary education, artisan, living with wife, social housing renter)

In line with other research (Forrest & Yip 2012, Manzo et al. 2016), our parents mostly affirmed that 'real' housing independence was reached with homeownership,[8] reflecting the context of high rates of homeownership in Italy (over 70% of the entire population). Both generations displayed the same attitudes towards homeownership, considering it an ideal life-goal, notwithstanding the rising difficulties for young people to buy a house and the awareness of the changes and constraints of the economic context.

Negotiating parental housing support

The research shows that young people and parents are embedded in a dense network of almost daily exchanges connected to housing support. The question is: how are these exchanges experienced and understood? As other studies point out, support comes in the form of a 'gift' or 'loan', with blurring boundaries between the two (Heath & Calvert 2013), and this is constantly negotiated between parents and adult children, with concerns regarding issues of *legitimacy* and *worthiness* of the request.

In our study, young people and parents considered financial resources and in-kind help as a 'normal' expression of parental duties towards their children: thus, parents' support was understood mainly in terms of gifts rather than loans. Both givers and receivers acknowledged these exchanges as the normal way to organize intergenerational relationships in the family, so a reciprocation of the received support would probably lead to a significant change in the relationships between the two generations.

Moreover, gifts turned out to be a way of 'socializing' adult children to particular values, such as orientation to saving, and ideals of 'sacrifice', 'soberness' and long-term thinking:

If my daughter asks me money for the university or for medications, then I'm the first to give her money. But if she comes to me and asks for money to go on holiday I say, 'Go to Riccione (i.e. cheap holiday destination on the Adriatic Riviera) instead of going to the Maldives!
(Family no. 7, Father, 62, retired, lower secondary education, living with his wife, his mother and his only daughter in his mother's owned house)

Data also show the importance of complying with the traditional under-standing of family, with parents supporting their adult children with *gifts* only in case of marriage and parenthood. For example, one father (*Family no. 4, 57, artisan, lower secondary education, living with wife and youngest son, social housing renters*) said that he might help his daughter once she got married to her current partner, with whom she was already living.

There were also parents who preferred to support their children with loans, even if these generally concerned extraordinary expenses, not related to housing (for example, cars, bikes, etc.). These kinds of support were justified as a way to avoid paying interest on money loaned from banks, and thus a way to save and keep the economic capital under the family's control.

Young adults instead preferred to consider the parental support as a loan in cases of conflictual familiar relationships. In that way, parental help did not come into conflict with their self-representation of independence. For example, a young woman (*Family no. 5, Daughter, aged 30, part-time employee, upper secondary education*) was living in her grandmother's home in loan for use. First, when asked who helped her when she left home, she did not overtly recognize the economic help she received in term of housing from her parents, with whom she had many quarrels in the past (especially with her father). On the contrary, she admitted being helped with money for her car repairs, emphasizing that she was repaying the money.

So far, our study highlights the existence of strong family ties, based on parental contributions and frequent – when not daily – exchanges of resources and negotiations of support, which constituted the pillars of a system of inter-generational solidarity among family members and reflected a traditional characteristic of the local working classes (Capecchi 1982). At the same time, it seems that this solidarity system also represented a strategic way of managing the socio-economic conditions of family members, who aimed to pool different kinds of resources in the hands of the family in order to maximize the chances of each member climbing up the social ladder, or at least to maintain the same social position as their parents. This resulted in the creation of a dynamic micro-economics system at the family level, as in the following example:

> *My mother helped me with my children (…). She was still working when I had my first daughter, then the baby fell ill and couldn't go to the kinder-garten, I didn't know what to do; I had to take a babysitter or stop working. Then my mother told me 'I will do it, otherwise, you will never get the pension in the future! So she quit her job. Then, I gave her some money 'cause there was my brother at home, and he had to finish his studies… well, we helped each other, indeed!*
>
> (Family no. 1, Mother, 62, retired, vocational training, living with husband, owner)

Our study reveals the presence of a generational contract involving both adult children and parents, and grandparents and siblings as well, characterized by a flow of exchanges going both ways, from the older generations to the youngest, and *vice versa*.

Furthermore, in a time of crisis such as the one these young adults were facing, the family solidarity system provided a safety net from risks deriving from unemployment and precarious jobs. Family can thus represent a reaction against the market, trying to compensate for the market's effects on young people, in relation to the difficult – if not impossible – access to the mortgage market. However, in the context of a familistic welfare system such as the Italian one, families could also find themselves facing the majority of the costs of the crisis, affecting their own savings and exposing future generations to higher economic deprivation risks. These costs do not only concern an economic aspect but also a psychological one, such as a growing lack of confidence in the future. This is the case of a young man who, after a period of private renting with his partner and the birth of their first daughter, moved into the house of the mother of his partner, since they could no longer afford the rent.

> *For me, living in a house which isn't mine, and I can't say anything 'cos I'm depending on others... it's really difficult. I'm angry with myself, I don't feel free to express myself! (...) to be honest now I don't feel to be myself any more. I'm changed (...) I feel unfulfilled, demoralized.*
>
> (Family no. 2, youngest son, 31, lower secondary education, manual worker, living with his partner and their daughter in her mother's owned home)

These feelings of discomfort might arise in situations of asymmetrical relationships between young adults and older generations, where a condition of protracted dependence on family may lead young people to have to cope with the 'shame of dependence' (Holdsworth & Morgan 2005; Sennett 2003), which can result either in the loss of emotional freedom and resignation, or in more or less explicit forms of resistance when not overtly in conflict, and a mismatched perception of intergenerational justice.

Conclusion

In this chapter, we considered the complexity of exchanges of parental housing support, and the negotiations of meaning attributed to it, within working-class families and across generations, in times of recession and financial crisis. We focused on three main aspects: young people's practices of housing autonomy, ideas of 'independence' and 'autonomy' of young people and their parents, and finally intergenerational negotiations of support.

Notwithstanding the limits of our research, in terms of class and ethnic heterogeneity, observing young people's struggles to achieve housing autonomy and meanings of parental support allowed us not only to understand the underlying processes which lead parents to help their children in leaving home, but also to unveil the process by which social categories such as working class 'are produced, experienced, reproduced, and resisted in everyday life' (McCall 2005, 1783). Once more, working-class family networks – despite the scarcity of financial resources – turn out to be a key factor in supporting transitions to independent living, and its functioning is still guided by the traditional strong attitude towards homeownership, notwithstanding the increasing difficulties for young people and their parents in reaching this life-goal. Similar to other countries with high rates of homeownership, in Italy working-class families pursue and manage access to an owned house as an insurance against the risks of the current society, considering it one of the most important markers of the achievement of a full social citizenship (Negri & Filandri 2010).

As discussed before, even if the Italian working class lacked liquid assets to support homeownership, until the 1980s they could rely on the possibility of taking advantage of low costs and non-market channels, such as self-building on a community base, which in other countries characterized only rural areas. As soon as these opportunities ceased, working-class families managed to help their adult children by providing in-kind support, such as a prolonged co-residence in the (owned) parental home or giving them property in loan for use. So, by delaying independent living and living longer in parents' houses, working-class young people prolonged the period necessary to accumulate resources to access homeownership, trying in this way to cope with the increasingly market-led logics in the Italian housing system.

Our findings show that financial resources and in-kind support appear to still be considered by young people and their parents as normal, and normative, expressions of parents' duties towards their adult children. This means that generally young people do not ask for parents' help. More exactly, they think of it as a right they are entitled to. In this context, intergenerational support is given as a *gift*, and any reciprocation of it could lead to a re-shaping of the social relationships between the two generations. Moreover, gifts do not imply simply an exchange of material commodities, but also entail moral transactions. Our research shows that through aid given mostly in the form of gifts, working-class parents try to affirm their own values and visions of social relations, stressing in particular the importance of orientation towards saving, and their ideals of 'sacrifice', 'soberness' and long-term thinking. Intergenerational support in the form of gifts is a deliberate attempt to 'socialize' adult children to such attitudes. However, sometimes family conflicts occur, and adult children often react to this, trying to avoid any moral obligations to their parents, choosing not to ask them for help or negotiating support in terms of a loan to be repaid.

In conclusion, the increasing struggles of young people in their housing transitions, mirrored by a prolonged co-residence with their parents, make the negotiation of intergenerational support more difficult, and raise issues concerning the legitimacy and worthiness of parental help. On the one hand, being helped by parents – sometimes even substantially – does not seem to be considered something to be ashamed of, nor does it diminish young people's feelings of independence. Parents recognize that adult children demonstrate their ability to cope on their own, in spite of the substantial difficulties when leaving home. On the other hand, there is evidence of an increasing discomfort among young people, due not to the impossibility of paying their parents back, but to the growing difficulties of attaining permanent independent living.

Notes

1 The four types of negotiations are a) intra-family financial partnership; b) small parental contributions; c) imbalanced support; d) advance inheritance (Druta & Ronald 2016).
2 In Northern Europe, on the contrary, there is a strong (even though not always linear) relationship between social class and level of homeownership in leaving home: middle-class households are more likely to live in owned houses compared to lower social classes (Filandri & Bertolini, 2016).
3 Since the beginning of the 1980s, there was in Italy a rapid increase in the average age of leaving home. This is not a brand-new phenomenon, as Barbagli et al. (2003) noted that, until the 1930s, young people (especially male) left the parental home at an average age of 30 years old. After a reduction occurred in the following years, it started again to increase for cohorts born at the beginning of the 1960s, realigning for cohorts born in the 1980s around the ages typical of the first decades of the 20th century (Schizzerotto & Lucchini 2004).
4 Source: Eurostat, last updated 11.05.2017, extracted on 22.05.2017, cf. http://app sso.eurostat.ec.europa.eu/nui/show.do?dataset=yth_demo_030&lang=en. As the fieldwork was carried out in 2013–2014, data refers to 2013 in order to give a picture of the situation of young people at the time of interviews, even if the situation in 2016 is almost the same, with young men leaving at an average age of 31.3 years old, while women leave around 29.0 years old.
5 None of our young adults was neither entitled to a council house nor ever applied for it, supposing that they would not match the criteria to benefit from it.
6 Naturally, this cash aid is also used to cover important medical costs (for example, dental treatments).
7 According to Albertini et al. (2007), transfers from parents to children are less frequent but more intense in the southern European countries.
8 Just a few respondents say that one can reach his or her own housing autonomy through renting, but only in the case of long-term renting contracts.

References

Albertini, M., & Kohli, M. (2012), The generational contract in the family: An analysis of transfer regimes in Europe, *European Sociological Review*, 9(4), 828–840.
Albertini, M., Kohli, M., & Vogel, C. (2007), Intergenerational transfers of time and money in European families: common patterns – different regimes?, *Journal of European Social Policy*, 17(4), 319–334.
Allen, J., Barlow, J., Leal, J., Maloutas, T., & Padovanim L. (2004), *Housing & welfare in Southern Europe*. Oxford: Blackwell Publishing.
Baldini, M., & Poggio, T. (2014), The Italian housing system and the global financial crisis, *Journal of Housing and the Built Environment*, 29(2), 317–334.

Barbagli, M., Castiglioni, M., & Dalla Zuanna, G. (2003), *Fare famiglia in Italia: Un secolo di cambiamenti* [Doing family in Italy: A century of changes]. Bologna: Il Mulino.

Bauman, Z. (2013). *Liquid times: Living in an age of uncertainty.* Cambridge: Polity Press.

Bernardi, F., & Poggio, T. (2004), *Home ownership and social inequality in Italy*, in Kurz, K. & Blossfeld, H.P. (eds), *Home ownership and social inequalities in comparative perspective.* Stanford, CA: Stanford University Press, pp. 187–232.

Billari, C. (2004), Becoming an adult in Europe: A macro(/micro)-demographic perspective, *Demographic Research*, SC3(2), 15–44.

Billari, F.C., & Liefbroer, A.C. (2010), Towards a new pattern of transition to adulthood?, *Advances in Life Course Research*, 15(2–3), 59–75.

Capecchi, V. (1982). *Famiglia operaia: mutamenti culturali: 150 ore* [Working-class family and cultural changes: 150 hours], Bologna,: Il Mulino.

Druta, O., & Ronald, R. (2016), Young adults' pathways into homeownership and the negotiation of intra-family support: A home, the ideal gift, *Sociology*, 51(4), 783–799.

Filandri, M. (2015). *Proprietari a tutti i costi: la disuguaglianza abitativa in Italia* [Owners at any cost: housing inequalities in Italy]. Rome: Carocci.

Filandri, M., & Bertolini, S. (2016), Young people and home ownership in Europe, *International Journal of Housing Policy*, 16(2), 144–164.

Finch, J. & Mason, J. (1993), *Negotiating family responsibility.* London: Routledge.

Forrest, R., & Hirayama, Y. (2009), The uneven impact of neoliberalism on housing opportunities, *International Journal of Urban and Regional Research*, 33, 998–1013.

Forrest, R., & Yip, N. (Eds.). (2012). *Young people and housing: Transitions, trajectories, and generational fractures.* London: Routledge.

Heath, S., & Calvert., E. (2013), Gift, loans and intergenerational support for young adults, *Sociology*, 47(6), 1120–1135.

Holdsworth, C., & Solda, M.I. (2002). First housing moves in Spain: An analysis of leaving home and first housing acquisition, *European Journal of Population*, 18(1):1–19.

Holdsworth, C. (2004), Family support during the transition out of the parental home in Britain, Spain, and Norway, *Sociology*, 38(5), 909–926.

Holdsworth, C., & Morgan, D. (2005), *Transitions in context: Leaving home, independence and adulthood.* Buckingham: Open University Press.

Istat (2017), *Rapporto annuale 2017.* Rome: Istituto nazionale di statistica.

Jones, G. (1995), *Leaving home.* Buckingham: Open University Press.

Kurz, K., & Blossfeld, H.P. (eds.), (2004), *Home ownership and social inequalities in comparative perspective.* Stanford, CA: Stanford University Press.

Lareau, A. (2003). *Unequal childhoods: Race, class and family life.* Berkeley, CA: University of California Press.

Manzo, L., Druta, O., & Ronald, R. (2016), *Supported home ownership and adult independence in Milan: The gilded cage of family housing gifts and transfers* (November), Houwel working paper series, http://houwel.uva.nl/working-papers/working-papers/working-papers/content/folder/hwp11.html

McCall, L. (2005), The complexity of intersectionality, *Signs: Journal of Women in Culture and Society*, 30(3), 1771–1800.

Mencarini, L., & Tanturri, M.L. (2006), *Una casa per diventare grandi. I giovani italiani, l'autonomia abitativa e il ruolo della famiglia d'origine* [A home to grow up. Italian young people, housing autonomy and the role of the family], *Polis*, 3, 405–430.

Mulder, C.H. (2009), Leaving the parental home in young adulthood, in Furlong, A. (ed.), *Handbook of youth and young adulthood: New perspectives and agendas.* London: Routledge, 203–210.

Neale, B., & Flowerdew, J. (2003), Time, texture and childhood: The contours of longitudinal qualitative research, *International Journal of Social Research Methodology,* 6(3), 189–199.

Negri, N., & Filandri, M. (2010). *Restare di ceto medio: Il passaggio alla vita adulta nella società che cambia* [Staying middle class: The transition to adulthood in a changing society]. Bologna: Il Mulino.

Patton, M.Q. (2002), *Qualitative evaluation and research methods.* London: Sage.

Poggio, T. (2009), Le principali dimensioni della disuguaglianza abitativa in Italia [The main dimensions of housing inequalities in Italy], in Brandolini, A., Saraceno, C., & Schizzerotto, A. (eds.), *Dimensioni della disuguaglianza in Italia: povertà, salute, abitazione* [Dimensions of inequality in Italy: poverty, health, housing]. Bologna: Il Mulino, pp. 273–292.

Schizzerotto, A., & Lucchini, M. (2004), Transitions to adulthood, in Berthoud, R. & Iacovou, M. (Eds.), *Social Europe: Living standards and welfare states.* Cheltenham: Edward Elgar, 46–68.

Sennett, R. (2003), *Respect in a world of inequality,* New York and London: WW Norton & Company.

Walther, A., Stauber, B., Biggart, A., du Bois-Reymond, M., Furlong, A., López Blasco, A., & Mørch, S. (2002), *Misleading trajectories: Integration policies for young adults in Europe?*Wiesbaden: Springer.

9 Young people, transition to adulthood and recession in Greece

In search of a better future

Alexandros Sakellariou and Alexandra Koronaiou

Introduction

Young people's transition to adulthood in times of crisis is a topic that has attracted scientific interest since the 1980s but came to the forefront again after the global financial crisis of 2008 (Beck, 1992; Bauman, 2000, 2007). The purpose of this chapter is to study young people's views, emotions and thoughts during a very crucial period of their lives and under exceptional circumstances, those of a deep crisis – economic, social and political – in Greek society. Based on a qualitative research study conducted at the peak of the economic crisis in Greece (2013), the main questions that we will try to answer are the following: How are young people affected by the crisis? How do they view Greek society under crisis and where do they see themselves in the future? What do young people think about the role of their family? Is this supportive and how does support take place? What are their opinions about politics, politicians and political parties? Our main goal is to study this important transition period in young people's lives through the prism of the crisis and to examine how young people responded to the crisis.

The importance of transition in young people's lives

Transition to adulthood is an important time in people's lives and has been studied under a variety of scientific perspectives mainly from psychological perspectives (Erikson and Erikson, 1997) but also from sociological ones (George, 1993). Transitions have been studied not only in western societies (Hutson and Jenkins, 1989; Goldscheider and Goldscheider, 1999; Corijn and Klizjing, 2001; Müller and Gangl, 2003; Holdsworth and Morgan, 2005) but on a global level as well (Lloyd, 2005; Gebel and Heyne, 2014) and in some cases with a special focus on vulnerable populations (Osgood et al., 2005; Stein and Munro, 2008).

As argued by Snee and Devine (2015: 544) career decisions are very important for young people's lives and could have a crucial impact upon their future. Employment choices and opportunities are interrelated with social class, and are subject to restructuring in times of economic recession. An important set of questions are posed by Snee and Devine relating to whether the longer run context is one in which upward social mobility is declining and downward social mobility increasing, and if disadvantaged young people have diminished opportunities (Snee and Devine 2015).

Within the European context in particular, young adults confront new challenges relating to work and to family formation within a context of a flexible and precarious labour markets and new pressures relating to the ability to form new households. Knijn and Plantenga argue that, in the move away from post-war welfare settlements, it is more necessary to plan and implement social policies with a particular focus on young people's future (Knijn and Plantenga, 2012: 210). During the last decade the labour market has faced serious crises and is shifting in almost all European societies meaning that young people look upon their future with uncertainty, especially in comparison to their parents' generation (Knijn and Plantenga 2012). Higher qualifications are no longer considered a guarantee for job stability and security. However, as research has shown (Knijn and Plantenga, 2012: 204) there are extensive differences among countries with regard to school- and university to work transitions.

Youth transitions, however, cannot be considered only in relation to employment and the labour market since in contemporary societies a variety of 'status indicators' (social, political, and economic) contribute to the formation and development of young people's trajectories (Jones and Wallace, 1992; Coles, 1995). Being in a relationship or not, moving from parental home, or being an active consumer, alongside an increasing access to social, political and economic rights all play a crucial role (France, 1996). Change in wider social and economic arrangements and in patterns of support across generations have had a direct impact on young people's lives. For example, there is growing evidence of a new 'boomerang generation' that leaves home but then returns because it faces difficulties during this transition (Wyn and White, 1997), along with wider evidence of difficulties securing independent housing (see Ch. 8, Mattioli and de Luigi this volume).

Regarding departure from their parents' home, according to recent European research young people leave later as compared to previous generations, with the only exceptions being France and Germany (Knijn and Plantenga, 2012: 211). Knijn and Plantenga state that young females leave the parental home at a later age than young males because they stay in education longer and because they experience more difficulties entering the labour market compared to their male counterparts (Knijn and Plantenga, 2012: 211). Transformations taking place in the labour market (flexible contracts, part-time jobs, low wages and working without social security) create a climate of uncertainty for young people leading them to postpone their departure from their parents' home and making them feeling insecure in their ability to support their own independent home or commence family formation (Knijn and Plantenga, 2012: 211). Not infrequently those who have already left the parental home decide to return to the family nest.

The crisis and its impact on Greek youth

The economic and social collapse that Greece has been experiencing since 2010 has indelibly marked both the society and the political system. The crisis, as well as the complete failure to tackle it effectively either on the national or European level brought to the surface, magnified and accelerated extensive and profound socio-political processes that have been developing during the last two decades. The long austerity period started officially in May 2010, when the first loan agreement was signed between the PASOK centre-left government of the time and the country's creditors in order to enable the Greek government to continue repaying the national debt. It has been characterised by wide public budget cuts, high salary and pension reductions, high taxation of incomes and the abolition of labour rights and welfare services, which in turn severely affected the entire economy plunging it into deep recession (INE-GSEE, 2011; INE-GSEE, 2017). The burst of unemployment, poverty, homelessness and suicides as well as the dismantling of the already anaemic social welfare services had a profound impact on the living conditions of the population, while young people were among the first and most severely affected parts of the population (Malkoutzis, 2011; Bank of Greece, 2012; Hauben et al., 2012; ELSTAT, 2013c; Petmesidou, 2013). In 2011 the unemployment rate for the 15–24 age group reached 49.9 per cent, while for the 25–29 age group it was 34.0 per cent (ELSTAT, 2013a); since then it has skyrocketed to 57.2 per cent for the 15–24 group and to 43.8 per cent for those aged 25–29 years old (ELSTAT, 2013b). More recent data show a decrease in youth unemployment. However, it is still at a high level of 45.7 per cent, the first place in the EU, followed by Spain (42.2 per cent) and Italy (37.9 per cent) (EUROSTAT, 2017).

The crisis had a very negative impact on education in Greece. According to a recent report (KANEP/GSEE 2017), since 2008 public spending on education decreased by 54.7 per cent (4.5 billion euros) while at the same time private spending also decreased by 31.8 per cent (1.7 billion euros), meaning that families can no longer afford to pay for the extra education of their children where needed (eg. foreign languages, preparation for university exams, private schools). Furthermore, a reduction in the teaching staff by 32,717 people from 2008 is reported, and new teaching staff are not being hired due to austerity measures. Universities in Greece faced similar problems since their public budgets were decreased by around 50 per cent during the years of the crisis. In this period of harsh economic conditions, particularly in some low-income areas, many children were not getting appropriate nutrition at school and were consequently facing health problems (eg. some could not attend sports classes; were fainting during the class). The government, in collaboration with a private institution, decided in 2012 to start offering free meals in those schools in order to confront the problem of 'food supply insecurity', and nowadays this project is expanding and includes other regions and schools around Greece with similar socio-economic problems. It is worth mentioning that according to UNICEF child poverty is on the rise. An average of one in five children in rich countries live in relative income poverty, among them Spain, the United States, Italy, Portugal and others, with Greece being a particular case after seven years of recession with 45 per cent of children living in conditions of deprivation of the basic essentials and services. Furthermore, the percentage of children living under the poverty limit increased from 20.9 per cent in 2009 to 55.1 per cent in 2014 (UNICEF, 2017).

At this point, it is important to sketch the educational system in Greece. Education in Greece is divided into two main categories. On the one hand there is public education which is free, and there is also private education which comprises a smaller part. According to the latest data from the Hellenic Statistic Authority (ELSTAT, 2017: 131–135) in the academic year 2014–2015 there were 5,171 public nurseries against 441 private ones; 4,398 public primary schools and 307 private; and 2,770 private secondary schools against 190 private ones. Accordingly the numbers of pupils are much higher in public compared to private schools. Education is compulsory for all children from six to 15 years old, a period which includes primary education (six years elementary school) and first-level secondary education (Gymnasium, three years). The second level of the secondary education (Lyceum, three years) is not compulsory and functions as a preparation period for those who wish to take the national exams in order to study at university level. However, the majority of young people continue at this second level regardless of their wish to study at university because obtaining at least the final school degree is considered a crucial qualification in order to find a job.[1]

At the tertiary level, all universities in Greece are public, i.e. without fees although in some cases and only when it comes to Master's degrees some of them have introduced fees during the last decade. However, despite the fact that education is free, there is a parallel private system which mainly includes the learning of foreign languages starting at a very early age (first grades of elementary school) and courses for the preparation for the university national exams (last three years of secondary education). There are also private support classes in parallel with public school, which cost families a lot of money. This exacerbates inequalities since not every family has the potential to follow this. In terms of early school leaving, it is interesting that during the last years of the economic crisis the numbers are decreasing and an interpretation given is that due to the high unemployment rates for young people both children and families find school a shelter. Since education is compulsory until the age of 15, the age that young people decide to leave school is between 15 and 17 years old.[2]

Another parameter of the current crisis is young people's emigration. During the years of the crisis (2008–2016) it is estimated that between 350,000 and 425,000 young people (25–39 years old) left Greece either for further studies (e.g. Master's degree or PhD) and/or for work. For the education of this generation – called variously Generation E (expats), Generation G (young, talented and Greek), or Generation We – the Greek state has paid around 8 billion euros and now it loses 12.9 billion euros from its GDP and 9.1 billion euros from taxes. In addition, according to recent studies 49 per cent of those employed and 43 per cent of the unemployed expressed the will to leave Greece and go to other countries (Endeavor, 2015: 16–17) while even school students (15–18 years old) expressed a similar wish (Labrianidis and Sykas, 2017). Other data seem to verify this trend, with 51 per cent of young people feeling compelled to study, undergo training or work in another EU country because of the crisis compared to the EU average of 26 per cent (Kraatz, 2015: 6). As most of them say, the reasons that lead them towards this decision are: low wages, high taxes, no future professional prospects, lack of a national development plan and lack of country prospects. This is considered one of the most important and negative effects of the crisis because the country loses a substantial part of its productive population.

Although for earlier years there are no official data available, since this phenomenon was not considered important, it is estimated (Labrianidis 2011: 177) that in the years 1962–1977 approximately 7700 graduates left the country permanently and 35,600 graduates left temporarily. In the following years according to the censuses of 1981 and 2001 it seems that most people who were already abroad decided to return to Greece (Labrianidis 2011: 178–179). Regarding the educational level of those emigrating it is evident that during the latter part of the twentieth century a significant change occurred. Labrianadis and Pratsinakis (2016) argue that until the 1980s those who decided to emigrate mainly held lower educational qualifications, but during the 1990s and especially from the 2000s onwards the majority of those going abroad held a university degree. This shift continued during the period of economic crisis, with graduates accounting for 75 per cent of those who emigrated from 2010 onwards (typically to Europe and other Western societies including the U.S., Australia or New Zealand) (Labrianidis and Pratsinakis 2016: 14–15). Another change noted by Labrianadis and Pratsinakis (2016) relates to the age composition of the emigrant population with people migrating later in the life course. After 2010 the mean age of emigrating was 30.5 years old, in the period from 2000 to 2009 it was 28.3 and in the 1990s it was 24.3 years old.

In harsh financial conditions family plays a crucial role in the support of young people. Family support is an element of Greece's traditional agricultural culture from the pre-war period but continues to play an important role and nuclear and extended family routinely offer material and psychological support to underemployed or unemployed family members. During the economic crisis this support became even more important because of high unemployment rates, especially among young people, cuts in social spending and more particularly cuts of social benefits and low wages in the labour market. In many cases the family and sometimes pensioners (the grandparents) support both their unemployed children and their grandchildren evidenced by a recent survey (Dianeosis 2017) according to which

48.2 per cent of young people (78 per cent aged 18–24 and 33.2 per cent aged 25–35) are receiving financial support from their parents or other relatives.

Although in Greece the provision of parental support has long been extensive compared to most other European societies (Tsekeris, 2015: 15–16) there is an historical deferral in the move to independent living for young people worldwide (Marvakis et al., 2013). It has been argued (Bell and Blanchflower, 2015) this historical pattern of deferral has taken place because of high prices in the housing market in relation to low wages and unemployment. According to research (Eurofound 2014:19), Greek youth leave the parental home at the age of 29, much higher than in Nordic and central European countries (eg. young people leave the parental home at 20 in Denmark and 23 in Germany). Based on the above it has been argued that "young Greeks are notoriously pampered by their family, due to a culture of strong family ties and Greek parents traditionally have a say in a young person's choices" (Ioannou, 2014, cited Tsekeris et al 2015, p. 15).

Financial and job insecurity and poverty impede young adults' efforts to create their own family, move to their own home and live independently (Narotzky and Besnier, 2014, as reported by Tsekeris et al 2015, see also Chapter 1, this volume). As argued in previous studies conducted in other contexts (eg. Hutson and Jenkins, 1989 in the UK), young people's unemployment might not become a major political problem because it is being coped within the privacy of the home and the intimacy of relationships. Contrary to that finding in the Greek case youth unemployment has clearly become a political and social problem, but at the same time family does play a crucial role in coping with it.

The methodology of the research

The purpose of this chapter is to examine how young people in Greece are dealing with the crisis at a crucial point in their life course, i.e. their transition to adult life. The following is based on the findings from a study we conducted as part of a large research project (MYPLACE-Memory, Youth, Political Legacy and Civic Engagement 2011–2015)[3] and more particularly on 60 semi-structured interviews with young people (15–30 years old) conducted at the peak of the economic crisis in Greece (2013). The objectives of this particular study followed the project's general objectives.[4] However, since our research took place during the crisis a special focus became the impact of this on young people's lives. As a consequence, the main objectives were to examine young people's socio-political activism and engagement; how history and political heritage affected their socio-political activism and participation; and the impact of the economic crisis on their lives as well as on their socio-political engagement. Due to the variety and plurality of the findings, in this chapter we only focus on a some of them, more particularly those related to the crisis and youth transitions.

The analysis that follows presents the findings and is divided into three main sub-sections: 1) The crisis (What young people think about the crisis – experiences; impact) 2) Politics and politicians (What they think about politics, politicians, and political parties in relation to the crisis); and 3) Society and the future (What young people think about social inequalities, Greek society and their place in it – emigration, family). The method of data analysis applied was discourse analysis and specifically classic thematic analysis (Maingueneau, 1991; Grawitz, 2001; Jorgensen and Phillips, 2002; Guest, 2012) of the collected material. After an initial reading of the empirical material for overall familiarisation, the interviews were studied in more detail in order to define the principal thematic categories and sub-categories of analysis, using the Nvivo software program for qualitative analysis.

The demographic profile of our respondents were as follows:[5] 36 of them were female (F) and 24 male (M). They were all Greek. There were 11 in the 15–18 age group; 34 in the 19–24 age group; and 15 in the 25–29 age group. All of them were single. 40 of them, the vast majority, were living with their parents; 11 were living independently alone and two with other relatives. 34 were at university; 11 in secondary education; 11 had completed university and four were studying at postgraduate level. Finally, regarding their employment status, 42 were in full-time education, eight were unemployed, seven were working and studying, two of them working part time and one was working full time.[6]

The crisis in the eyes of young people

As anticipated, when respondents were asked to describe what is going on in Greece that affects people the most, they identified the economic crisis as the crucial factor. However, most of them argued that the crisis is not just economic; it affects all sectors of society and that makes it multidimensional: 'It is a crisis of values; it's a social crisis, a human crisis, a social and economic crisis; and of course political' (Periklis, M, 21).[7] Others focussed mainly on the moral side for example saying that: 'I think it is basically a moral and spiritual crisis and that particular aspect of it has led us to the point we are now' (Michos, M, 25). Another approach presented by some respondents was to compare it to a small-scale civil war, as it has led to increased antagonism among people and caused serious problems in interpersonal relationships. As one respondent said:

> To be honest, I don't think that we are far from a civil war; what we are living now may not be a war with guns and armed hostilities, but it is an economic war that makes us turn against each another
>
> (Gianna, F, 24)

The crisis was characterised as universal and of the capitalist system, not only of Greek society. Many of the respondents acknowledged that the crisis is not new as its foundations may be found many decades ago. Only two underlined a positive aspect of the crisis, which could be an opportunity for changes and reconstruction to be made (Menandros, M, 21).

The representation of the crisis

Besides the respondents' detailed answers about the economic crisis, it was interesting to analyse what was the first thing that comes into their minds when they hear the word 'crisis'. Not surprisingly, all of their answers had negative connotations, as in the following example: "There is no hope" (Aris, M, 25). The most common feelings that were expressed by our respondents were pessimism about any possible end to it and the tough road ahead in order to get there, and rage, not only at those seen to be responsible for the current situation but also at their inability to bring about significant change. Bearing in mind that since the time of the research (2013) four years have passed, the pessimism expressed during the interviews seems justified.

When asked to describe what kind of image(s) came to mind when they heard the word 'crisis', images of impoverishment were the most frequent responses. Respondents said that when they heard the word 'crisis' they immediately thought about the homeless people that sleep on the streets; the food rations increasingly organised by several municipalities, the church and others; poverty and unemployment. Intense images were dominant in the young people's minds; images that indicate chaos, disaster and collapse, but also social unrest, people fighting for their rights in demonstrations and occupations:

> *I think of people being sad but I also imagine people who are on the streets and they go to demos and people on the streets fighting for their demands. I mean I don't have only negative images about the economic crisis, but I think of people demonstrating, mainly young people, because they can't stand this situation any longer.*

(Efthalia, F, 20)

All of these primarily negative representations make young people feel old as they have lost their hopes for the future and they have to deal with a lack of perspective resulting from living in a social context that they think is characterised by moral decline. It is worth mentioning that only one respondent replied that she feels optimistic about the evolution of the crisis (Afroxilanthi, F, 16) arguing that at some point it will come to an end because young people have visions and because they have many new things to offer to society.

The consequences of the crisis

The vast majority (42) of the respondents contended that the most serious and intense consequences of the crisis were psychological ones. They referred to feelings of insecurity and uncertainty about their future plans; they described a generalised depression caused by the lack of hope about individual and social futures, and anxiety and increased stress about their future studies and the outcome of the current situation. They said they felt disillusioned and frustrated when they considered the increased rates of unemployment and the poor prospects for securing paid employment when they finished their studies. This is related to the demographic data of the respondents of whom only one was working in a full-time job. The possibility of going abroad to continue their studies and hopefully find a job intensified their already strong feeling of distress and fear. The extract that follows illustrates the aforementioned psychological situation in which most of the young people found themselves:

> *Psychologically we all feel depressed and disillusioned. We cannot dream and make plans because generally when you make plans God laughs at you and he laughs even more in our society.*
>
> (Loukia, F, 24)

Moreover, a significant number of respondents (34) concurred that there were many financial consequences that had a range of impacts on their everyday life. One respondent said:

> *I experience [the crisis] daily because my mother is unemployed and only my father works and basically things at home are tough because we have frequent quarrels due to our financial state and this affects me a lot.*
>
> (Rodanthi, F, 16)

The majority of the young people we interviewed live at home with their parents and were not in the labour market. This exacerbated an already difficult situation as their parents had often suffered salary cuts or were unemployed. Most of them admitted that they go out less often to have a coffee or go to the cinema; they buy only absolute necessities; and that this situation has a negative impact on how they feel about the future, meaning that a vicious circle is created.

Many of the respondents described how they saw the impact that the crisis has had on society as a whole. Some said that people have become more self-centred and try to help only themselves; this results in a decline in collectivity and solidarity among people. Others argued that many problems arise in interpersonal relationships due to feelings of despair and unease, while others noted growing social inequalities and the fact that the middle class had become poorer. In order to highlight these feelings of depression, it is probably worth mentioning that just three out of 60 participants claimed that the crisis had not affected them either emotionally or economically. From the above it is clear that young people in Greece are living in very uncertain social and financial conditions, not knowing what the future will bring and what exactly they will do after finishing school or university. This uncertainty cultivates a climate of fear for the future and this, along with feelings of depression in an important life course phase, make young people vulnerable and in many cases pessimistic.

Those responsible for the crisis: Politics and politicians

During the discussion about the crisis and its impact, young people were asked to mention who they consider to be responsible for the crisis. Politicians and political parties were the first to be mentioned. They were highly critical of mainstream politics and political parties, and this was a field that did not attract them to participate. Fourteen of them identified politics with corruption, having in mind the economic scandals that have been made public about Greek politicians, and perceiving the majority of them as liars who took advantage of their power for their own interests, ignoring the common good and eventually leading the country to a major economic recession. As one respondent argued, "I associate Greek politics with a state of corruption and clientelism. With what else? People that came into power and embezzled state money, public wealth" (Lida, F, 19). Many of the respondents argued that when they think about politics, they spontaneously think about political parties, parliament, the state and its citizens, while others felt that politics has nothing to do with the political parties, as politics is a collective responsibility and refers to the way of dealing with social problems: "politics provides the means for the evolution of society" (Lakis, M, 25).

Views about the political system and politicians

The overall attitude towards politics and politicians was negative and young people were disappointed with the system. One respondent said: "Basically, I have zero hope of the political system" (Periklis, M, 21) while another argued that:

> [Politicians are] a bunch of fellows wearing suits and they sit in that marvellous room that we visited at school, the Parliament, and they discuss about us, making decisions about us without taking into consideration what we think; and they make all those great speeches full of promises that they are not going to keep [...]
>
> (Myrana, F, 16)

The respondents thought that politicians were corrupt and that consequently the majority of institutions were dysfunctional, leading to intense feelings of insecurity and disillusionment. Furthermore, since some of them argued that the government had taken on a merely executive role following detailed guidelines by external institutions (i.e. the European Commission, the

International Monetary Fund and the European Central Bank), they concluded that the government's role was at the least inefficient in dealing with social problems (Myrana, F, 16) and that the government "doesn't give a shit about us" (Litsa, F, 19). All of these negative views and emotions about the political system and politicians led one respondent to say that the current situation may be worse than the period of the 1967–1974 dictatorship, seeing in the present only a facade of democracy. But some recognised the fact that politicians were not the only ones responsible for the current social and economic conditions. The Greek people were to blame as well:

> *I see both sides of the coin, we cannot blame just one, we must blame many people because we voted for them, we gave our support to these political parties all these years, and these politicians. We voted for them once, twice, so we are responsible as well.*

(Violeta, F, 17)

The rejection and disappointment of the respondents towards the political system and the institutional political actors evident from the analysis is manifest also in their views about political parties. Many of the respondents argued that all the political parties are the same since their basic goal is to ensure financial profits and power for their members, not taking into account the best interest of the country. Thus they expressed an intense distaste for political parties. One respondent characteristically said: "[...] I believe that all of them are phonies and money and only money governs everything. So I prefer not to vote for anyone than choose one of them" (Rodanthi, F, 16). Some focussed on critiquing the two major political parties, the socialists and the conservatives,[8] saying that they have fooled the people because "[...] they had power for so many years because people voted for them and they did nothing at all" (Lemonia, F, 18).

While there is debate in Greek society about which generation is responsible for the crisis, our interviewees never accused their parents. Perhaps they perceive the older generations as having responsibility but this has to do primarily, if not exclusively, with those who governed Greece during the previous four decades. This said, scepticism and rejection of politics and politicians was not unique to Greek young people; it was a main finding in the whole MYPLACE project (Pilkington and Pollock, 2015).

Young people's perceptions of Greek society

Within this climate, respondents were asked and expressed their views about specific issues in Greek society, including: social conflicts and social inequalities; the positive and negative characteristics of Greek society; views about the future and what individuals can do in order to improve the current situation, and the way they think of their own future.

When asked about social conflicts, the majority of young people replied that they could identify a range of different current conflicts in Greek society. Those most frequently mentioned were: political conflicts; conflicts in everyday life; and racial conflicts. They also mentioned class conflicts, intergenerational conflicts and family conflicts. This last point follows on from the discussion in the previous section: that family is not considered responsible for the crisis and conflicts are not created. On the other hand, the lack of intergenerational conflicts is mainly explained by the role the family plays in Greek society historically. As a consequence, even though some young people blame their parents and previous generations for the current crisis, the support that the family provides under these circumstances is very important and potentially works against the formation of generational subjectivities or even conflict.

When they referred to everyday conflicts respondents meant that the years of recession and austerity measures have left people feeling pressurised and this impacted on their everyday relationships. For example, one respondent mentioned that a fight broke out on a bus because someone gave his ticket to another person (Ersi, F, 21), while others mentioned a similar kind of behaviour on public transport (Fokion, M, 21; Evdokia, F, 21; Aris, M, 25). Another respondent mentioned that people are very tense and fight even over a parking spot (Menandros, M, 21). As young people explained, the current crisis has made people unhappy in a way that impacts on their everyday life, and reveals how young people read everyday events through the prism of the crisis.

Racial conflicts noted by respondents were also explained as a consequence of the crisis. As one respondent said:

> *I mean conflicts, to the degree that... I know people, basically kids of my age that are going and beating up foreigners, for no obvious reason, they just hunt them and beat them.*
>
> (Lemonia, F, 18)

This is a very common response to socio-political crises and Greece too has witnessed the growth of public discourse that describes immigrants as thieves, murderers, rapists, and people who steal jobs from the Greek people. This kind of dominant discourse has been very influential over the last few years and has become part of the collective consciousness of large parts of the population, such that the 'other', the foreigner, has become the scapegoat for almost all of the problems that Greek society faces.

When it comes to inequalities due to the crisis, financial inequalities were the dominant response (30). The majority of the respondents mentioned the widening of the gap between the rich and the poor in Greek society. As one of them said, "the rich people are getting richer and the poor are getting poorer" (Thrasyvoulos, M, 21).

Positive and negative views about Greek society

Young people were asked to express their personal views about the positive and negative characteristics of Greek society. Of 41 recorded responses, 28 were negative and 13 positive. The most common answers regarding positive aspects were: solidarity, hospitality, positive attitudes in the face of adversity and Greek history and culture. As some respondents said, "I believe that Greeks are more humanistic compared to other countries" (Erato, F, 22); "The Greek will look after his fellow citizen, when he is in need; he is not individualist, he is not going to look after himself alone, something that is happening for example abroad" (Litsa, F, 19). Of course, solidarity goes hand in hand with hospitality: "Hospitality is one of our basic characteristics from ancient times through to today. Maybe you have nothing to eat, but you will share your bread" (Periklis, M, 21). It is worth mentioning that some respondents (7) could find no positive characteristics to refer to.

However, as noted above, the majority of the characteristics were negative. Most frequently cited were: individualism, conservatism, racism and xenophobia; lack of respect, organisation and cooperation between people, corruption and clientelism. It is critical to underline that the crisis to some extent has influenced young people's opinions about society. For example, as one said:

> *[P]eople don't see that the common good will help them too. They think that if they take care of themselves alone, they will prosper, but the opposite happens and that is why this disaster [the crisis] took place.*
>
> (Loukia, F, 24)

Some others talked about "social cannibalism" (Markos, M, 25) and "individualism without limits" (Thanos, M, 25). A key finding here was that young people seemed to understand and recognise the negative characteristics of society, and this may encourage them to follow a different path in their own lives. It is important to note also that, even though young people mentioned more negative than positive characteristics, they do not perceive social relations exclusively in primary colours. However, some of the positive characteristics seemed to be quite stereotypical and reproduced from generation to generation such as hospitality or history and the country's cultural heritage.

Young Greeks' emigration

As mentioned at the beginning of the chapter, one of the most important issues is that of the emigration of young Greeks to other European or western countries, and this was extensively discussed during the interviews. With the unemployment rate standing at more than 60 per cent in the 15–24 age group, and more than 35 per cent in the 25–34 age group at the peak of the crisis, it was no surprise that many of them thought about leaving the country, not only to study but in order to find a job and thus stay abroad for years. Of course, even though this is a very strong trend, there are also young people who wish to stay in Greece and fight for a better future. As a consequence, respondents' views fell into two main categories: those who wished to stay in Greece (26); and those who wanted to leave (22). Some respondents (7) remained unsure as to whether they wanted to stay or leave. This highlights the pressure young people feel and the difficulty of deciding about their future. Only one respondent talked about internal migration, arguing that young people should leave the big cities and especially Athens and return to the provinces and their villages.

Some declared their wish to stay and fight in Greece: "We are living under a very difficult period but I am not going to leave now, because now my country needs me" (Afroxilanthi, F, 16).

> *The only reason to leave would be if I couldn't manage to have the basics here, to survive, to the major degree. In general, I disagree with abandoning your country for any kind of reason. I disagree with migration, unless you are a migrant for economic reasons.*
>
> (Themistoklis, M, 25)

Some had not contemplated emigration because it was not an option for them (Efi, F, 20) while others said they could not go because their family was here (Rodanthi, F, 16; Ariadni, F, 25). It should be noted that even among those young people who said they wanted to stay in Greece, almost all had thought about and discussed the possibility of leaving for two reasons: to study and then return, or as a last resort if things got so bad that all the doors were closed here and they did not have even the basic necessities for survival. As one of them put it:

> *I want to work here for my country, the country that I love; I was born here, and I want to live the rest of my life here; I like it here very much even with all these difficulties and the austerity.*
>
> (Periklis, M, 21)

This does not mean that those who wished to leave Greece had no hesitation: "Yes, I think of it [leaving] and I have made some first moves, I have sent some CVs; I have taken some steps to move abroad" (Triantafyllos, M, 25). Some of them were thinking of their family, while others said that they like their country but did not see a future in it. However, their main goal was to go abroad for postgraduate studies in the first place and probably to work for some time before deciding whether to come back or stay abroad permanently: "if I can yes, I will stay there for work. I think about it" (Pavlos, M, 23).

Of course, there were those who did not want to stay in Greece for any reason:

> *I think it is very strange those saying that they want to stay here. You are going to destroy your life here, or at least you are going to put in a lot of effort but not achieve what you want. Maybe I am wrong and I am a traitor for doing this [laugh] but I believe that everyone should first try to survive himself and then do some things like every human being and if he manages to stand on his own two feet, then return here, probably stronger, and do many things.*
>
> (Stathis, M, 21)

Another respondent said:

> *I think that every one of us thinks about it. Of course, there is the romantic opinion, some who say that if we all leave what will happen, only the old people will stay. On the other hand, we must be more realistic. I don't think that if you have no future, and a door opens for you abroad, no matter how difficult it would be to stand on your own two feet, to adjust to society, to a different way of life, because what are you going to do here? What are you going to do in Greece? Stay for the sea and the sun? I don't think so.*
>
> (Liakos, M, 19)

As is clear from these responses, any decision to emigrate either for studies and/or for work is not easy. Even among those who seem set to leave, many think that they have something of a moral obligation to stay in Greece not only for the country but also because of their family. The main reason to stay in Greece and fight for a better future is their family, which as we have mentioned earlier is supportive of young people and with which young people maintain strong bonds. Furthermore, not all of those declaring that they were likely to leave were very sure of what they wanted to do in the future and of course not all of them were satisfied that things had turned out this way. Emigration is never easy, and this is something that most young people seemed to understand well. As Knijn and Plantenga (2012: 202–203) argue, it has become evident that it is mainly the younger generations of male and female adults who suffer from the lack of prospects of steady jobs and incomes, as well as the opportunity to start family life, although not to the same degree everywhere. Although no figures are available, many – particularly higher-educated – Italian, Spanish, Portuguese, and Irish young adults declared their intention to emigrate, or have already done so. In sum, many countries of the 'old continent' face serious challenges in offering their young adults a promising future and this is certainly the case for Greece. However, regarding young people's perspectives on the future Brannen and Nilsen (2002: 63) have suggested that some young people view the future as a risk to be calculated and controlled, and perhaps even as a positive challenge, and this is a finding that comes out from our research as well.

Conclusion

In an attempt to sum up the chapter, our first finding is that young people in Greece are indeed living under very different circumstances compared to those of their parents when they were young. Stability and a given future – study and a stable job – was the main pattern for the majority of young people ten years ago. However, after the onset of the crisis the situation changed dramatically and now young people find themselves living under uncertainty and continuous risk. Within such social and economic conditions, young people experience their transition to adult life as a difficult period and their future as very precarious. The only response to this dire situation seems to be emigration to other western societies; and this is a second finding that emerged from our research, since all of our respondents have thought of emigration regardless of their final decision or of their rejection of emigration as a solution to the crisis. This, however, does not imply that it is a desired solution for either those who had decided to leave or those who wished to stay or were unable to leave for various reasons (familial, financial and ideological etc). Current circumstances forced young people in that direction. When discussing whose responsibility the current situation in Greek society was, young people seemed to target the political system, political parties and politicians, because they had failed to create a viable society and provide them with the same opportunities the older generations had benefitted from. Despite their negative views about politics and politicians, though, young people were not apathetic and indifferent. They seemed to have been awakened by the crisis. One final finding is that young people in Greece found shelter in their family which they considered essential, especially under times of crisis. Even though they blamed their parents for supporting and voting for the political parties that had created the current situation, they recognised that the family was their safety net and from our analysis no explicit intergenerational conflicts were found. In a sense, the family was the only stable and safe harbour in a completely unstable situation in which future prospects, both personal and for the country, were unknown if not completely negative. To sum up, it could be argued that the crisis that runs in its seventh year, and its consequences, will influence Greek society for at least a decade into the future, and will have a clear impact on young people's transition from school/university to adult life in respect of labour market opportunities and family formation, and, for many, new migratory pathways.

Notes

1 For example, in 2016 only 6.5 per cent of those studying in Gymnasiums did not continue their studies at the level of the Lyceum. See www.avgi.gr/article/10839/

8019988/to-scholeio-kataphygio-gia-tous-mathetes-sten-krise   [20   July   2017].
Regarding access to university, usually around 50 per cent of the Lyceum students
decide to take the national exams to enter university.

2   Early school leaving declined from 13.7 per cent in 2010 to 6.5 per cent in 2016. For
information on this, see www.avgi.gr/article/10839/8019988/to-scholeio-kataphygio-gia-
tous-mathetes-sten-krise [20 July 2017] (in Greek). For more information regarding
education see https://ec.europa.eu/education/sites/education/files/monitor2016-el_en.pdf
and http://ec.europa.eu/eurostat/statistics-explained/index.php/Europe_2020_indicators_
-_education [20 July 2017].

3   For more information about the project, visit https://myplaceresearch.wordpress.
com/ and www.fp7-myplace.eu/ [20 July 2017].

4   For the specific objectives of the project, see www.fp7-myplace.eu/concept.php [22
July 2017].

5   The selection of the sample was based on the preceding large-scale survey that was
part of the project. During the survey, participants were asked if they would like to
take part in the following qualitative phase in order to discuss further the issues
raised in the questionnaire. All of the participants were from Athens since this was
the region selected for the survey, and more particularly two distinct municipalities
with different socio-political and economic backgrounds. The fieldwork took place
from March 10, 2013 and ended on April 28, 2013. For more information on the
selection strategy of two regions, please see www.fp7-myplace.eu/documents/D5.3%
20Greece.pdf [21 July 2017].

6   Since specific social class information was not available, it is not possible to give
particular numbers. Such information was available only in the preceding survey
but we were not allowed to relate the questionnaires to the interviews because the
first ones were anonymous. However, bearing in mind the social background of
the two selected regions it could be argued that the respondents were from the
lower middle and working class in the one case and from the upper and upper-
middle class in the other. For more details on this particular research, see the full
project report at www.fp7-myplace.eu/documents/D5.3%20Greece.pdf [21 July
2017].

7   All names used are pseudonyms.

8   PASOK is the socialist party and New Democracy the conservative party.

References

Bank of Greece (2012) *Social policy and social cohesion in Greece in conditions of financial crisis*, Athens: Bank of Greece (in Greek).
Bauman, Z. (2000) *Liquid modernity*, Cambridge: Polity Press.
Bauman, Z. (2007) *Liquid times: Living in an age of uncertainty*, Cambridge: Polity Press.
Beck, U. (1992) *Risk society*, London: Sage.
Bell, D. N. and Blanchflower, D. G. (2015) 'Youth unemployment in Greece: measuring the challenge', *IZA Journal of European Labor Studies*, vol. 4, no. 1, pp.1–25.
Brannen, J. and Nilsen, A. (2002) 'Young people's perspectives on the future', in Brannen, J., Lewis, S., Nilsen, A. and Smithson, J. (eds.) *Young Europeans, work and family: Futures in transition*, London: Routledge, pp.48–68.
Coles, B. (1995) *Youth and social policy: Youth citizenship and young careers*, London: UCL Press.
Corijn, M. and Klizjing, E. (eds.) (2001) *Transitions to adulthood in Europe*, Dordrecht: Springer.

Dianeosis (2017) *Cultural factors of financial self-efficiency and entrepreneurship*, Athens. [Online], Available: www.dianeosis.org/wp-content/uploads/2017/07/anergia_neoi_17.7.2017_updated_final.pdf [21 July 2017] (In Greek).

ELSTAT (Hellenic Statistical Authority) (2013a) *Labour force survey – 4th quarter 2012* (press release), Piraeus. [Online], Available: goo.gl/we8H9q [2 May 2017].

ELSTAT (Hellenic Statistical Authority) (2013b) *Labour force survey – 3rd quarter 2013* (press release), Piraeus. [Online], Available: goo.gl/Ns2Ywa [2 May 2017].

ELSTAT (Hellenic Statistical Authority) (2013c) *Statistics on income and living conditions 2012 (Income reference period 2011). Risk of poverty (press release)*, Piraeus. [Online], Available: goo.gl/RVQVqk [2 May 2017].

ELSTAT (Hellenic Statistical Authority) (2017) *Greece in numbers*, Piraeus: ELSTAT (in Greek).

Endeavor Greece (2015) *Creating jobs for young people*, Athens: Endeavor (in Greek).

Erikson, E. H. and Erikson, J. M. (1997) *The life cycle completed*, New York: Norton.

Eurofound (2014) *Mapping youth transitions in Europe*, Luxemburg: Publications Office of the European Union.

EUROSTAT (2017) *Unemployment statistics*. [Online], Available: http://ec.europa.eu/eurostat/statistics-explained/index.php/Unemployment_statistics [2 May 2017].

France, A. (1996) 'Youth and citizenship in the 1990s', *Youth and Policy*, vol. 43, pp.28–43.

France, A. (2007) *Understanding youth in late modernity*, Maidenhead: Open University Press.

Gebel, M. and Heyne, S. (2014) *Transitions to adulthood in the Middle East and North Africa: Young women's rising?*, Basingstoke: Palgrave Macmillan.

George, K. L. (1993) 'Sociological perspectives on life transitions', *Annual Review of Sociology*, vol. 19, pp.353–373.

Goldscheider, F. and Goldscheider, C. (1999) *The changing transition to adulthood: Leaving and returning home*, Thousand Oaks, CA: Sage.

Grawitz, M. (2001) *Les méthodes des sciences sociales*, Paris: Editions Dalloz.

Guest, G. (2012) *Applied thematic analysis*, Thousand Oaks, CA: Sage.

Hauben, H., Coucheir, M., Spooren, I., McAnaney, D. and Delfosse, C. (2012) *Assessing the impact of European governments' austerity plans on the rights of people with disabilities*, European Report, European Foundation Centre. [Online], Available: www.enil.eu/wp-content/uploads/2012/12/Austerity-European-Report_FINAL.pdf [2 May 2017].

Holdsworth, C. and Morgan, D. (2005) *Transitions in context: Leaving home, independence and adulthood*, Buckingham: Open University Press.

Hutson, S. and Jenkins, R. (1989) *Taking the strain: Families, unemployment and the transition to adulthood*, Milton Keynes: Open University Press.

INE-GSEE (2011) *Greek economy and employment: Annual report 2011*, Athens: INE-GSEE (in Greek).

INE-GSEE (2017) *Greek economy and employment: Annual report 2017*, Athens: INE-GSEE (in Greek).

Ioannou, T. (2014) 'Most young Greeks still living with mom and dad', *Times of Change*, 27 January 2014 (in Greek).

Jones, G. and Wallace, C. (1992) *Youth, family and citizenship*, Buckingham: Open University Press.

Jorgensen, M. and Phillips, L. J. (2002) *Discourse analysis as theory and method*, London: Sage.

KANEP/GSEE (2017) *Basic numbers of the Greek education*, Part B, Athens: Centre for the Development of Educational Policies/General Secretariat of Greek Workers (in Greek).

Knijn, T. and Plantenga, J. (2012) 'Conclusions: Transitions to adulthood, social policies and new social risks for young adults', in Knijn, T. (ed.) *Work, family policies and transitions to adulthood in Europe*, Basingstoke: Palgrave Macmillan, pp.202–215.

Kraatz, S. (2015) 'Youth unemployment in Greece: Situation before the government change', Brussels: European Union. [Online] Available: www.europarl.europa.eu/ RegData/etudes/BRIE/2015/542220/IPOL_BRI%282015%29542220_EN.pdf [21 July 2017].

Labrianidis, L. (2011) *Investing in leaving: The leak of scientists from Greece in the era of globalisation*, Athens: Kritiki (in Greek).

Labrianidis, L. and Pratsinakis, M. (2016) *Greece's new emigration at times of crisis*, London: The Hellenic Observatory of LSE.

Labrianidis, L. and Sykas, Th. (2017) 'Why high school students aspire to emigrate: Evidence from Greece', *Journal of International Migration and Integration*, vol. 18, no. 1, pp.107–130.

Lloyd, B. C. (ed.) (2005) *Growing up global: The changing transitions to adulthood in developing countries*, Washington DC: National Academies Press.

Maingueneau, D. (1991) *L'analyse du discours*, Paris: Hachette Supérieur.

Malkoutzis, N. (2011), *Young Greeks and the crisis: The danger of losing a generation*, Athens: Friedrich Ebert Stiftung. [Online], Available: http://library.fes.de/pdf-files/id/ ipa/08465.pdf [2 May 2017].

Marvakis, A., Anastasiadou, M., Petritsi, I. and Anagnostopoulou, T. (2013) *Youth shows the way – but whither? Youth and extreme right in Greece*. Athens: Friedrich Ebert Stiftung. [Online], Available: www.academia.edu/4152314/Youth_and_Right_ Extremism_in_Greece [2 May 2017].

Müller, W. and Gangl, M. (eds.) (2003) *Transitions from education to work in Europe: The integration of youth into EU labour markets*, Oxford: Oxford University Press.

Narotzky, S. and Besnier, N. (2014) 'Crisis, value, and hope: Rethinking the economy', *Current Anthropology*, vol. 55, no. S9, pp.S4–S16.

Osgood, D. W., Foster, E. M., Flanagan, C. and Ruth, R. G. (eds.) (2005) *On your own without a net: The transition to adulthood for vulnerable populations*, Chicago: The University of Chicago Press.

Petmesidou, M., (2013), *Austerity and the spectre of 'immiseration' on the periphery of Europe*, CROP Poverty Brief, CROP, August 2013. [Online], Available: www.crop. org/viewfile.aspx?id=479 [2 May 2017].

Pilkington, H. and Pollock, G. (2015) *Radical futures? Youth, politics and activism in contemporary Europe*, Chichester: Wiley-Blackwell.

Snee, H. and Devine, F. (2015) 'Young people's transitions to employment: Making choices, negotiating constraints', in Wyn, J. and Cahill, H. (eds.) *Handbook of children and youth studies*, Singapore: Springer, pp.543–555.

Stein, M. and Munro, R. E. (eds.) (2008) *Young people's transitions from care to adulthood: International research and practice*, London and Philadelphia: Jessica Kingsley Publishers.

Tsekeris, Ch. (2015) *Young people's perception of economic crisis in Greece: A social psychological pilot study*, Athens: ELIAMEP.

UNICEF (2017) *The state of the children in Greece Report 2017: The children of the crisis*, Athens: Hellenic National Committee for UNICEF.

Wyn, J. and White, R. (1997) *Rethinking youth*, London: Sage.

10 Kinship, community and the transition to adulthood

Geographical differences and recent changes in European society

Patrick Heady

Introduction

Family ties play a central role in the transition to adulthood. In fact, they play two distinct roles: as part of the process, and as part of the outcome. During the process of transition, young people's families of origin offer influence and practical support. And a successful outcome to the transition process almost always includes the establishment of the young person's own family of reproduction. However, although both these aspects of the familial transition to adulthood are virtually universal, the way in which they are carried out varies greatly between different parts of Europe, and has also changed over time. These variations have been intensively studied in several different disciplines, including sociology, demography, history and anthropology – generating a literature that both describes the differences and tries to explain them.

In this chapter I will summarise the main geographical differences, and some of the explanations that have been proposed – looking particularly at possible connections with economic life and the operation of different welfare-state systems. At the same time, I will raise what seems to me to be a fundamental question: Can the different patterns of familial transition be seen simply as pragmatic responses by young people and their close relatives to an exogenous system of economic and institutional constraints? Or does an additional dimension need to be taken into account: namely, the ways in which individuals when making their personal transitions are simultaneously renewing, or transforming, the communities in which they live? If this dimension is important, we will need to look explicitly at processes of community building, and at the influence of the wider community on the choices made by young people and their families.

The structure of this chapter is as follows. The first section presents basic statistics on geographical variation, covering the extent of parental support and young people's success in setting up their own families of reproduction. It defends the validity of treating sub-replacement fertility as an indication of failure in this respect. The following section asks whether the current geographic distributions of fertility and parental support can be explained by the pragmatic responses of individuals and their immediate families to exogenous constraints – and concludes that, on the basis of the data considered so far, they can.

However, the third section complicates the picture by presenting additional data on partner choice, the spatial structure of kinship networks, and on gender roles – and by relating all the variables to urban-rural differences. This suggests an alternative explanation of residential patterns, and of below-replacement fertility, as responses to the historic move from agricultural to urban systems of economic subsistence. The analysis developed in the fourth section shows that neither residential nor fertility patterns can be entirely explained as the outcome of pragmatic decision-making by individuals and their immediate families.

In response to this, the fifth and sixth sections develop an alternative analysis, which views residence and marriage choices as means of affirming collective relationships – involving practical cooperation and the social control of reproduction.[1] Theoretically, the key idea is an anthropological notion of kinship as a structural framework which draws on descent and marriage ties to integrate families into encompassing communities. In terms of data, the section draws on an ethnographic account of the use of residential and marriage ties to construct a sense of local community.

A short concluding discussion attempts to draw the threads together, placing them in the context of the book as a whole.

The basic statistical picture

Family ties in the transition to adulthood

In 2008, the year of the worldwide economic crisis, Eurostat (the European Statistical Office) issued a publication entitled *The Life of Women and Men in Europe* – describing different phases of the life-cycle and the transitions between them, on the basis of official statistics for most European countries. Table 10.1, which is based on data from that publication, provides information on a central aspect of the transition to adulthood: the act of leaving the parental home.[2]

There is a gendered difference: in all countries women leave home earlier than men. However, just as striking is the difference between the major European regions. Looking at the figures for 25 to 29 year olds we see that, taking the 'northwestern' and 'central' regions together, around 25 per cent of 25- to 29-year-old men are still living with their parents – while the comparable figure for the southern and eastern macro-regions is about 65 per cent. The same picture emerges when these facts are looked at from the parental point of view. SHARE, a comparative study of the life course of elderly people in northwest, central and southern Europe, shows that the proportion of over-50s who are living with an adult child is highest in Mediterranean countries and lowest in Scandinavia (Kohli et al. 2010). Similar findings are produced by the ISSP (International Social Survey Programme, cited by Murphy

Table 10.1 Percentages of young adults living with their parents in 2005

Region	Country	Age Group			
		18–24		*25–29*	
		Women	*Men*	*Women*	*Men*
Northwest	Denmark	33	48	2	5
	Netherlands	55	75	8	20
	United Kingdom	50	67	14	24
Central	France	56	70	11	23
	Germany	56	72	12	25
	Austria	63	77	20	38
South	Spain	81	90	49	62
	Italy	90	94	53	71
	Greece	68	76	47	68
East	Croatia	84	95	43	82
	Czech Republic	78	87	31	52
	Poland	–	–	–	–
	Romania	74	91	31	60

Source: Eurostat (2008) Statistical Annex: Table A9

(2008)) – which also include Russia, and shows that the Russian figures are very similar to other parts of eastern Europe.

Figure 10.1 provides complementary findings from another source, which I will refer to a number of times in this chapter. The data are derived from kinship network interviews carried out between 2005 and 2007 in different parts of Europe – as part of the KASS (Kinship and Social Security) study.[3] 570 interviews were carried out altogether – an average of 30 in each of 19 local field sites – with two or three sites (always including at least one rural and one area) in each of eight different countries. Although the field sites were not statistically representative of the countries concerned, the samples for interview were representative of the local field sites – and the data on inter-generational co-residence is broadly consistent with the macro-regional patterns described in the previous paragraph (Heady & Kohli 2010; Heady & Schweitzer 2010). For this reason we can use the additional data about kinship networks, collected during the KASS interviews, to add an extra dimension to our picture of European kinship.

Figure 10.1 shows that the macro-regional differences are not just a matter of the age at which young adults leave home. In some cases young couples continue to live with the parents of one of the partners – so that, when they have their own children the household contains three generations of the same family. These multi-generational families are most common in southern and

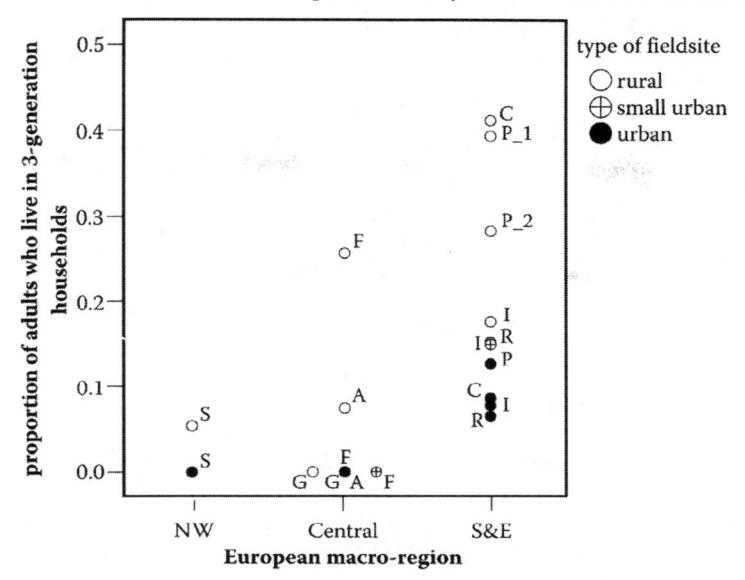

Figure 10.1 Intergenerational co-residence by European macro-region and area type
Icon labels: A Austria; C Croatia; F France; G Germany; I Italy; P Poland; R Russia; S Sweden.
Source: KASS network interviews

eastern Europe – the same regions in which young adults generally stay longest in the parental home. (Figure 10.1 also shows that multi-generational households are most common in rural areas – and in fact they are particularly characteristic of families who are involved in farming. I will return to this point later on).

A second finding that emerges from the KASS interviews is that the co-residence of parents and adult children (whether or not the latter have children of their own) implies particularly intense forms of intergenerational exchange. This involves both domestic work and, implicitly, financial subsidies. Table 10.2 shows that a substantial proportion of young adults who lived with their parents were effectively living rent-free. It is likely that they also received implicit subsidies for their food and perhaps other expenses.

Birth rates

The next set of results refer to the final stage of the transition to adulthood: the establishment of one's own family of reproduction. In what follows, I will treat birth rates (specifically the achievement of replacement-level fertility) as an indicator of success. In doing so I am not arguing that replacement-level fertility is necessarily a good thing: in an over-populated planet, there is a good deal to be said for birth rates that permit a gradual

Table 10.2 Proportion of individuals who made no contribution to household expenses of ego's household by number of adult generations in the household, age group, and sex.

	Male			*Female*		
Age group	20–44	45–64	65+	20–44	45–64	65+
1 generation: proportion of non-contributors	*4%*	*3%*	*0%*	*8%*	*6%*	*4%*
N	63	40	31	73	34	27
2 or more generations: proportion of non-contributors	*34%*	*4%*	*9%*	*58%*	*18%*	*5%*
N	90	70	18	74	78	28

Source: KASS network interviews

Base: people aged 20 or over living in ego's household – restricted to households with at least one man and one woman, and with adequate information on contributions to household expenses.

reduction in current population levels. What I *am* arguing is that below-replacement fertility is an indication that parents have failed to attain their own reproductive objectives.

This contradicts an alternative view – advocated particularly by Lesthaeghe – that the low levels of fertility currently experienced in most European countries reflect a change in cultural values brought on by educational and economic change, which has led an increasing number of people to prefer a single child or to opt out of parenthood altogether (Lesthaeghe 1995; Surkyn & Lesthaeghe 2004). There certainly have been cultural changes in recent decades (Grandits 2010b; Sobotka 2008), but nevertheless there is an obstinate fact that undermines Lesthaeghe's argument. This is the fact that, when asked to state their preferred number of children, potential parents in nearly all European countries continue on average to opt for target family sizes of at least two children (Sobotka & Beaujouan 2014). So below-replacement fertility is an indication that parents and would-be parents are missing their own targets.

The figures in Table 10.3 – taken from the same Eurostat volume that was cited earlier – suggest that this was indeed happening, even before the financial crisis of 2008. Looking at the figures for the year 2005, in the final column of Table 10.3, we see that birth rates in all parts of Europe were below the two-child ideal – but that the problem was least severe in northwest Europe and in France. The birth rates in southern and eastern Europe varied between 1.2 and 1.4 children per woman.

A slight qualification is in order here. The birth rates presented in Table 10.3 are Total Fertility Rates (TFRs for short) which are in fact estimates – representing the average number of children that women *would* have over their

Table 10.3 Fertility rates per woman of child-bearing age

Region	Country	Total Fertility Rate (TFR)	
		1990	*2005*
Northwest	Denmark	1.7	1.8
	Netherlands	1.6	1.7
	United Kingdom	1.8	1.8
Central	France	1.8	1.9
	Germany	1.5	1.4
	Austria	1.5	1.4
South	Spain	1.4	1.3
	Italy	1.3	1.3
	Greece	1.4	1.3
East	Croatia	1.7	1.4
	Czech Republic	1.9	1.3
	Poland	2.0	1.2
	Romania	1.8	1.3

Source: Eurostat (2008) Statistical Annex: Table A8

life-time, if the age-specific fertility levels observed in the year concerned continued to apply. The TFR values for particular years can be influenced by a number of factors – including changes in the timing of births – which may not affect women's life-time fertility levels. However, by 2005 the low TFRs had persisted for too long to be explained by effects of this kind. A comparison with the figures for 1990 (in the first column of Table 10.3) shows that the low TFRs in Germany, Austria and southern Europe had persisted more or less unchanged for at least a decade and a half. By 2005 the only plausible interpretation was that average life-time fertility had also fallen well below replacement level.

This point is confirmed by Figure 10.2, which presents national figures for the eight countries covered by the KASS project.[4] It compares the TFR in 2005 with the life-time fertility of the cohort of women (born in 1965) who reached the age of 40 in that year. As noted already, the TFR was below replacement level in all eight countries (though only marginally so in France and Sweden). The key point is that completed life-time fertility in Italy, Austria, Germany and Russia had also fallen far below replacement level. This had not yet happened in Croatia and Poland – but it is worth noting that, in those countries, many of the births to the 1965 cohort of mothers would have occurred before the sharp falls in TFRs following the collapse of communism. By 2005, TFRs had been very low for a decade or more – and it was likely that they too would ultimately lead to life-time fertility rates that were well below replacement level.

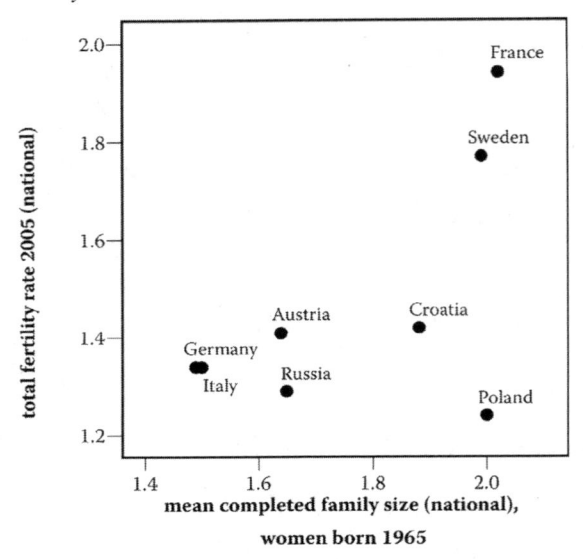

Figure 10.2 Total national fertility rate (2005) by mean completed family size (women born in 1965)

Overview

So the overall situation just before the onset of the financial crisis was that in France and northwestern Europe, young adults were relatively independent of their own parents, and, as parents themselves, were averaging nearly two children per family. In southern and eastern Europe, where the residential break with the family of origin occurred later and less completely, fertility levels were well below the desired level of two children per family. The following sections will consider possible explanations for this geographic pattern.

A pragmatic explanation: levels of assistance from the welfare state

One possibility is that both the shortfalls in fertility, and the differing levels of support from close relatives, are responses to varying levels of assistance from the welfare state. The argument runs as follows.

A fundamental practical constraint is that young people must found their families of reproduction in the first part of their adult lives. Although the maternal age at first birth varies a good deal, there are biological limits – and most births must take place between the mothers' 20th and 35th birthdays. This means that the material capital of reproduction – notably a home and a secure income – must also be secured early in adult life. Housing in particular is not cheap, and it is very unlikely that parents-to-be could save enough money to pay the full purchase cost of their own home before the first child arrives. This in turn means that the young couple must receive help from somewhere: perhaps from their parents (in the form of accommodation in the parental home, or by receiving a house as a parental gift, or by financial support with house-purchase); perhaps from the market (in the form of rented accommodation, or commercial loans for home purchase); or finally from public authorities (in the form of rented accommodation, financial support to young families, or publically provided childcare that enables the mother to continue earning).

Given this overall constraint, different levels of assistance from the welfare state (and different degrees of access to housing finance) could have a double impact. A shortfall in support from public institutions could increase the need for support from the couple's own families of origin – delaying the departure from the parental home. And if the increase in support from their own families only partially compensated for the lack of public support, the shortfall could also reduce the total resources available to the young couple – reducing the number of children they could afford to raise. This would be consistent with the tendency for low fertility to occur in countries where departure from the parental home is also delayed until a comparatively late age.

It would also fit what is known about different welfare-state systems. Here we have to be a bit cautious, because there is no single agreed measure of the young-parent-friendliness of different welfare systems. However, it is generally agreed that, in western Europe, support for young parents is highest in Scandinavia and in France, and lowest in Mediterranean countries (Esping-Andersen 1990; Naldini 2003). It is also well known that state welfare provision in the former eastern bloc was radically reduced following the fall of communism. So in broad terms at least, both the variation in residence patterns and the variation in birth rates, recorded by Eurostat for the year 2005, could be explained by differing levels of public institutional support.

This is a powerful argument, but it is not universally accepted[5] – and even if correct it may only be part of the picture. The next section will provide additional statistical material on which to base a different interpretation of the relationships between fertility and residence patterns during the transition to adulthood.

An enhanced statistical picture

This section presents additional data on the transition to residential adulthood – including partner choice, the spatial structure of kinship networks, and gender roles. It also relates all the variables, including fertility levels, to differences between urban and rural environments.

To start with, let's look at the residential side of things. As we have already seen, Figure 10.1 shows that multi-generational households are most common in rural areas. This urban-rural difference applies in all parts of the continent. But the absolute levels of intergenerational co-residence, in both the countryside and the towns, are highest in the south and east. Interestingly enough, the same geographic pattern applies to several other aspects of the transition to residential adulthood – both to the processes involved and to the outcome.

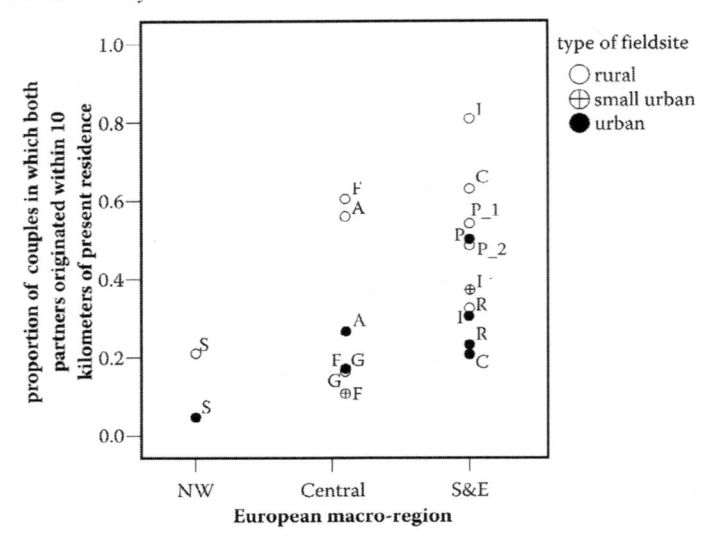

Figure 10.3 Spatial endogamy (local marriages and partnerships) by macro-region and area type
Icon labels: A Austria; C Croatia; F France; G Germany; I Italy; P Poland; R Russia; S Sweden
Source: KASS network interviews

Figure 10.3 refers to an important aspect of the transition process – namely, the choice of marriage partners. It shows that in rural areas – and also in southern and eastern Europe – people are more likely to choose partners whose families of origin live near their own. Taken together, these residential and marriage choices have an additional consequence which is illustrated in Figure 10.4, namely that kinship networks tend to cluster together physically. In fact, the extent of kinship clustering illustrates the underlying geographic patterns particularly clearly. Kinship networks are most clustered in rural areas and in southern and eastern Europe. Relatives are least likely to stick together in northwest and central Europe, and in towns and cities.

There is one other residential variable that follows a similar geographic pattern: the division of labour between men and women within the household. As Figure 10.5 shows, the division of domestic labour is strongly correlated with spatial clustering (Pearson's $r = .71$), and is sharpest in rural areas.

However, in the case of birth rates there is a different geographic pattern. Figure 10.6 is based on official population statistics for the local administrative districts in which the 19 KASS field sites were situated – and uses the ratio of children to young adults to provide approximate estimates of local fertility rates. Urban birth rates are lower than in rural areas – but urban and rural fertility also follow different macro-regional patterns. Rural birth rates are close to replacement level in nearly all the KASS field sites – showing little macro-regional variation. But urban birth rates vary

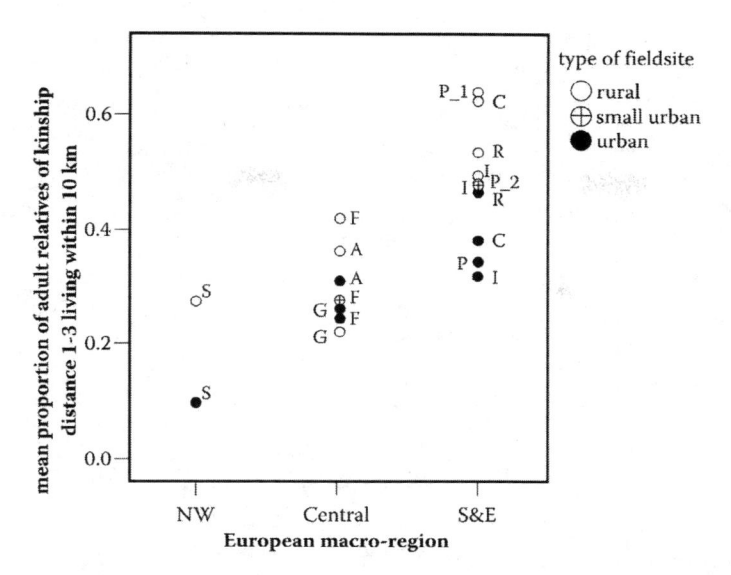

Figure 10.4 Spatial clustering of relatives by European macro-region and area type
Icon labels: A Austria; C Croatia; F France; G Germany; I Italy; P Poland; R Russia;
S Sweden
Source: KASS network interviews

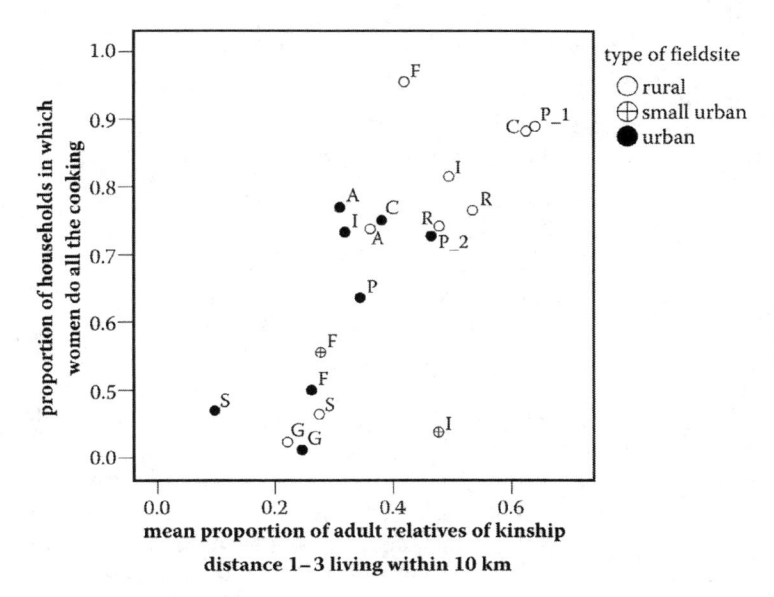

Figure 10.5 Gendering of domestic tasks by spatial clustering of relatives
Icon labels: A Austria; C Croatia; F France; G Germany; I Italy; P Poland; R Russia;
S Sweden
Source: KASS network interviews

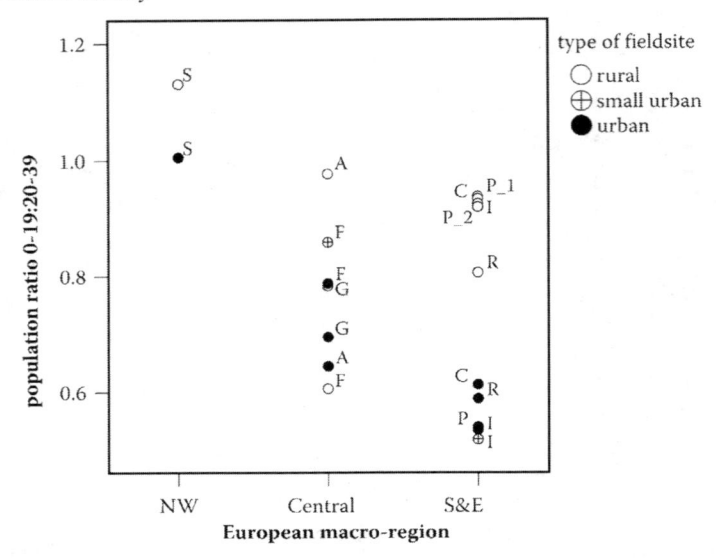

Figure 10.6 Ratio of children to young adults, by European macro-region and area
type
Icon labels: A Austria; C Croatia; F France; G Germany; I Italy; P Poland; R Russia;
S Sweden
Source: Official population statistics for KASS field site areas

dramatically – and are lowest in the south and east, where residential and
marriage ties are closest.

A circumstantial explanation: the move from farming to urban life

Over the last two centuries, all European societies have moved from a situation in which most people worked on farms, to a more diversified economic
structure in which only small proportions of the working population are still
employed in agriculture. This economic shift out of agriculture has been
accompanied by a spatial movement from the countryside to towns and other
urban areas. The shift took place earliest in northwest and central Europe,
where it was largely complete by the middle of the twentieth century. However, in most Mediterranean countries and in eastern Europe, almost half the
population was still occupied in agriculture in 1950. All of these countries
experienced a massive shift from agriculture to urban life in the latter half of
the twentieth century (Gruber & Heady 2010) – so in southern and eastern
Europe this shift was still a living memory in the years leading up to the
financial crisis of 2008.

Might this difference in recent historical experience help to explain the
macro-regional differences in the transition to residential and reproductive
adulthood discussed above? And, if so, could the explanation be framed in
terms of pragmatic decision-making by individuals and their families?

Residential patterns

Let's start by looking at residential patterns: meaning by this the two transition-process variables, intergenerational co-residence and partner choice – and the two outcome variables, spatial clustering and gender roles within the household.

The urban-rural differences do seem to make pragmatic sense. In the case of co-residence and partner choice, a more detailed investigation of the data shows that the two "close" options – continuing to live in the parental household, and choosing a partner from the same area – were particularly common in farming families. Both these transition choices make good practical sense, since farm land is often passed on by inheritance – and farming families often draw on practical help from relatives and neighbours. The more scattered pattern of family connections in urban areas (and among rural non-farmers) would have the advantage of allowing them to move in pursuit of employment opportunities. The comparative rarity of three-generation families in urban areas may also reflect the character of the urban housing stock.[6]

The association between spatial clustering and the gendered division of labour also makes a kind of sense – since it is easier for women to take exclusive responsibility for cooking, or other domestic tasks, if they can draw on help from female relatives living in the same household or nearby. Conversely, given that families in urban areas tend to be more scattered, a greater readiness for men to take on domestic tasks would make practical sense – and that is confirmed by the data in Figure 10.5, though the difference between urban and rural areas in the same country is often rather slight.

Overall, it looks as though the urban-rural differences can be explained in terms of the pragmatic actions of individuals and their families – though, as we will see later, that need not mean that they have to be explained entirely in this way.

What about the macro-regional effects? The fact that the overall residential pattern is most urban-looking in the countries that urbanised first, and most rural-looking in those where large-scale involvement in agriculture persisted until recently, suggests that the macro-regional differences reflect the length of time the societies concerned have had to adapt to urban conditions. Does that mean that the national differences can also be explained in pragmatic terms?

This might be possible – but there are two difficulties. Firstly, the fact that the three distinct variables – co-residence, marriage-choice, and gender roles – always move together suggests that we may be dealing with a single cultural complex, rather than with separable pragmatic motives. Secondly, the delay itself poses a problem. If behaviour is simply a response to externally given conditions, shouldn't the adaptation to urban circumstances be virtually instantaneous? Unless the delay is due to institutional rigidities – welfare state or market institutions that are still adapted to more rural conditions – it could suggest that ordinary people have a continuing cultural attachment to the rural residence complex. Some implications of this point will emerge when we consider the changes in fertility patterns.

Fertility patterns

Might the recent move from agriculture to an industrial and service economy also explain the very low fertility levels in southern and eastern Europe? There are several pragmatic reasons why it might lead to a fall in fertility, including the increased cost of child rearing due to the need to invest in educational capital, and the extra opportunity-cost of motherhood due to the availability of increased employment opportunities for women in the modern economy (Caldwell 1980, 2005; Becker 1993). However, these costs apply in all of Europe's modern economies – so they do not explain the particularly low fertility levels in southern and eastern Europe.

Another possibility is that these exceptionally low fertility levels result from delays in the adaptation of institutional arrangements and family behaviour to the new urban conditions. This might mean that in southern and eastern Europe, people are attempting to deal with the realities of a modern urban economy while still equipped with attitudes and institutions that are more adapted to the rural past.

The low support for young parents in Mediterranean welfare states could be one example of this. There would have been little need for such support in rural environments where families clustered together and help was available from relatives – either in the same household or living close by. But the move, with urbanisation, to a slightly less clustered pattern of family ties would have the effect of lessening the availability of family-based support. If welfare-state support did not increase sufficiently to compensate for this, then the increased overall cost of parenting might lead to a declining birth rate.

A similar effect might occur if the rigid gender roles, formerly characteristic of rural life, persisted in the new urban environment – with its increased availability of employment opportunities for women and reduced levels of support from family networks. In these circumstances the opportunity costs of motherhood would be particularly high – providing another reason for fertility to fall below the levels in the longer-established urban economies of northwest Europe (McDonald 2000).

Though both explanations would be consistent with the distribution of urban birth rates shown in Figure 10.6 – only the first can be explained as the result of purely pragmatic action. In the case of the gendered division of labour, it would obviously make pragmatic sense if young urban couples who wished for two children redistributed the household tasks, so that the husband took on more of the load. The continuing influence of earlier gender patterns suggests that something more than family-level pragmatism is involved.

Social influence on fertility

Confirmation that more than family-level pragmatism is involved comes from some remarkable ethnographic and historical studies of ways in which women influence each other's fertility decisions. Krause (2005) carried out anthropological research in central Italy in the 1990s, at the time when she herself was a young mother. She records the pressure that she experienced to meet approved standards of childcare – in terms of both time committed and material living standards. This happened both directly – receiving friendly 'advice' from a neighbour about ensuring that her daughter's clothes were clean – and indirectly when groups of friends criticised the performance of other young mothers who happened not to be with them at the time.

In an oral history study of child-bearing in the Ukrainian city of Kharkiv in the mid-twentieth century – at a time when fertility there was far below replacement level – Hilevych (2016) obtained accounts of how female work mates would help each other to obtain abortions. This help – which was generally sought by women who already had one child – was not unbiased. It was often combined with advice that the woman should have an abortion – in order to be able to look after the child which she already had, and to maintain the living standards of her family.

In both these cases, it is clear that decisions about fertility are not the business of the family alone but also reflect a degree of community control. This raises the question of how the community is constituted – and that in turn requires a new approach to the statistical data on the transition to residential adulthood.

Community building and the transition to residential adulthood

In statistical terms, the new approach involves a change in the implicit causal order. Instead of treating the different levels of spatial clustering, shown in Figure 10.4, as mere by-products of residential and marriage choices, the different spatial patterns are assumed to be the results which the other elements of the residential transition are intended to achieve – because they constitute the framework for different, and contrasting, systems of community relationships. In this context, the differences in gender roles also take on a new meaning.

Theoretically, the key to this approach is a kind of conceptual re-focussing, away from the sociological notion of 'family', which centres on the conjugal pair, and onto the anthropological notion of 'kinship' – which is concerned with the ways in which the basic ties of parenthood and marriage partnership can be used to constitute ongoing social units, and to connect them into an encompassing community. Two classic statements of kinship theory (Murdock 1949; Lévi-Strauss 1969 [1949]) assign a central role to the transition to adulthood – emphasising the very themes discussed above: post-marital residence, the choice of marriage partner, and the different roles of men and women.

The underlying idea of classical kinship theory is that ties between parents and adult children constitute descent groups, while marriages between members of different descent groups connect the groups concerned into a single encompassing community. Descent relationships tend to be expressed by residential closeness, and are most commonly traced through men. Lévi-Strauss famously argued that marriage is typically thought of as the gift of a woman from one male descent group to another. An implication of this is that women are, in some sense at least, the property of men. While this account is over-simplified, something like it does apply in many parts of the world.

To be clear, I am not saying that the sociological view is wrong, or that the Lévi-Straussian model applies exactly to any European society. But what I am suggesting is that societies in northwestern Europe place more stress on the separate existence of distinct conjugal families, while some aspects of Lévi-Strauss's analysis can help us to understand the implications of kinship and community ties in much of southern and eastern Europe.

To give an idea of the differences between the two systems, I will briefly recount some of my own impressions – as someone who, having been raised in the conjugal family system of middle-class north London, chose to study a rather different system of family and community relationships in northern Italy.

Ethnography

Between 1989 and 1991 I carried out PhD fieldwork in Carnia, an alpine region near Italy's border with Austria (Heady 1999). In the valley where I worked, people lived in small villages, and agriculture (supplemented by sea-sonal emigration) had been an important part of most families' livelihood until the early 1970s. Since then, rising living standards in Italy generally had meant that local agriculture in the rather difficult mountain terrain was no longer economically attractive – and most men now worked as employees in construction, forestry, local factories or non-manual occupations (women's employment levels were a good deal lower). People remembered the agricultural days as a time of cooperation, both between families and by each village as a whole – but also as a time of intense rivalries and quarrels. People used to marry locally. To take the example of Ovasta (a community of 175 people on which I focused particularly), in just over half of the couples who had married before 1960 both the husband and the wife originated in Ovasta itself. By the time I got there it was no longer usual to marry someone from the same village, but kinship ties between fellow villagers were still very dense: everyone living in Ovasta in 1991 was either born into an Ovastan family, or was married to someone who was. People lived in large houses, often divided into separate flats – and in several cases three generations of the same family occupied a single building, though usually in separate flats.

Ovasta clearly fits the pattern of intergenerational co-residence and locally concentrated marriage ties, characteristic of southern Europe. In what ways might it also approximate a Lévi-Straussian system?

One of first things that impressed me as different from what I was used to back in London was that the local word for house, *cjasa*, was also used to refer to the family. Houses had names, not chosen by the residents, but bestowed informally by the local community – and these names were also used to refer to the family who lived there. Some *cjasa*-names referred to individuals, but these were never the present occupants – instead, the houses were named after notable ancestors a couple of generations back. Until recently, houses had been inherited almost exclusively by sons. So it seems that for local people a patrilineal family was implicitly linked to a specific house, in an ongoing relationship with other house-families within the village community.

By bringing his wife to live in this parental house, the son assured the physical continuity of his own patrilineal family – but also, in many cases, affirmed its connections to the village as a whole. The unifying role of marriage ties was expressed in a village ritual that took place during the winter months. The exact date varied from village to village – but 31st December, and *Epifania* ('Twelfth Night') were popular choices. The ritual involved young unmarried men (sometimes young women and children as well) visiting every house in the village (where they received food, drink and small money payments) and then at dusk lighting a bonfire on the slope above the village, at which they lit wooden disks which were thrown down towards the village – accompanied by a shouted dedication to a supposedly courting couple, and with a witty comment which could be friendly but might also be critical of the individuals concerned.

This representation of social unity built on future marriage ties, under the leadership of men, can be seen as an application of the basic Lévi-Straussian framework to the circumstances of European village life (Heady 2003). Consistent with the standard Lévi-Straussian set-up, older people said that the young men had thought of the village girls as their property. One way this was expressed was by the young men collecting a (fairly small) bride-price from the husband-to-be when one of 'their' girls married a young man from another village, and another was the occasional use of threats to discourage outside suitors. The subordinate status of women was also expressed in the pattern of domestic labour. Houses were definitely places in which women looked after men – and people explained that male house ownership implied authority over women and children.

The winter courtship celebration was valued by villagers of all ages, but I was told that there were several villages in which it had been temporarily abandoned. This occurred around 1970, at the same time as villagers were cutting back on agriculture and ceasing to choose marriage partners from their own village. If we think back to the time before 1970, we can see that this complex of implicit ideas about families, houses and community – together with the village ritual of courtship – fits in well with the actual patterns of residence and marriage, as well as with the reality of a farming-based economic system that also called for village cooperation. All the elements of the transition to adulthood presented in the earlier statistical analyses played their part in constituting and renewing the cooperative local community. That did not mean, however, that it was capable of entirely over-riding practical economic motives. When the local economy changed – effectively ending the need for agricultural cooperation – so did the marriage pattern, and the commitment to the ritual that expressed it was also weakened.

Ethnographic findings and macro-regional systems

Of course, the conclusions of a single ethnography cannot simply be extrapolated to an entire European region. However, it is worth noting that young people's rituals resembling the one described here have been reported in village communities right along the southern European mountain chain from Iberia to Romania (Heady 2003). The verbal equivalence of house and family is not unique to the Carnian dialect, as can be seen by checking the words *casa* and *casato* in a good Italian dictionary. The stem *casa* also appears in *accasare*, one of the Italian words for 'to marry', as it does in Spanish and Romanian – implicitly suggesting that marriage is also a matter of establishing a spatial location.

The decline of agricultural employment coincided with a loosening of kinship ties in other parts of Italy as well. One form this took was a sharp decline, during the second half of the twentieth century, in the proportion of young couples who started married life in one of their parental home. However, as in Carnia, this was a loosening rather than an abandonment of local kinship ties. The decline of actual co-residence was matched by an almost equal rise in the frequency of close residence – in which the young couple established a separate home near to one of their parental homes. (Colclough et al. 2010; Viazzo & Zanotelli 2010).

Even this somewhat loosened system of local kinship ties formed a sharp contrast to the transition to residential adulthood as I and my friends had experienced it in north London about 20 years before. There was a very clear expectation that once we had completed our education young people would leave home. In general, we wanted to do so – but if for any reason we delayed, we experienced distinct parental pressure to go. Although my own residential transition is now quite distant in time, this social stress on individual autonomy is consistent with the Eurostat figures for 2005 displayed in Table 10.1. As the KASS network findings show, early departure from the parental home is correlated with geographic mobility, and forms part of a transition system that tends to generate delocalised networks of independent conjugal families.

There is, however, one way in which the Carnian and north London systems resemble each other. In neither case is the transition to residential adulthood simply a response to externally given economic constraints. In both cases it is largely, though not entirely, shaped by social norms. In Carnia these were overtly intended to perpetuate a highly valued system of local social ties. In London the overt goal was simply independence – but a consequence, intended or not, was to rule out the kind of kin-based local solidarity characteristic of much of southern and eastern Europe.[7]

Communities as regimes[8] of reproductive control

In geographically immobile communities, parents find themselves in competition for their children's future access to local resources – in terms of both material subsistence and social status. This is an issue for any kin-based local community, but the problem is particularly severe for farming communities which need to maintain a balance between population and land – and it used to be sharpest of all in mountain areas where usable land was scarce (Viazzo 1989). In these areas the local community had to impose some form of reproductive control.

In some alpine communities – particularly in the eighteenth and nineteenth centuries – this was achieved by legal rules that imposed a property qualification for marriage (Lanzinger 2003). But rules of this kind were probably a reaction to incipient economic change – and merely formalised a previous system of informal control. Informal pressures of this kind, in which local public opinion monitors both the economic status and the respectability of every family, have been reported in many ethnographic studies of kin-based local communities in southern Europe.

So contemporary social pressures that discourage would-be parents, as reported by Krause and Hilevych, can be seen as a continuation – in different circumstances – of an intrinsic feature of the former rural kinship model. Operating in the changed environment of an industrial city, or the post-agricultural countryside, it seems that the resulting pressures are in effect misfiring – and contributing to the prevailing pattern of below-replacement fertility.

But this leaves us with a final puzzle to resolve. If social pressure to control fertility now generates below-replacement fertility – and this pressure also existed in the past – why did it not have the same effect in the cooperative rural past? A clue to this is provided by what local people say about the ways in which their social life has changed. Carnia provides a useful example, since at the time of my fieldwork, approximate estimates suggested that the TFR in the area where I worked had declined to little more than one child per woman.

Carnia in 1990 was not a happy place – since the end of the cooperative relationships that underlay local agriculture had left a sense of social dislocation. People felt that prosperity had made people selfish – and that relationships had been better when people had needed each other's help. Indeed, this equation between prosperity and selfishness is something of a cliché in contemporary Italy.

This might be dismissed as merely typical nostalgia by the middle-aged and elderly, were it not for the fact that in a few instances an ethnographer has studied a particular village community both before and after the transition from an agricultural to a quasi-urban system of economic life. Two studies of Spanish communities report the same shift from collective to individualistic patterns of interaction that Carnians report about themselves. The objective changes were accompanied by the same complaints about the loss of solidarity, and coincided with the onset of Spain's decline towards sub-replacement fertility. (Lisón Tolosana 1966, 2004; Collier 1997).

On the basis of these findings I have argued that the experience of cooperation itself was a source of social and emotional capital, that enabled many potential parents to resist the discouraging effects of the constant mutual criticism. With the decline of agricultural work, the cooperative basis of the local community fell apart – leaving only the downward pressure from mutual criticism and social competition, and resulting in drastic fertility decline (Heady 2017a).

Although there is a sense in which this decline can be thought of as a result of individualism, it should not be confused with the view, advanced by Lesthaeghe and various colleagues, that recent falls in fertility have been due to a value shift which has led potential parents to prioritise self-fulfilment over parental duties (Lesthaeghe 1995; Surkyn & Lesthaeghe 2004). One problem with Lesthaeghe's approach was pointed out above – namely, the continuing commitment to a two-child ideal. Another problem arises from the geography of fertility in present-day Europe: namely, that the individualistic values that Lesthaeghe expected to be associated with lower fertility are actually more widespread in the northwest European countries where fertility is comparatively high (Sobotka 2008).

The key to the difference is, I think, that individualism, in the sense of personal autonomy if not in the more recent sense of self-realisation, has long been accepted as a *value* in northwest Europe – and is associated with a geographically mobile kinship regime in which there would be no reason for the downward social pressures on local fertility discussed in this section. This is quite different from the effect of individualistic *behaviour* in a system where the underlying model is one of mutual involvement based on kinship and local ties.

Concluding discussion: pragmatics, community and economic stress

This chapter has been based on statistical comparisons, and extrapolations from an ethnographic case study. It has argued that the transition to residential and reproductive adulthood needs to be understood from two perspectives. In terms of the pragmatic efforts of young people and their immediate families to establish the material basis for a family of reproduction – and as a set of social actions which confirm and renew the communities in which they live – these communities exercise an important degree of social control on economic cooperation and reproduction, and themselves adapt over time to changes in systems of economic subsistence.

Much of the discussion has been framed in terms of an over-simplified contrast between a system based on local kinship ties (adapted to agricultural conditions), and another in which kinship ties are much more scattered (adapted to urban life). Crude though it is, this contrast does enable us to make relevant comparisons at the level of Europe as a whole. Both systems can, in their favoured environment, lead to replacement-level reproduction, though their implications for gender relations are very different. However, the process by which formerly rural societies adapt to urban conditions is slow – and the resulting mismatch can place obstacles in the way of young people's attempts to found and complete their families of reproduction.

The data which I have discussed stops in the year 2007, and so this chapter has had nothing directly to say about the impact of the 2008 crisis and the subsequent period of recession and cutbacks in official welfare systems. Nevertheless, the analysis may have implications for later developments. One recent study suggests that the impact of recession on family formation has been greatest in southern Europe (Goldstein et al. 2013) – the area in which this chapter has identified a mismatch between community and economic systems. Awareness of long-standing differences in kinship and social systems, and of the massive social impact of the economic transformations in the second half of the twentieth century, may also reduce the risk of overstating the impact of recent economic difficulties on phenomena whose ultimate roots reach much further back in time.

Notes

1 The approach developed here, which derives from anthropological ideas, converges in several ways with Irwin's (2000, 2003) sociological concept of Reproductive Regimes.
2 See Billari (2004) for a more detailed treatment of the age at leaving home.
3 The KASS findings were published in three volumes: Grandits 2010a; Heady & Kohli 2010; & Schweitzer 2010.
4 See Frejka and Sobotka (2008) for comparable data on Europe as a whole.
5 Demographers tend to be particularly cautious about making inferences of this kind. This is not because they think that the welfare-state argument is definitely wrong, or because they believe that fertility behaviour is inherently unpredictable. There are many robust results about the determinants of fertility at the individual level. The problem is that it is much more difficult to evaluate hypotheses about causal processes that might operate at the national level. There are relatively few nation states, and there are a very large number of factors that might generate variations. Added to that, in the case of fertility, is the difficulty – discussed above – of distinguishing differences in the level of births from differences in the timing of births. So, although there are a large number of suggestive analyses, they are very rarely conclusive in statistical terms (Balbo et al. 2013).
6 The KASS urban samples contained a high proportion of apartment blocks.
7 Goody (1983) and Mitterauer (2003) have argued that the present system of family relationships in northwestern Europe, and the values associated with it, arose from a millenium-long series of successful struggles to weaken kinship ties in order to strengthen state and market institutions. See also Heady (2017b).
8 I have borrowed this term from Irwin (2000).

References

Balbo, N., Billari, F., & Mills, M. (2013), Fertility in advanced societies: a review of research. *European Journal of Population* 29: 1–38

Becker, G. (1993), *A treatise on the family (enlarged edition)*, Cambridge, MA: Harvard University Press.

Billari, F. (2004), Becoming an adult in Europe, *Demographic Research*, Special Collection 3, article 2, pp. 15–44, www.demographic-research.org/special/3/2/, doi:10.4054/DemRes.2004.S3.2

Caldwell, J. (1980), Mass education as a determinant of the timing of fertility decline. *Population and Development Review* 6(2): 225–255.

Caldwell, J. (2005), On net intergenerational wealth flows: an update. *Population and Development Review* 31(4): 721–740.

Colclough, N., Ghezzi, S., Capello, C., & Lorenzini, C. (2010), Three Italian localities, in P. Heady & P. Schweitzer (eds.), *Family, kinship and state in contemporary Europe. Vol. 2: The view from below: Nineteen localities*. Frankfurt and New York: Campus, pp. 269–330.

Collier, J. (1997), *From duty to desire: Remaking families in a Spanish village*. Princeton, NJ: Princeton University Press.

Esping-Andersen, G. (1990), *The three worlds of welfare capitalism*. Princeton, NJ: Princeton University Press.

Eurostat (2008), *The life of women and men in Europe: A statistical portrait*. European Statistical Office, online publication. ISBN: ISBN 978-92-79-07069-3, http://ec.europa.eu/eurostat/documents/3217494/5698400/KS-80-07-135-EN.PDF/101b2bc8-03f8-4f49-b4e4-811fff81b174

Frejka, T., & Sobotka, T. (2008), Overview Chapter 1: Fertility in Europe: Diverse, delayed and below replacement (part of Special Collection 7: Childbearing Trends and Policies in Europe). *Demographic Research* 19: 15–46.

Goldstein, J., Kreyenfeld, M., Jasilioniene, A., & Örsal, D. (2013), Fertility reactions to the 'Great Recession' in Europe: recent evidence from order-specific data. *Demographic Research* 29: 85–104.

Goody, J. (1983), *The development of the family and marriage in Europe*. Cambridge: Cambridge University Press.

Grandits, H. (ed.). (2010a), *Family, kinship and state in contemporary Europe. Vol. 1: The century of welfare: Eight countries*. Frankfurt, New York: Campus.

Grandits, H. (2010b), Introduction: The reshaping of family and kin relations in European welfare systems. In H. Grandits (Ed.), *Family, kinship and state in contemporary Europe. Vol. 1: The century of welfare: Eight countries*. Frankfurt: Campus. pp. 23–46.

Gruber, S., & Heady, P. (2010), Kinship in transformation – Measures and models. In H. Grandits (Ed.), *Family, kinship and state in contemporary Europe. Vol. 1: The century of welfare: Eight countries*. Frankfurt: Campus, pp. 363–390.

Heady, P. (1999), *The hard people: Rivalry, sympathy and social structure in an alpine valley*. Amsterdam: Harwood Academic.

Heady, P. (2003), Conscripts and Christians: representing kinship and affinity in the Carnian Alps. *Journal of the Royal Anthropological Institute*, 9(1): 77–95.

Heady, P. (2017a), Feeling secure to reproduce: economy, community and fertility in southern Europe. In P. Kreager & A. Bochow (eds), *Fertility, conjuncture, difference: Anthropological approaches to the heterogeneity of fertility declines*. New York and Oxford: Berghahn, pp. 133–163.

Heady, P. (2017b), A 'cognition and practice' approach to an aspect of European kinship. *Cross-Cultural Research* 51(3):285–310.

Heady, P., & Kohli, M. (eds). (2010), *Family, kinship and state in contemporary Europe. Vol. 3: Perspectives on theory and policy*. Frankfurt and New York: Campus.

Heady, P., & Schweitzer, P. (eds). (2010), *Family, kinship and state in contemporary Europe. Vol. 2: The view from below: Nineteen localities*. Frankfurt and New York: Campus.

Hilevych, Y. (2016), Later if ever: family influences on the transition from first to second births in Soviet Ukraine. *Continuity and Change* 31(2): 275–300.

Irwin, S. (2000), Reproductive regimes: changing relations of interdependence and fertility change. *Sociological Research Online* 5(1).

Irwin, S. (2003), Interdependencies, values and the reshaping of difference: gender and generation at the birth of twentieth-century modernity. *British Journal of Sociology* 54(4): 565–584.

Kohli, M., Albertini, M., & Künemund, H. (2010), Linkages among adult family generations: evidence from comparative survey research. In P. Heady & M. Kohli (Eds.), *Family, kinship and state in contemporary Europe. Vol. 3: Perspectives on theory and policy.* Frankfurt: Campus, pp. 225–248.

Krause, E. (2005), Toys and perfumes: imploding Italy's population paradox and motherly myths, in C. Douglass (ed.), *Barren states: the population "implosion" in Europe.* Oxford: Berg, pp. 159–182.

Lanzinger, M. (2003), Toward predominating primogeniture: changes in inheritance practices in Innichen/San Candido, 1730 to 1930, in H. Grandits & P. Heady (eds.), *Distinct inheritances: Property, family and community in a changing Europe.* Münster: LIT Verlag, pp.125–144.

Lesthaeghe, R. (1995), The second demographic transition in Western countries: an interpretation, in K. O. Mason & A.-M. Jensen (eds.), *Gender and family change in industrialized countries.* Oxford: Clarendon Press, pp. 17–62.

Lévi-Strauss, C. (1969 [1949]), *The elementary structures of kinship.* London: Eyre and Spottiswoode.

Lisón Tolosana, C. (1966), *Belmonte de los Caballeros.* Oxford: Oxford University Press.

Lisón Tolosana, C. (2004), *Invitación a la Antropología Cultural de España.* Madrid: AKAL.

McDonald, P. (2000), Gender equity, social institutions and the future of fertility. *Journal of Population Research,* 17: 1–16.

Mitterauer, M. (2003), European kinship systems and household structures: medieval origins, in H. Grandits & P. Heady (Eds.), *Distinct inheritances: Property, family and community in a changing Europe* . Münster, Germany: LIT Verlag, pp. 35–51.

Murdock, G. (1949), *Social structure.* New York: The Free Press.

Murphy, M. (2008), Variations in kinship networks across geographic and social space. *Population and Development Review,* 34: 19–49.

Naldini, M. (2003), *The family in the Mediterranean welfare states.* London: Frank Cass.

Sobotka, T. (2008), Overview Chapter 6: The diverse faces of the Second Demographic Transition in Europe (part of Special Collection 7: Childbearing Trends and Policies in Europe). *Demographic Research* 19: 171–224.

Sobotka, T., & Beaujouan, E. (2014), Two is best: the persistence of a two-child family ideal in Europe. *Population and Development Review* 40: 391–419.

Surkyn, J., & Lesthaeghe, R. (2004), Value orientations and the second demographic transition (SDT) in northern, western and southern Europe: an update. *Demographic Research,* Special Collection 3, Article 3, pp. 45–86, www.demographic-research.org/special/3/3/default.htm, doi:10.4054/DemRes.2004.S3.3

Viazzo, P. (1989), *Upland communities: Environment, population and social structure in the Alps since the sixteenth century,* Cambridge: Cambridge University Press.

Viazzo, P., & Zanotelli, F. (2010), Welfare as a moral obligation: changing patterns of family support in Italy and the Mediterranean, in H. Grandits (ed.), *Family, kinship and state in contemporary Europe. Vol. 1: The century of welfare: Eight countries.* Frankfurt and New York: Campus, pp 47–92.

Index